CLIMBING ROSES
OLD AND NEW

NEW EDITION

WRITTEN AND ILLUSTRATED
BY

GRAHAM STUART THOMAS

OBE, VMH, DHM, VMM

Gardens Consultant to the National Trust

With 8 pages of water colours,
8 pencil drawings and 16 photographs

With a chapter on the botany and
derivation of Climbing Roses by

GORDON D. ROWLEY

J. M. DENT & SONS LTD
LONDON   MELBOURNE   TORONTO

In association with the Royal Horticultural Society

© Graham Stuart Thomas, 1965, 1978, 1983
Printed in Great Britain by
Biddles Ltd, Guildford, Surrey
for
J. M. DENT & SONS LTD
Aldine House, Welbeck St, London
First published 1965
Second impression 1967
Revised edition 1978
New edition 1983

British Library Cataloguing in Publication Data

Thomas, Graham Stuart
Climbing roses old and new.—New ed.
1. Climbing roses
I. Title
635.9'33'372   SB411
ISBN 0–460–04604–7

Contents

Illustrations 7

Acknowledgments 9

Introduction 11

1. The Characters and Uses of Rambling and Climbing Roses   15
   Notes in Regard to the Descriptions 23

PART 1. RAMBLERS DERIVED FROM THE MUSK OR
SYNSTYLAE SECTION OF THE GENUS *Rosa*

2. Synstylae—the Wild Ramblers of the Musk Rose Section and
   a few Close Hybrids 27
3. The Mystery of the Musk Rose 48
4. Old and New Garden Ramblers 58

PART 2. RAMBLERS AND CLIMBERS DERIVED FROM
THE MUSK ROSE OR SYNSTYLAE SECTION, INTER-
MARRIED WITH THE OFFSPRING OF THE CHINA
AND TEA ROSES

5. The Luciae Group of Ramblers 79
6. The Noisette and Tea Roses 87
7. Large-flowered Climbers of Hybrid Tea Style . . . 111
8. The New Climbers 128

PART 3. SOME RARE SPECIES AND THEIR HYBRIDS,
TOGETHER WITH A CHAPTER ON THE BOTANY OF
CLIMBING ROSES

9. The Banksian, Macartney, and Cherokee Roses; their Forms
   and Hybrids 145
10. The Botany of Climbing Roses and the Derivation of Some
    Garden Climbers, by Gordon D. Rowley . . . 155

PART 4. PRACTICAL POINTS

11. Cultivation, Pruning, and Training 163

12. Display 168
13. Selections of Ramblers and Climbers for Various Positions
    and Purposes 181

    Bibliography 187
    Addenda for 2nd Edition, 1978 190
    Addenda for 3rd Edition, 1983 190
    Index 193

Illustrations

Between pages 64 and 65

COLOUR PLATES FROM WATER-COLOURS: SCALE REDUCED
7:4 APPROX.

I. Sempervirens Ramblers: 'Adélaïde d'Orléans', 'Félicité et Perpétue', and 'Spectabilis'
II. Multiflora and Wichuraiana Ramblers: 'Violette', 'Veilchenblau', 'Rose-Marie Viaud', 'Bleu Magenta', and 'Goldfinch'
III. Boursault Roses: 'Madame de Sancy de Parabère' and 'Amadis'
IV. Luciae Ramblers: 'Auguste Gervais' and 'Alexandre Girault'
V. Noisette Roses: 'Alister Stella Gray', 'Blush Noisette', and 'Céline Forestier'
VI. Tea Roses: 'Mrs Herbert Stevens' and 'Lady Hillingdon'
VII. Modern Climbers: 'Lawrence Johnston' and 'Cupid'
VIII. Modern Climber: 'Dream Girl'

Between pages 112 and 113

PENCIL DRAWINGS: SCALE REDUCED 3:2 APPROX.

1. *Rosa brunonii* 'La Mortola'
2. *Rosa longicuspis*
3. *Rosa moschata*, the original Autumn-flowering Musk Rose
4. 'Autumnalis', closely related to R. *moschata*
5. *Rosa wichuraiana*
6. 'Bobbie James'
7. 'The Garland'
8. 'Vicomtesse Pierre du Fou'

Between pages 160 and 161

PHOTOGRAPHS

1 & 2. *Rosa filipes* 'Kiftsgate'
3. *Rosa brunonii* 'La Mortola'
4. 'Kew Rambler'
5. 'May Queen'
6. 'Paul Transon'
7. The climbing form of 'Cécile Brunner'

7

8. 'Claire Jacquier'
9. 'Lamarque' (*Photo: Edwin Smith*)
10. 'Madame Alfred Carrière'
11. 'Sombreuil' (*Photo: Dorothy Stemler*)
12. Devoniensis' (*Photo: Dorothy Stemler*)
13. 'Dream Girl'
14. A Musk Rose climbing into yew trees
15. Training of roses at Bagatelle, Paris
16. Training of roses at the Roseraie de l'Haÿ, near Paris

A Note on the Illustrations

Although this book seeks to cover my selection of old and new climbing and rambling roses, I have not included illustrations of modern varieties, since these have received unlimited publicity in books and catalogues of recent years.

DIAGRAMS

1. Wires stretched through vine-eyes 169
2. Large-headed nail and leather or plastic strap . . . 170
3. Metal bracket to support lattice 170
4. Traditional arches for doorways 171
5. Lattice to support a plant enhancing a plain window . . 172
6, 7. Various fences of open wood-work 172
8. Arches or arbours at junction of paths 173
9. Detail of rustic arches 174
10. Examples of different materials for posts 175
11, 12. Construction of pergolas 176
13. Pillars 176
14. Pyramid of wooden lattice 177
15. Tripod and simple arch of stout poles 177

Acknowledgments

FROM anyone who seeks to write a book such as this there must flow unbounded gratitude to all those writers of the past who have contributed so richly to our knowledge of THE ROSE; in my search for facts I have made much use of the Lindley Library at the Royal Horticultural Society's offices in London, and have been accorded ever-ready help by the librarian, Mr P. F. M. Stageman, and his staff.

Among present workers in the genus my principal thanks go to Mr Gordon D. Rowley who, with unhesitating kindness, agreed to sift the chapters for any taxonomic and botanical 'bricks' I might have dropped; his helpful criticisms have been incorporated in the book and he has, once again, been good enough to contribute a chapter, this time on the botanical aspect of the Synstylae Section, together with some illuminating genealogical tables. Dr William T. Stearn and Mr C. D. Brickell have very kindly helped with identifications of some species.

I am also grateful to Mr E. B. LeGrice and to Mr Leonard Hollis for several useful comments on the roses in Chapters 7 and 8. Mr John Render has skilfully interpreted my rough sketches and I record my thanks to him for the resulting diagrams in Chapter 12. Permission for the inclusion of the verse on page 87, an extract from the poetical works of Robert Bridges, is gratefully acknowledged to the Clarendon Press, Oxford, and for the extract on page 30 from *On the Eaves of the World* by Reginald Farrer to Edward Arnold (Publishers) Ltd. To Mrs Dorothy Stemler and Mr Edwin Smith I wish to record my appreciation for permission to use their copyright photographs, numbers 11 and 12, and 9 respectively.

There remain the many kind friends and enthusiasts who have given freely from their experience on a number of small points; to them I am also very grateful. One can do little without the help of others.

Introduction

You violets that first appeare,
By your pure purple mantles known,
Like the proud virgins of the yeare,
As if the spring were all your owne,
What are you when the Rose is blown?

Sir Henry Wotton, 1568–1639.

IN MY LAST book, *Shrub Roses of Today*, I expressed the hope that I should be able to write a survey of the climbing and rambling roses. Here is the result, a collection of miscellaneous jottings which have been welded into a series of chapters in which I hope I have covered both old and new climbers fairly impartially. Many of my readers know that I could not be wholly impartial about them; the older roses make an appeal to me which I have never been able to explain. Except, of course, that I prefer their colours, their scents, their shapes, their graceful abundance, and their longevity! Yet I should not like it to be thought that I can see no beauty in modern roses; they have their appeal--and it is a very strong one—and their undoubted place in the garden. They are mostly fragrant, extremely shapely, brightly coloured, and vigorous. Why then do I continue to stress the value of the older varieties?

The reason is that I like to pass on the pleasures I have enjoyed by growing all sorts of roses. It is not until one can hold in one's hand such diverse beauties as 'Cécile Brunner', 'Madame Hardy', 'Reine des Violettes', 'Spek's Yellow', the double white Burnet, 'Mrs John Laing', 'Roseraie de l'Haÿ', 'Lady Hillingdon', 'Lilac Charm', *farreri persetosa*, 'Madame Abel Chatenay', 'Souvenir de la Malmaison', 'Frühlingsmorgen', 'Josephine Bruce' . . . but I had better stop (I could with little trouble name another fourteen of equally divergent beauty); it is not until we contemplate such a handful that we can claim to know THE ROSE. These fourteen vary in width of bloom from one inch to five inches; in colour, from white through yellow, salmon, pink, crimson, maroon, purple, and lilac; in scent, indefinable and indescribable; in shape, rounded, globular, angular, cupped, flat or reflexed, single with five petals only, or double with sixty or more; so that we may say they cover the principal variations of the rose, in both wild and cultivated forms.

The above are bush or shrub roses. It will be quite easy to name fourteen climbers and ramblers with as much variation: 'Adélaïde d'Orléans', 'Guinée', 'Gloire de Dijon', 'Sanders' White', the single yellow Banksian, 'Violette', 'Mermaid', 'Madame de Sancy de Parabère', 'Alister Stella Gray', 'Mrs Herbert Stevens', 'Étoile de Hollande', 'Madame Alice Garnier', 'Kiftsgate', and 'Danse du Feu'. Here are scramblers—in more ways than one—for every position and task; to the categories of qualities listed above they add a further variation, for in height they may achieve from six feet to forty feet on supports, and an equal width.

I like to grow these varying kinds because only by so doing can I feel that I am appreciating to the full the bounties offered by the genus. Of what use is it to be so besieged by novelties and bright colours that one has neither time nor space to grow the established favourites? And by this I do not mean the favourites of yesterday, but of the last hundred or more years, the best of which stand out like lightships in the drowning waste of the thousands of second-rate varieties that have come and gone. It is a shattering thought that we mortals have made and named during the last hundred and fifty years some ten to fifteen thousand varieties of roses that are completely lost and forgotten.

Raisers of roses have always named their best seedlings and distributed them; just a few have achieved such popularity that they have been preserved through changing fashions—ready for emergence when some new fashion or economic or social change brings them forth again. This is what happened to the Old Shrub Roses after the Hitler war. It may well happen all over again when good-style roses become neglected. It is illuminating to read how Dean Hole, the celebrated rosarian of the late nineteenth century, and founder of our National Rose Society, cast aside the old ramblers. He was mainly interested in the bigger and better roses of the day for the show-bench; he loved the brighter and more

spectacular roses which were then founding the race of Hybrid
Teas. His 'Maréchal Niel', 'Gloire de Dijon', and 'Charles
Lefèbvre' were to him the apotheosis of the rose; he gracefully
recalls (in 1870) how 'many years have passed since I laid "The
Garland", as an Immortelle, upon the tomb of "Madame
d'Arblay"'. Thirty-two years later, with the turn of the horticultural tide from artificiality to a truer appreciation of natural
beauty, Gertrude Jekyll found them just the thing to create
graceful festoons of scented blossom over her arches, walls, and
shrubs. The principal message of her excellent book *Roses for
English Gardens* (1902) is this use of the carefree rambler.

Unless we are going to specialize in the modern accepted style
of rose, and to grow only Hybrid Teas and Floribundas, we are
not qualified to judge roses without having become acquainted
with their main ancestors. But after becoming acquainted with
them, first grounded or graduated as it were on the wild species
themselves, we begin to realize how much we lose by growing
modern varieties only. I like, therefore, to sift the newcomers
well, before writing about them; occasionally a new horticultural
break will occur—examples in recent times are 'Mermaid',
'Nevada', and the onset of the new colour 'pelargonidin' which
has brought intense neon-brilliance to roses of today typified by
'Super Star'. These examples are part of rose history; we live in
the midst of evolution; at any moment something may happen
which will ensure the rose of the season going down to posterity
while its companion hundreds will be lost to cultivation in ten
years.

It is not everyone that will wear scarlet stockings, or picture-
shirts; the rage for gaudy plastic articles may pass; already the
natural beauty of wood is achieving a new popularity, and I think
it is not only a pleasure but a duty to bring forward the gracious
things of the past and range them alongside some of their more
worthy modern counterparts.

As far as I am aware, no book devoted solely to rambling and
climbing roses has appeared in Britain before, though two have
appeared in the United States. Practically all rose books devote
chapters to them, but that is all. It is no longer fashionable to
address the 'gentle reader', but we must be gentle, open-minded,
and appreciative of all grace and beauty in assessing wild species

and man-made hybrids. As with all plants we must also be patient, waiting for the soil and the weather to help our roses to give of their best. When our culture is right and the weather perfect, and above all when the placing of the plants and their companions is right, then, at a certain moment of the year, for perhaps a day or two or even a week, any rose in our gardens can be so beautiful that we shall stop weeding and fussing and drink deeply of that unfathomable, incalculable 'rich power that breeds so many and many a flower'. Though that moment may never come again with the same rose plant, it will enrich our lives with a precious memory of welcome colour, intangible fragrance and natural grace— qualities which seem to become yearly more scarce. And it is to the wild species and certain ramblers that we must turn for the greatest refreshment, with their supreme contributions of grace, fragrance, and plenitude of flower.

G. S. THOMAS.

Woking, Surrey.

'The true blessedness of mankind
is not to arrive but to travel.'
R. L. Stevenson.

I

The Characters and Uses
of Rambling and Climbing Roses

The morning rose that untouch'd stands
Arm'd with her briers, how sweet she smells!
But pluck'd and strain'd through ruder hands,
Her sweets no longer with her dwells.
Sir Robert Aytoun, 1570–1638.

THERE COMES a day in June when the popular rose 'Chaplin's Pink' begins to open, and all over the South of England at least its vivid cerise-pink shows over garden walls. Because of its brilliance and ubiquity it heralds the beginning of the rose season. With it two much older but less spectacular roses usually open, 'Paul's Carmine Pillar' and 'Gloire de Dijon'. Apart from some early flowering species of *Rosa*, such as the Banksian and certain shrub roses, these are the first. They are closely followed by 'Albertine', 'American Pillar', and 'Paul's Scarlet', and later by 'Dorothy Perkins', 'Excelsa' and 'Dr van Fleet'. What household words these have become! And what sheets of bloom they give, effervescing up house walls, foaming over arches and garden fences, and even cascading down banks or surmounting the wrecks of posts or trees that they have overpowered!

They come at a time when we have already feasted on the season's fullness. The rhododendrons and azaleas, the cherries, lilacs, laburnums, and many other favourite genera are over, each adding to the year's pageant of beauty. The rose can easily hold its own with them, and particularly is this true of the ramblers and climbers; each plant can give a greater quantity of blossom at one time than any other type of rose. Most of them bring a wonderful perfume—and also prickles. (A list of roses without prickles is given at the end of this book, for the benefit of the less courageous.)

But first let us consider our terminology and define what is meant by the horticultural groups 'ramblers' and 'climbers'. According to the dictionary they are the same, but they have come to mean two quite different classes of roses, and are comparable in their looseness and synonymy with the two terms for lower growing roses—'shrub' and 'bush'. Just as 'shrub' roses have come to mean the wild species and bigger roses bred closely from them, and the 'bush' or 'bedding' roses mean the highly bred, large-flowered Hybrid Teas and Floribundas, so among the taller roses the 'ramblers' are the wild species and closely allied garden forms—flowering once only in the summer, as is normal with most species—and the 'climbers' are the large-flowered, highly bred, mainly repeat-flowering varieties.

These are very superficial terms. To begin with, no rose really climbs in the sense that self-clinging or twining plants like ivy or honeysuckle will climb. The rose, like the blackberry, usually bears hooked prickles which help to secure its branches to the support, but almost all roses need tying and helping upwards or outwards. The botanists term them 'scramblers'; we might call them 'drooping roses', or 'roses that need support'. These terms might be misunderstood, and so throughout this book I shall adopt the accepted distinctions as outlined above.

Thirty years ago it would have been comparatively easy to describe the difference between the two groups of roses, the ramblers and the climbers, but with increased hybridization they come nearer together in the search for a large-flowered rose that will bloom through the summer and into autumn, be hardy, fragrant, and graceful. A few, like 'Mermaid', 'New Dawn', and 'Pink Cloud', are getting near to this ideal.

Species and Hybrids

This book is concerned as much with species of roses as with garden hybrids, and a list of the wild species mentioned in these pages which can be classed as ramblers or climbers is given below, arranged in their taxonomic sections. All roses mentioned in these chapters owe part of their parentage to one or more of these species; they are all natives of the Old World, except one, and mostly of the Far East.

SYNSTYLAE
Rosa *arvensis*
    brunonii
    cerasocarpa
    crocacantha
    filipes
    helenae
    henryi
    longicuspis
    luciae
    maximowicziana
    moschata
    mulliganii
    multiflora
    phoenicea
    rubus
    sempervirens
    setigera
    sinowilsonii
    soulieana
    wichuraiana

LAEVIGATAE
Rosa *laevigata*

BRACTEATAE
Rosa *bracteata*

BANKSIANAE
Rosa *banksiae*

INDICAE
Rosa *chinensis* (not in cultivation)
Rosa *gigantea*

The species of the Laevigatae, Bracteatae, and Banksianae Sections have made little groups on their own, and have had no appreciable influence on our garden ramblers and climbers; moreover, together with R. *gigantea*, they would not be reliably hardy except on sunny walls in the warmer parts of these islands. Therefore we turn to the members of the Synstylae Section, and among these the most prolific of hybrids has been R. *wichuraiana*, with R. *multiflora* and the old R. *moschata* a good second and third. R. *phoenicea* and the old R. *moschata* are believed to be parents of the Old Shrub Roses, and R. *arvensis* and *sempervirens* had their little day as founders of a few old ramblers grown a hundred years ago; the last two species are not grown in gardens and their hybrids are now seldom seen. The chapters devoted to each Section contain fuller details.

The members of the Synstylae, the Laevigatae and the Banksianae are all once-flowering ramblers; likewise R. *chinensis* (the wild species) and R. *gigantea*. R. *bracteata* flowers from summer till autumn, and therefore qualifies, in this abstract horticultural classification, as the only 'species-climber'. Practically all the climbers in cultivation owe their status of 'climber' to four original hybrids of R. *chinensis* and R. *gigantea* which were introduced as garden plants from China between 1792 and 1824, as outlined by Dr Hurst on pages 75–80 of my first book, *The Old Shrub Roses*, and supplemented on pages 115–16 of its sequel, *Shrub Roses of Today*.

The wild roses of the Synstylae Section are, almost all, preeminent in fragrance, both on account of their strength and their carrying power in the air. With a richness unsurpassed among roses, and indeed in the floral world, in this character they are nearly unique. In spite of the size of growth of so many of them and their short season of flowering, their fragrance should ensure their being planted everywhere. They take their place with the lime and the philadelphus, the clover and the bean, bringing midsummer to a climax of scent which is not equalled during the rest of the year out of doors.

Before we consider hybrid ramblers and climbers, I will recall those roses of lax growth which are perhaps not of sufficient length of shoot to be classed as ramblers, and which are also probably too bushy for training on supports. These can be classed as sprawling shrubs—even carpeters—and all those which create dense ground-cover, either flat or mounding themselves up into wide hummocks, have been described in *Shrub Roses of Today*. To keep all these roses in view, I include a list of them in this book on page 182. If a climbing or rambling rose has no support it will obviously make either a loose arching shrub or collapse on the ground, according to how sturdy are the branches; if it is dense in growth it qualifies for a position among labour-saving ground-covering plants. But if it does not make a dense mass, however beautiful it may be sprawling about, it will not make satisfactory ground-cover, and to try to weed or otherwise tend the ground among trailing and arching prickly growth is not a desirable occupation; the growths should be given proper support and kept under control.

So far the classification would seem obvious and easy, but when it comes to hybrid climbers it is a very different matter. The oldest recurrent or perpetual hybrid climbers belong to the Noisettes and Bourbons; somewhat later in the general trend are the Tea-Noisettes and Hybrid Perpetuals. 'Blush Noisette' and 'Aimée Vibert' are two important originals, shewing the firstfruits of the combined influences of the China and the Musk Rose towards perpetual-flowering climbers.

In addition to the great bulk of large-flowered, recurrent, climbing sports of Hybrid Teas belonging to this century are the repeat-flowering climbers in their own right, so to speak—varieties raised from seed like 'Allen Chandler' and 'Golden Showers'. Conversely, some climbing sports are very shy of later blooms, like 'Peace', and there are some splendid large-flowered climbers, raised from seed, which flower only at midsummer. We also have climbing sports of bush Polyanthas and Floribundas, and I know of a plant of 'Frensham' which has reached some 12 feet in rich soil against a wall, yet it has not 'sported' a climber. This is just an example of how, with the warmth and protection of a wall, shrub and other roses may grow to unexpected heights.

We are dealing with such a complex race of plants that anything may happen when new varieties are raised from seed. The China Rose hybrids are at the back of everything; to them may be traced not only practically all our perpetual or recurrent-flowering climbing roses of today, but the overwhelming majority of hybrid shrub roses and dwarf bush roses as well. Only two or three wild species are recurrent, and these have not yet entered into the parentage of our modern roses except recently through R. *kordesii*. Those roses which flower from June to October, among which may be numbered several old roses and many new, raise the genus *Rosa* to a high pinnacle among hybridized genera. Glad we may be of this, but the mere recurrence of flower should not blind us to the beauties of the wild species and the many well-tried favourites which give to our gardens unsurpassed grace and free fragrance. Very few of the large-flowered climbing roses make any pretence of shedding fragrance to the degree achieved by the species in the Synstylae group.

Scent and grace, to me, are important points. When they are combined, as occasionally happens among the ramblers, then I would choose them in preference to a graceless plant with big double blooms. There is something a trifle vulgar about having huge growth *and* huge blooms, however desirable it may appear at first sight; and yet I have only to meet a big plant of some climbing Hybrid Tea sport, smothered with fragrant, large, beautiful flowers, to realize that I would rather have those than any number of small blooms *without scent* on a graceful rambler. And it must be admitted that a few ramblers have no scent, or have only an apology for it.

A knowledge of the various groups mentioned above is necessary when it comes to pruning, though it is better not to prune climbers and ramblers at all than to prune them wrongly. I have included some hints in Chapter 11; the elementary rules are easy to grasp.

Uses of Ramblers and Climbers in Gardens

This brings us to another point: how do we most enjoy our ramblers and climbers? Their use in our gardens really depends upon whether we are tidy—or, shall I say, untidy—gardeners; putting it perhaps more subtly, it depends on whether we impose our will on the roses or let them display their personalities to us.

The first method entails training and pruning so that the stiffer, more modern varieties with their large blooms may make a curtain of blossom one foot from a house wall or trellis; so that the shorter-growing varieties may make a cylinder of close bloom up a post or pillar; and so that the strong pliant ramblers may be trained to outline neatly the curve of arch or swinging chain or rope. In these ways the roses become part of the architecture of the garden, and give neat displays, often more closely smothered with bloom than any other garden plant. The best place to see a display such as this is at Bagatelle or at the Roseraie de l'Haÿ, near Paris (photographs, Plates 15 and 16). The French are methodical, and what is achieved by the careful gardeners there needs to be seen to be believed; stretching away into the distance are flat, circular or Gothic arches, swags and festoons, pillars, umbrellas and fountains of roses, impeccably pruned, trained, and drilled, with prim beds beneath filled with dwarf roses. The endless variety of cross vistas and the great treillage of ramblers is an example of floral gardening which it would be hard to surpass. Moreover it is an example of English and French gardening of almost a hundred years ago.

Two of the best English displays of ramblers and climbers are found in or near London. At Queen Mary's Rose Garden in Regent's Park very high and widely spaced pillars connected with swinging ropes taxed the resources of the Superintendent to the full—only the best cultivation and careful selection of most vigorous varieties have made it the success it is. At the Royal Botanic Garden, Kew, we can see a pergola of stout brick pillars connected with beams above, providing homes for many varieties. Here again, on gravel as opposed to the clay of Regent's Park, the size of the arches is proving a test in covering the pergola successfully. At Wisley, on poor sandy soil, larch poles with their side-shoots left at a discreet length provide wide pillars of blossom, and a similar method is used at Powis Castle in North Wales, while at Polesden Lacey, Surrey, on shallow soil overlying chalk, an Edwardian rose garden has a long larchwood pergola covered with roses of the period—'Dorothy Perkins', 'American Pillar' and all their clan. The effect is delightful, but of course, fragrance is mainly lacking. At Bodnant, the climbers and ramblers are mixed with other things, which is how I prefer them.

Plate 14 is a photograph of a rose growing in a natural way, its main shoots secured for safety to firm supports, and their branches spilling forward and weighed down with beauty. This is how I prefer my climbing and rambling roses, and most of my experience, my thought and aim in growing them, has been with this style in mind. This is one reason why I like the older varieties; from my remarks on page 114 it will be understood that hybridization in the main has given us the recurrent-flowering habit at the expense of grace.

There is a great variety of suitable supports for rambling and climbing roses, and I have tried to make their selection and erection easier in Chapter 12. In addition to the more formal supports, there is a simple stout post about six feet high to which one ties the main shoots of a rambler; thereafter it is allowed to grow outwards and downwards, making a lax bush or fountain of blossom.

Ramblers are useful plants to cover unsightly sheds and fences and stumps and stems of dead trees, but none of these methods, neat or natural, on artificial or existing supports, can rival the beauty of a rose trained on a living support, allowing it freedom of growth. A rose can grow through a living tree without harming it, giving it midsummer beauty.

It is the *falling spray* of ramblers that is most beautiful, not those which are trained upwards. This is the lesson I have learnt and want to try to pass on, and some of the methods described above may help. To see and smell the long trail of blossoms hanging from a growing leafy host-tree is one of the great pleasures of summer.

This brings me away from the garden varieties and hybrids of ramblers back to the species themselves. The gardening public has not yet realized what giants these wild roses can be. It is no good putting them into the usual ornamental or fruit trees of our gardens; RR. *brunonii, rubus, helenae*, together with 'Kiftsgate' and 'La Mortola', *longicuspis*, and 'Paul's Himalayan Musk Rambler', are tremendous growers and suitable for really big supports. I have enlarged on this in the chapter devoted to them (see page 30). It is enough to say here that there is a wealth of garden beauty and fragrance available in strong and very strong rambling species and varieties to add greatly to our gardens in June and July.

So far we have been considering the uses of ramblers and once-flowering allied roses. The hybridized climbers require rather different treatment. Some are tractable and easy to train, and will make great lax bushes like those visualized above; others, particularly the climbing sports of Hybrid Teas, are stiff and awkward to train and are apt to get lanky at the base. I think these stiffer-growing roses have two main uses; to grow up high walls so that their blooms look in at the bedroom windows, while below we can plant something smaller to hide their nakedness; or to grow as lanky shrubs among the greater inmates at the back of the large borders with a stake or two to make them safe. I especially like the combination of a great Hybrid Tea flower growing mixed with a small-flowered rambler; the two different types of growth support one another. When fully established, the big wood of the climber would support some of the rambler's trails, while the latter, as the years go by, develops a thicket of growth and helps to bolster up the climber. Almost all pruning would be omitted, leaving the general effect to be enjoyed rather than quality of bloom. Personally, in a large garden I like a *smother* of roses, a great mounding up of blossom and scent, contrasting in shape and size, using the stiff shrubby growers to provide solidity for a tangle of ramblers; it is all in keeping with summer's bounty.

It will be understood from what I have written that my favourite methods of growing climbing and rambling roses are not suitable for very small gardens. This should not, however, discourage owners of such from growing them; they will reap great enjoyment when their roses are trained over arches and along fences. A rose is always beautiful, anywhere.

Notes in Regard to the Descriptions

Names in large capitals denote species.

Names in small capitals denote sub-species and recognized botanical varieties.

Names in bold type and quotes denote garden forms, varieties, and hybrids, called 'cultivars'.

Wherever possible the name of the raiser and the date of introduction have been given, together with synonyms and parentage.

All references are to artists' coloured illustrations, unless otherwise stated, and they are not in any particular order. The immense increase in colour illustrations from photographs of late years in books and catalogues gives a good idea of the general trend in colour-breeding, but the illustrations are for the most part concerned only with the flower, often omitting altogether the leaves, prickles, and stems, and I have therefore included only a few references from these, where I consider them worthy.

For details of books consulted, see Bibliography, page 187.

The figures in the descriptions denote the approximate height or length to which the stems may grow in Surrey, but all such measurements vary with local conditions.

A 'sport' ('mutation' in genetic parlance) is a shoot which is different in growth from the parent plant; these shoots usually remain constant when vegetatively propagated.

A 'clone' is the vegetatively propagated progeny of a single individual.

A 'perpetual' rose flowers more or less continuously during the growing season. 'Remontant' or 'recurrent' or 'repeat-flowering' roses usually have two crops, or flower intermittently towards autumn after the main crop, but are not necessarily 'perpetual'.

PART 1

Ramblers Derived from the Musk or Synstylae Section of the Genus *Rosa*

2

Synstylae

THE WILD RAMBLERS OF THE MUSK ROSE SECTION AND A FEW CLOSE HYBRIDS

> I know a bank where the wild thyme blows,
> Where oxlips and the nodding violet grows,
> Quite over-canopied with luscious woodbine,
> With sweet musk-roses and with eglantine.
>
> Shakespeare, *A Midsummer Night's Dream.*

THE NAME Musk crops up in many garden flowers denoting a special scent supposed to be like that obtained from the male Musk Deer. The little Musk plant was a strain of *Mimulus moschatus* which ages ago developed this fragrance and which it has since lost. *Rosa moschata*, the Musk Rose,[1] is a noted member of the Synstylae Section, and in fact, many of the roses of this Section are so closely related in general appearance and their sweet fragrance that they may well be termed collectively the Musk Roses, especially as another species, R. *arvensis*, is, I consider, the original English Musk Rose of the poets (see Chapter 3).

The roses of this Section grow wild in a chain of countries and districts across the Old World, extending from Madeira, North Africa and Southern Europe, Western Asia (R. *moschata* itself) to the Himalayas (R. *brunonii*) through Western and Central China (RR. *longicuspis*, *mulliganii*, *helenae*, etc.), to Japan and Korea (R.

---

[1] Quite distinct from R. *centifolia muscosa*, the Moss Rose—all very confusing to the novice.

multiflora), while R. *setigera* is the sole representative in the New World. Except poor forms of R. *multiflora* and its sport *watsoniana*, all are of considerable beauty, some superlatively so.

All wild species of roses are best classed as shrubs except those enumerated in this book, and it so happens that practically all the roses of our gardens—and particularly the ramblers—owe all or part of their ancestry to the species in this botanical Section, the Synstylae, if one is ready to accept that R. *phoenicea* is a parent of the Damask Roses. The term at once indicates their botanical character; it is their speciality of having their little bunch of styles in the very centre of each flower tightly aggregated into a brief column, not spread out as in other species. (The Old Shrub Roses sometimes have a green pointel in the centre, but this is quite a different phenomenon.)

Though the Section as a whole is so distinct, its members are not so easily separated. If I wanted to give someone a life-task I would assign to him the botanical unravelling of these roses; I would ask a good friend to do it, for the fragrance and beauty of these Musk Roses are unsurpassed, and would be a wonderful companionship for full enjoyment over the years. The task would consist of importing plants or seeds of these roses from their native countries, and from as many districts in those countries as they are to be found; to grow them for some years to maturity in a warm and sunny field, and to write us a new botanical 'key' to the Section. On the completion of this task, he should then be able to decide to what species belong all the numerous roses that masquerade in our gardens under the specific names contained in this Section.

I must confess I find them more confusing and difficult to name than all the other species, and being mostly such large plants they are seldom seen about the country; moreover they germinate well from seeds and hybridize very easily in cultivation; many hybrids are found in gardens. Only by fresh importation and study can we be certain, I think, of correct identification. While some of the species, i.e. RR. *setigera*, *soulieana*, *arvensis*, *sempervirens*, and *sinowilsonii*, are readily recognizable, many of the others seem to merge into one another. There are several more closely related species enumerated in botanical books which are rare and obscure and not seen in gardens, and for this reason I have omitted them;

among others they include RR. *maximowicziana*, *leschenaultiana*, *glomerata*, and *crocacantha*. These four are natives of the Far East.

The descriptions in botanical works are based on the original specimen—usually in a herbarium—collected by the discoverer. The plants we grow in our gardens may have been propagated vegetatively from first or second or later generations of seed and may be more or less hybridized. The resulting plants will grow quite differently in varying soils and conditions, and the particular plants we know under various established names may be different from those grown in another country. Be this as it may, the plants I grow and describe are all distinct horticulturally; all have been propagated vegetatively from established specimens, and these clones have been widely distributed.

All of the species in this Section, then, are ramblers achieving anything up to 40 feet with support—some only 12 feet perhaps— with clusters of flowers borne rambler-fashion on short shoots all along last year's long summer growths; the flowers are single, with five petals only, creamy white with yellow stamens and a delicious fragrance; the only exceptions in colour are RR. *setigera* and *multiflora*, which have pink forms. All normally have seven leaflets. R. *soulieana* and R. *setigera* are shrubby in growth rather than climbers, and accordingly I included them in *Shrub Roses of Today*; they are, however, excellent when allowed to clamber through and over bushes, low trees, and hedgerows. The remainder need much space and are unsuitable for small gardens. Those who look for less rampageous ramblers with equally fragrant single flowers and the 'wild' look, should choose 'Kew Rambler' and 'Francis E. Lester'.

Taking the smallest first, there is little R. *multiflora watsoniana*, which is more of a curiosity than a plant of garden value. The next least vigorous of those in the present chapter are R. *multiflora* and R. *wichuraiana*. The former has rather small flowers but an unforgettable scent; in addition it has value in other ways which I will mention under its own heading later in this chapter. R. *wichuraiana* is a most valuable plant for many purposes, for ground-cover on banks and borders, or as a·dense rambler, and it does not flower until summer is well advanced and the eucryphias are in flower. R. *luciae* is closely related.

Some of middle strength are RR. *helenae*, *henryi*, *longicuspis*,

mulliganii, and *sinowilsonii*, together with a few hybrids such as
'Wedding Day' and 'Polyantha grandiflora'. We can expect all
these except one to climb at least 25 feet; R. *sinowilsonii* is somewhat
of an exception as it is not really hardy in England and needs the
shelter of a wall, where its magnificent foliage, the best provided
by any rose, will create more beauty than its flowers. The Old
Musk Rose R. *moschata* is probably all the better for a wall also.
This leaves us with the big hybrid version of R. *moschata* and R.
brunonii, R. *rubus*, and R. *filipes*, all achieving 40 feet in favourable
conditions. R. *sempervirens* and R. *arvensis* are not normally grown
in our gardens, but I have included them as they are ancestors of
some garden ramblers.

Some of these great roses may be seen smothering small trees
in certain gardens, as at Kiftsgate Court, Gloucestershire; at
Highdown, Sussex, they have even seeded themselves in the chalk
cliff, and give visitors an excellent example of their use in a bold
way in the landscape; many are trained up trees at Knightshayes
Court in Devon, and at Sissinghurst and Hidcote.

In his book *On the Eaves of the World*, vol. ii, Reginald Farrer
gives a description of one of these musk roses growing wild in
Kansu, Western China. We do not turn instinctively to Farrer
for information on roses, but his pen is one of the very few that
can give us a real picture of the prolificity and all-pervading fragrance of these roses. He writes of R. *filipes* ('Barley Bee' is his
adaptation of the name of the local village):

'In June Barley Bee has yet a further attraction, for all its
hedges are filled with a gigantic rambler rose, which casts abroad
twelve-foot slender sprays (beset with rare but very vigorous and
ferocious thorns), which in their second season are bowed into
arches by the weight, all along their length, of huge loose bunches
of snow-white blossom unfolding from buds of nankeen yellow;
and carrying on their glory far into the early winter in showers of
round berries, finer than the finest mountain ash, that ripen of a
rich orange and develop to soft crimson-scarlet with a delicate,
faint bloom. But this is not its chief merit when it submerges
Barley Bee in a surf of snow, for now the scent is so keen and
entrancing that all the air quivers with the intoxicating delicious-
ness of it for half a mile round the village in every direction, and
the toils of the climb ended sweetly indeed, as I lay out upon the

flat roof through the soft summer dusk and dark, lapped in waves of that warm fragrance, staring up to where the dim bulk of the mountain overhead again and again leapt into a vivider darkness, with the wide flares of sheet-lightning flickering out behind . . . .'

Looked at historically, some natives of the Old World have been in cultivation a long time. R. *moschata* is recorded in books from the sixteenth century onwards; R. *arvensis* is a native of Britain and gave rise to the Ayrshire roses, dating from the early nineteenth century. R. *sempervirens* was mentioned first in the seventeenth century, and has given rise to a few hybrids also. R. *brunonii* reached us in 1822, while R. *multiflora* arrived from Eastern Asia in 1862, and from this species stem all the early ramblers like 'Crimson Rambler', 'Goldfinch', and 'Blush Rambler'. The other most potent species, R. *wichuraiana*, which provided the hybrids of the 'Dorothy Perkins' clan and, through its relative R. *luciae*, the far superior strain modelled on 'Albéric Barbier', arrived with R. *soulieana* just before the turn of the century.

With the great plant collectors busy in China during the first two decades of our century a flow of new species arrived: RR. *sinowilsonii, helenae, rubus, filipes, longicuspis, mulliganii*, and others.

It is believed that, prior to all of this, in days before history started—perhaps aided by man, who may have grown them together and was thus instrumental in the exchange of pollen— R. *phoenicea* from Asia Minor and the old original R. *moschata* of Herrmann, from South Europe and North Africa, were ancestors of the Summer and Autumn Damask roses. The old R. *moschata* enters our strains again through the Noisettes, and perhaps, together with R. *multiflora*, through the Hybrid Musks. This last species is also a parent of the Dwarf Polyanthas, and thus through to the Floribundas and our newest roses. The older species of the Synstylae therefore have played a considerable part in the production of garden roses through the centuries, and it remains to be seen what effect the comparatively new introductions will have.

ARVENSIS. A native of Britain and Europe, rare in Scotland, and a characteristic of many of our hedgerows, where it flowers rather later than the Dog Brier, R. *canina*, in the hotter weather of July. Then its creamy, wide-open flowers with their rich yellow stamens are most welcome, as the grasses fade and we reach high summer. It is very fragrant, the flowers being borne in small clusters along the lengthy trailing branches. In their first year these branches are sparsely leaved and of purplish hue, and this tone together with the dark leaves and creamy flowers puts it into a class of its own. The fruits are oval or rounded, bright red. It is not to be recommended for any but the wildest of gardens, for it makes long, unmanageable trails, eventually creating a dense thicket, but its influence may be sought among the so-called 'Ayrshire Roses', of which a few linger in old gardens. For these please see the next chapter, and for its possible connection with the Musk Rose see page 49.

> Then will I raise aloft the milk-white Rose,
> With whose sweet smell the air shall be perfumed.
>
> Shakespeare, *2 Henry VI.*

Redouté, vol. i, Plate 89.
Andrews, Plates 1 and 2. White and pink forms. Unnatural. Plate 3. Double pink Ayrshire.
Willmott, Plate 11. Excellent.
Lawrance, Plate 86. 'The White Dog Rose.' Poor.
Botanical Magazine, t.2054. The figure is of R. *arvensis*, and hence the editor's inability to distinguish the Ayrshires from R. *arvensis*.
Journal des Roses, Décembre 1907. 'Thoresbyana', a double white Ayrshire.
Sowerby, vol. iii, Plate 476.
The Garden, vol. lvi, p. 233. A good monochrome photograph of a spray and also a plant in full flower.
Jekyll, photograph of a plant in full flower, facing p. 30.

Hybridized with a China rose, R. *arvensis* gave R. *ruga*. This was a beautiful rose, according to illustrations, but I have found it to be scentless.
Botanical Register, t.1389.
Willmott, Plate 55.

'Bobbie James'. See page 47.

BRUNONII. The Himalayan Musk Rose. It is a native of the Himalayas, and, according to Miss Willmott, is found from Afghanistan to Kashmir, Simla, Garhwal, Kumaon, and Nepal. It flowered in this country in 1823 and was originally classed as a variety of R. *moschata*, R. *m. nepalensis*. It is a very vigorous species with big hooked prickles, sending canes over a building or into trees up to 30 or 40 feet. The leaves are greyish, downy, of extreme drooping elegance, with narrow leaflets. The flowers are borne on downy stalks in a rather tight and inelegant corymb. The heps small, oval. Heavy fragrance. Apt to suffer in cold winters.

This rose could not be confused with R. *moschata* of Miller and Herrmann, and I am at a loss to know why there should ever have been any doubt as to its identity. The picture became confused in later years and today the old R. *moschata* is practically unknown, its place having been taken by the spurious Musk Rose. (See under R. *moschata*, and also Chapter 3.)
Willmott, Plate 37.
Andrews, Plate 82. R. *napaulensis*. Possibly incorrect, as the prickles shown are straight instead of hooked.
Botanical Magazine, t.4030.
Botanical Register, vol. x, Plate 829. R. *moschata nepalensis*, the Nepal Musk Rose. The information given is controversial.
Flore des Serres, vol. iv, Plate 366. Reverse of plate in *Botanical Magazine*.

BRUNONII 'La Mortola'. 1954. A particularly fine form of R. *brunonii*, which was brought by E. A. Bunyard from the famous garden whose name it bears; I secured it from Kiftsgate Court, where the late Mrs J. B. Muir had planted it, and introduced it, with her permission, under this name. Over a wall and outbuilding at Kiftsgate it has made a splendid mound some 30 feet high by 40 feet across. Foliage long, limp, greyish and downy; large pure white flowers in good clusters, the petals having distinctly mucronate apices; medium-sized oval heps. Richly fragrant. Apt to suffer in cold winters. Unquestionably the most ornamental of the *brunonii* group. (Fig. 1; also photograph, Plate 3.)

CERASOCARPA. Introduced in 1914. Discovered by

Augustine Henry in the district near Ichang, Central China, where also grows R. *chinensis*. Long, pointed, rather leathery leaves and panicles of small white fragrant flowers borne on markedly glandular pedicels. Globose fruit, dark red. I have not grown this.

Botanical Magazine, t.8688. Shows attractive flowers.

FILIPES. Western China. Introduced in 1908. Though seldom seen in gardens this species should take a high place. The only form that I have grown or seen is one secured, probably from the Roseraie de l'Haÿ, by the late E. A. Bunyard, but so far I have found no record of it in his writings. A plant was purchased from him by Mrs Muir about 1938, and still grows strongly at Kiftsgate Court. It makes shoots 20 feet long in a season, is about 100 feet wide and is steadily invading bushes and trees within reach, including a copper beech, in which it has achieved a height of about 50 feet. I have heard of another old plant of this growing in Yorkshire. The young shoots are richly tinted with brown and copper, and the leaves are of light green with 5 to 7 leaflets. When in flower or fruit it is a most astonishing sight: the corymbs of blossom may be 18 inches across, composed of a hundred or more small, cupped, creamy white flowers with yellow stamens, borne on thread-like stalks. These slender stalks give it the name of 'filipes'. Small oval heps. Its fragrance is equally remarkable, and it is undoubtedly a very fine type, and should be grown wherever space can be given to it.

This particular form is being distributed by nurseries as 'Kiftsgate', thus distinguishing it from other possibly inferior forms of R. *filipes*, and also drawing attention to the garden where it thrives so well. Together with R. *longicuspis* it flowers rather later than most in this group, often remaining in beauty until late July in the south of England. It takes some years to become established, and disappoints the impatient; for them I recommend R. *longicuspis*, but for those who garden on good soil in a reasonably sheltered area, I would choose 'Kiftsgate' provided there is room for it. (Photographs, Plates 1 and 2.)

Botanical Magazine, t.8894. A plate and description of the wild species. The Kiftsgate rose appears to be very near if not identical.

HELENAE. Central China, whence it was introduced in 1907. Reaching 15 or 20 feet, this is another of the big scrambling roses for growing over hedgerows and trees; its main characters, to distinguish it from its relatives, are the strong hooked prickles, and leaves having 7 to 9 leaflets pubescent beneath or at least on the veins. The flowers are creamy white, borne in a fairly regular, round-topped, umbel-like corymb. The dark green of the leaves shows up the flowers to great advantage, and it is as fragrant as any. It is spectacular when in bloom, as the flowers are in dense snowball-like heads, and is a plant of extraordinary beauty in fruit, the closely held bunches of small, oval heps being conspicuous at a distance. Though the flowers are held aloft, the fruits droop in graceful bunches from their own weight, and are extremely attractive in late autumn. After the severe winter of 1962–3 it produced no flowers at Sunning-dale, although its growths had not suffered.

Hu, vol. ii, t.77. A line drawing.

R.H.S. *Journal*, vol. xlvii, Plate 195. (Monochrome photograph.)

HENRYI. Central and Eastern China. Introduced in 1907. Bears some resemblance to R. *helenae*, but has glabrous leaves and orbicular fruits. For many years I have grown what was given to me as R. *gentiliana* (R. *henryi*) and distributed it, but on examination my plant proved to be the hybrid 'Polyantha grandiflora' (see page 43).

LONGICUSPIS. Prior to 1915. Sometimes considered synonymous with R. *sinowilsonii* and R. *lucens*. Western China. Like the Kiftsgate R. *filipes*, this species flowers after most of these Musk Roses are over, and is therefore doubly valuable. Its young shoots are reddish, becoming green, extremely vigorous, reaching 20 feet in length in one season, with hooked thorns, and bearing rather sparsely dark green glossy leathery leaves with 7 leaflets. Like all these roses, in the second year the flower shoots appear in every leaf axil, bearing in this species large open corymbs containing up to one hundred and fifty blooms on the principal shoots. The flowers are deep cream in bud opening to milk-white, with conspicuous yellow stamens and a glorious fragrance of bananas. R. *mulliganii* is similar to this species. A very satisfactory garden rose often growing well where 'Kiftsgate' will not thrive, but not quite so overwhelmingly vigorous as that variety. The hundreds of tiny heps are attractive though not so conspicuous as those of R. *helenae*. (Fig. 2.) See also page 190.

MOSCHATA. The Musk Rose. Its native countries are variously given as Madeira, North Africa (Barbary), Spain, and Southern Europe to Western Asia, and it is supposed to have been brought to England in the early years of the first Elizabethan Age, as recorded by Hakluyt. Its name was recorded by Bauhin in 1671, and it was described by Herrmann in 1762 and by Miller in 1768. It grows to about 12 feet, has glabrous leaves, oval rather than elliptic, with downy stalks and downy veins on the reverse, and downy flower stems and calyx. The flowers are borne in wide branching heads, cream, single, the petals reflexing often by noon on the day of opening, deliciously fragrant (of Musk), and are *not produced until late summer,* carrying on until autumn. Thus it is an outstanding and valuable garden plant, and as a progenitor of our garden roses and for further hybridizing it is noteworthy. Redouté records that it was used for distilling perfumes in Tunis. Miller records that it 'varies with double flowers'. (Fig. 3.)

Andrews, Plate 93. A good portrait.

Lawrance, Plate 64. The 'Single Musk Rose'. Not unrecognizable.

Redouté, vol. i, Plate 33. Good.

As may be read in Chapter 3, the above rose was almost extinct, its place having been taken in botanic gardens by a well-known plant, perhaps a hybrid. Bean (*Trees and Shrubs*) admits to some confusion and also states that the green-leaved form in cultivation was hardier than that with glaucous leaves. He was no doubt describing the splendid old plant which used to grow in the rose dell at Kew, and which was identical with the enormous specimen which achieved a height of 40 or 50 feet on the Austrian pines on the island at the Botanic Garden at Cambridge. Both of these venerable plants have been destroyed to make way for improvements. Both had a basal stem about a foot through, and the Kew plant made a thicket some 50 feet across. It was a great delight to stand to leeward of it at flowering time, and to savour its fragrance in the air. This 'botanic garden form' of R. *moschata*, if I may so call it in the absence of a proper name, has been widely distributed as R. *moschata* by nurseries (including my own until 1964) for many years, and is a spectacular garden plant. It is of course possible that this was the rose described by Ray as R. *moschata major*, a summer flowering plant, but so far I have found no figure of his plant for comparison.

This plant has greenish brown young wood, nearly straight prickles, limp, long, attenuated leaves, glabrous above, downy on the midrib below, somewhat purplish when young but turning to grey-green or light green later, with 5 to 7 leaflets. Flowers usually in corymbs of about seven, 2 inches wide, followed by small oval heps. The scent is powerful and delicious, particularly in the evening, and carries well in the air. The colour of the leaves and the white of the flowers gives a cool fresh appearance to this rose, which is lacking in others of this Section, excepting R. *brunonii* and R. *soulieana*. Its lightness makes it particularly suitable for growing over yew or holly trees, or other shrubs of dark colouring. In common with R. *brunonii* it should be given full sunshine and a position somewhat sheltered from cold winds, as its long summer growths continue to grow until the autumn, and are sometimes spoiled by winter frosts.

Willmott, Plate 33. This portrait has the general appearance of the old R. *moschata* of Herrmann, but lacks the reflexing petals and the oval leaves; I conclude therefore that it is the present rose.

MOSCHATA PLENA. R. *moschata semi-plena*, R. *m. minor flore pleno*. This, the 'Coroneola that beareth in Autume' of Parkinson's *Theatrum Botanicum*, is recorded by many old writers as indistinguishable from the single type, except by its extra petals; Herrmann states that it also differs from the type in not having semi-pinnate calyces; Thory, not quite so strong-growing and with smaller prickles; Andrews, that it is a sport occasionally produced by the single type. As recorded in Chapter 3, my double form occurred on one-year-old plants propagated from the old type plant at Myddelton House, which had produced only five-petalled flowers during the previous season. I am satisfied that this present sport, if such it be, is identical with the Redouté drawing. Thory in Redouté describes it as a native of Indostan. He records as historical fact a legend found in many books, that the Mogul Princess Nour Jehan was the first to notice an oily substance floating on a stream of rose-water which had been contrived to flow through the royal garden at a time of fête, and from this discovery started the industry of extracting Attar or Otto of roses. By attributing this discovery to R. *moschata plena* Thory poses a query: Had this rose been introduced from Europe to Kashmir and was it grown commercially to produce rose-water in copious quantity, or should we understand that R. *brunonii* was used, a native of Northern India? (Fig. 3.)

Redouté, vol. i, Plate 99. R. *moschata flore semi-plena*. A superlatively beautiful and accurate portrait of the Double Musk Rose, shewing the characteristic reflexing of the petals, which is not shewn in the following drawings.

Andrews, Plate 94. The Double Musk Rose. A good drawing, but flowers are not characteristic.

Lawrance, Plate 53. The Double Musk Rose. Poor.

Jacquin (*Plantorum Rariorum*). Exaggerated.

Roessig, Plate 27. 'Le Rosier Musqué.' A semi-double form, described as R. *corymbifera alba hispanica*—a doubtful and confusing appellation. A poor drawing.

MOSCHATA **'Autumnalis'.** I include this rose with some hesitation, since I cannot vouch for the name; it is not in any book I have consulted, but occurs in a Daisy Hill Nursery catalogue dated 1912. It is strange that it is so little known, for it is a pretty plant, with a few hooked thorns; light yellowish-green small leaves, limp and matt, and does not flower until August, carrying on until the autumn. Dainty sprays of small semi-double blossoms on softly downy stalks; silky petals, deep creamy buff on opening from pink-tinted yellowish buds, fading to cream, with yellow stamens and a delicious fragrance. It is apt to be damaged in hard winters and should be given the shelter of a wall. The thornless branchlets proceed in zigzag fashion from leaf to leaf. Possibly a Noisette of very early origin, such as 'Muscate Perpetuelle' or perhaps one of the 'autumn-flowering Musk Roses' mentioned in old books. The zigzag shoots are also present in another Noisette, 'Alister Stella Gray'. *Addendum 1983 Edition*: I incline more and more to the likelihood that this 'Autumnalis' rose is really Mrs. Gore's 'Princesse de Nassau' of 1897; see my notes in the Royal National Rose Society's *Annual* for 1983.

MOSCHATA NASTARANA. R. *pissartii*. A geographical form of R. *moschata*, Herrmann, reputedly introduced from Persia in 1879, and always described as more vigorous than R. *moschata*. The plate in Willmott's *The Genus Rosa* shows a semi-double form, although I have found no mention of this doubling elsewhere. I have not seen this rose.
Willmott, Plate 39. Semi-double. Highly doubtful.
Revue Horticole, 1880, pp. 314, 315. Line drawing and account, showing a single-flowered rose.

MULLIGANII. Introduced from Western China in 1917–19. A beautiful rose similar to R. *rubus*, R. *longicuspis*, and others, equally fragrant and floriferous. Dark plum-coloured young wood and reddish prickles; glossy, rich green leaves.

MULTIFLORA. R. *polyantha*, R. *multiflora thunbergiana*. Japan, Korea. Recorded by Plukenet in 1696 and introduced in 1862, this species has had a profound influence on garden roses in many ways. Though I had known it as a stock for nursery budding for many years, my first real acquaintance with it as a garden plant was at Nymans, Sussex, where it had been allowed to grow naturally, arching its smooth long stems over the path, and bearing freely the narrow somewhat pubescent leaves with usually 9 leaflets and pyramid-shaped trusses of tiny blooms which are so well known throughout the old Rambler group of roses, of which it was the main ancestor. The flowers are single, creamy fading to white, with bright yellow stamens and a powerful fruity fragrance, which is carried freely in the air. It can best be described as an arching shrub, although its shoots will ramble into trees as high as 20 feet. Normally it makes a dense thicket of interlacing lax shoots much like a blackberry. So dense is it, indeed, that when planted closely as a hedge it is rabbit-proof, and so thickly do its stems grow that

it is becoming increasingly popular in the United States and
also in Britain as a roadside plant, for its resilient thicket can
hold a car which runs off the road. What a use for a rose! On
the other hand, how lucky we are to be able to provide so pretty
and sweet a shrub for such a use. It is claimed in America that
it is 'horse high, bull strong and goat tight', and Mr Shepherd
records that over five hundred miles have been planted in Ohio
alone. It is not a greedy shrub; it is a haven for wild life, prevents erosion, holds embankments, and serves as a windbreak
or snow-fence.

After the clusters of flowers are over in July, the heps develop,
reaching maturity in late summer, and lasting through the
autumn into winter. They are about the size of a small pea,
bright red, very dainty, and most useful for cutting. The long
arching sprays may be cut in flower or fruit without damaging
the plant, just as one may cut any rambler, thus encouraging
fresh strong growth which will flower in later years. There are
few easier roses for growing in semi-wild parts of the garden,
and certainly nothing cheaper. If interspersed with something
more flamboyant, like R. *highdownensis* or *moyesii*, a hedge of
interest for a very long period will be achieved, with crops of
flowers and fruit of the respective plants alternating through
summer and autumn.

It is very often seen in gardens without the owner having
any idea of its identity, except that they know it is an understock
which has remained at the expense of its scion, and of course it
is utterly unsuited for a rose bed. The forms known as R.
multiflora japonica (thorny) and R. *m. simplex* (thornless) are
those used most often as understocks for budding, and differ
but little from a horticultural point of view; either will make a
charming plant, but both are rather small-flowered. Another
understock, 'Cress and Danieli', is undoubtedly the best of all
forms to grow for its beauty. The flowers, trusses, and foliage
are all of a high order. It was raised in the United States.
Willmott, Plate 23. Excellent.
Step, vol. ii, Plate 79.
Botanical Magazine, t.7119.

Yet another understock, known as R. *multiflora* 'De la
Grifferaie', is also sometimes used for budding, and as a

consequence it is also often seen in gardens, having outlived its scion. It is one of the 'old-fashioned roses' which are most often sent in for naming, being lusty, vigorous, prolific, and highly scented. The flowers are fully double, opening bright cerise and fading to pale lilac-pink (reminding one of R. *multiflora platyphylla*), and may often be mistaken at first glance for an old French rose to which it may well be related. Its scent and vigour will ensure its remaining in cultivation long after it has been completely given up as an understock. I have been unable to trace its origin, and it may not be related to R. *multiflora* in spite of its name, but possibly connected with R. *setigera*.

Jamain and Forney, Plate 52. Poor.

Leroy, Plate 2. Excellent.

MULTIFLORA CARNEA. A double form of R. *m. cathayensis* which I have not seen, but which was introduced in 1804 and was a favourite for many years.

Botanical Magazine, t.1059. Poor.

Redouté, vol. ii, Plate 67. Exquisite.

Roses et Rosiers, Plate 41. A poor copy of part of the Redouté portrait.

Duhamel, vol. vii, Plate 17.

Drapiez, vol. ii, Plate 113. Poor.

Reeves, vol. ii, Plate 38 possibly refers.

MULTIFLORA CATHAYENSIS. A variant with single pink flowers which was brought from China in 1907. Like its type-species it is vigorous and thrifty, and these characters together with its scent might keep it in cultivation. White flowers, blush-tipped; downy backed leaves of dull blue-green, rather coarse and reminiscent of 'Seven Sisters'.

Journal des Roses, Juin 1886. Nos. 3 and 4 may apply.

Hu, t.76. A pen drawing.

MULTIFLORA NANA. I have found no record of its origin, but it is available from seedsmen as R. *multiflora polyantha* or R. *carteri*, flowering in two months or so from date of sowing the seeds. A pretty, dwarf, bushy mutant or hybrid, not climbing, bearing sprays of palest pink or creamy-white single blooms all the growing season, followed by tiny red heps. The white is usually taller than the pink; both are sweetly scented.

MULTIFLORA PLATYPHYLLA. 'Seven Sisters Rose.' R. *cathayensis platyphylla*. A double pink rose introduced by Sir Charles Greville from Japan between 1815 and 1817, and probably a hybrid of R. *multiflora*. In the days when there were no coloured ramblers it was highly prized, and it is still grown on account of its origin, floriferousness, vigour, and charm of colouring. Its very name recalls its supposedly 7 flowers in the truss (usually many more) each of a different tint according to age; they open a bright deep cerise-purple, and fade to palest mauve or ivory white before dropping. Large, broad, light green leaves. It is somewhat fragrant, in the R. *multiflora* tradition, but with an admixture of the 'fresh-apple' fragrance of R. *wichuraiana*. Although a vigorous plant achieving 18 feet in a season, its canes sometimes suffer from early autumn frost, and it does best in full sun on a wall. It shows affinity with 'Crimson Rambler'. The name 'Seven Sisters' is sometimes erroneously given to 'Félicité et Perpétue' (see page 66). Like all Multifloras it roots easily from cuttings.

Journal des Roses, Juillet 1886. A Japanese portrait, but too bright a colour and not showing the normal variation.

Botanical Register, vol. xvi, Plate 1372. Shews the varying colour well.

Redouté, vol. ii, Plate 69. Flowers not typical.

MULTIFLORA WATSONIANA. This strange little rose can scarcely be considered as an ornament for gardens, but rather as a curiosity. It carries very narrow leaflets, almost linear and spotted and marbled with grey, on its trailing or arching stems, and makes a plant rather like a weak R. *multiflora*, of which it is counted a chimerical mutant or sport. Small flowers, single, pale pink, and round red fruits seldom containing fertile seeds. It was first recorded from a garden near New York in 1870, but is also grown in Japanese gardens, and is therefore probably a Japanese cultivar.

Willmott, t.53. An admirable portrait.

PHOENICEA. Turkey, Syria. Tiny flowers and a rambling habit like that of R. *multiflora*. Its only claim to fame horticulturally is that it is thought to be a parent of the Damask Rose. It is not hardy in Surrey.

'Polyantha grandiflora'. Bernaix, 1886. The name is certainly descriptive, but is not really permissible since it infringes the International Code of Nomenclature; R. *polyantha* is a synonym of R. *multiflora* and is, besides, used as a group-name for the Poly-poms. I have for many years distributed this rose as R. *gentiliana* in error; it is probably R. *multiflora* hybridized with a garden rose—a common occurrence where that species is concerned—as its styles are not united. In all other respects it might be taken for a species in the Synstylae Section; the leaves are smooth, lustrous, richly tinted while young, becoming deep green, with rather deep veins, laciniate stipules, and prickles on the reverse. It bears a few large reddish prickles on its trailing stems, which will reach 20 feet or more, climbing into trees. At midsummer it is covered with creamy white single flowers, opening from creamy yellow buds and with conspicuous orange-yellow stamens, borne on glandular-hispid flower stalks, in clusters of a dozen or so. It has a powerful fragrance of orange. Bunches of medium-sized, oval, orange-red heps last usually through the winter, creating a greater show than any of the true species in this Section except R. *helenae*. In spite of the information given in several books this rose bears little resemblance to R. *moschata* or R. *brunonii*.

Willmott, Plate 34. This does not show the glandular-hispid flower stalks, and the drawing of the heps seems grossly exaggerated.

RUBUS (R. *ernestii*). Central and Western China. Like R. *helenae*, to which it is closely related, it was introduced in 1907 and is even stronger growing, with large hooked prickles; leaflets usually 5, more or less pubescent beneath, and flowers 1½ inches across in dense heads. The buds are often pinkish in colour, deep cream when open with a suffusion of orange-yellow towards the base of the petals. As the stamens are of orange, a freshly open spray gives richer colour effect than other roses in this Section. Powerful *multiflora* fragrance. Early flowering in this Section. Small oval heps. 30 feet.

There are two fairly distinct types of R. *rubus* in cultivation, one quite glabrous and the other downy. According to the latest classification, they should be distinguished as R. *rubus*

rubus (R. *rubus velutescens*) for the original downy type, while the glabrous form, which is the superior garden plant described above, should be called R. *rubus nudescens* (R. *rubus*). R. *r. velutescens* has long-pointed leaves and a short flowering period. Willmott, Plate 507. Line drawing.

SEMPERVIRENS. From Southern Europe and North Africa, this rose is seldom seen in our gardens, being somewhat tender, nearly evergreen, white-flowered, and only slightly fragrant. Leaflets 5 to 7. Its evergreen character has been transmitted to a race of old ramblers of which we still find in gardens 'Félicité et Perpétue', 'Spectabilis', and 'Adélaïde d'Orléans'. (See Chapter 4.) They are freely pictured in *Roses for English Gardens* by Gertrude Jekyll. Supposedly a parent of the Ayrshire Roses. (See page 58.)

Redouté, vol. ii, Plate 15.
Redouté, vol. ii, Plate 49. R. *sempervirens latifolia.*
Roessig, Plate 32, 'Rose toujours verte'. *Rosa sempervirens.*
Willmott, Plate 5.
Andrews, Plate 89.
Lawrance, Plate 45. Good.
Botanical Register, vol. vi, Plate 465.
Duhamel, vol. iii, Plate 13. Poor.

SETIGERA. The 'Prairie Rose' of the eastern United States. A shrubby species which I have described in *Shrub Roses of Today*. Being of considerable hardiness it was used by breeders, notably Horvath in the United States, in an effort to obtain hardy climbing roses for cold districts, but they are mostly insufficiently distinct to be popular for the British climate. I have grown 'Doubloons' (a good yellow), 'Jean Lafitte', and 'Long John Silver'; Komlosy has illustrations of two older hybrids, 'Beauty of the Prairies' and 'Queen of the Prairies'; to these may be added 'Baltimore Belle'. 'American Pillar' also has R. *setigera* in its parentage.

Willmott, Plate 71. The colour is far too near to salmon, and shews none of the mauve tinting of the original.
Meehan's Monthly, vol. viii, Plate 5. Poor.
Redouté, vol. iii, Plate 71. R. *rubifolia*. This is not recognizable.

SINOWILSONII. Western China. Considerable confusion surrounds the botanical status of this rose and R. *longicuspis*. They have been considered synonymous, but as grown at Kew and Bodnant, and at Wakehurst and Borde Hill, Sussex, R. *sinowilsonii* is quite distinct from any other rose I have seen. The plant is most conspicuous in the summer on account of its shining red-brown angled shoots, thorns of the same colour, and the seven broad but long-pointed leaflets, deeply veined and corrugated and coarsely toothed, of lustrous dark green above while beneath they are of glossy, rich, purplish red-brown. The flowers are white, borne several together, but not in the first rank of beauty. *No rose is so handsome in leaf*, and it would be worth a place on any warm sunny wall for this character alone; it is not particularly hardy, and will only otherwise thrive in sheltered gardens. Introduced in 1904.

SOULIEANA. A Chinese species with greyish leaves and white flowers, and bushy growth. Described in *Shrub Roses of Today* as it is more of a shrub than a climber—though it can produce shoots 12 to 15 feet long in a season when established.
Willmott, Plate 57.
Botanical Magazine, t.8158. Too yellow.

WICHURAIANA. This trailing evergreen rose has had great influence on rose-breeding during this century but as a species it has remained in obscurity, usually being found only in botanic gardens in this country. It was introduced in 1891 from Japan, but is also found wild in Korea, Formosa, and Eastern China. Known as the 'Memorial Rose' owing to its use in cemeteries in the United States.

It lies prostrate on the ground, which it covers with trailing stems, rooting as they grow, and bears numerous small, shining, dark green leaves, with 7 to 9 blunt-ended leaflets. These make a splendid ground-cover and background to the clusters of flowers, which are small, single, white with rich yellow stamens, borne in small pyramid-shaped clusters, very sweetly scented, and do not appear until late summer, usually in August. The flower branches bear 3-lobed leaves and numerous bracts. Tiny heps follow. It can of course be trained upright on supports, and its few hooked prickles help it to scramble through bushes and trees up to 15 feet or so, after which, if left to itself, it will form cascades of trailing shoots.

During the decades when roses were judged only for the size and brilliance of their flowers, it is remarkable that this insignificant plant was ever deemed worthy for hybridization. But today when a new appreciation of plants—as opposed to flowers—is developing, it is obvious that this species is a plant of very great garden value. For instance, it is most unusual to be able to number a rose among first-class ground-covering plants, and especially an *evergreen* rose. Then again, few roses are at their best in August. I know only two others that do not actually start to flower until that month, and those are R. *moschata* and the plant I grow as R. *moschata* 'Autumnalis'. The scent of R. *wichuraiana* is delicious. (Fig. 5.)

R. *luciae* is very closely related, with somewhat smaller flowers and fewer leaflets, and occurs wild in the same districts, but has not proved so hardy in cultivation. According to the latest taxonomic ruling, if one considers the two species as synonymous the name *luciae* takes priority; as *wichuraiana* is so well known it will be simplest to continue using it in the following chapters, with reservations in Chapter 5. Conspicuous among descendants of these two roses respectively are the rambling roses of the 'Dorothy Perkins' and the 'Albéric Barbier' groups. R. *wichuraiana* has further claim to fame, having been one of the parents of the new tetraploid species R. *kordesii*. See also page 191.

Revue Horticole, 1898, pp. 105, 106. Line drawings.
Willmott, Plate 19. Very good.
Botanical Magazine, t.7421 (R. *luciae*). Exaggerated.
Journal des Roses, Mai 1902. Poor.
Jekyll, facing p. 7 (photograph), as a ground-cover.

WICHURAIANA VARIEGATA: I have been unable to trace the origin of this pretty little plant. So far it has not flowered with me, and it is very much less vigorous than the species. The shoots of my plants have not exceeded 3 feet. The dainty leaves and the growing stems show much creamy variegation, some extremes of the branches being wholly without green colouring, and the growing tips and unfolding leaves are often coral-pink.

Delightful for cutting, but hardly a good garden plant, and requires a sheltered position with a little shade at the hottest time of the day.

'Bobbie James'. Sunningdale Nurseries, 1960. An unnamed foundling which it was my privilege to name in memory of one of the grand old men of gardening, the Honourable Robert James, a friend and correspondent of many years, who preserved many lovely roses and other plants in his beautiful garden at St Nicholas, Richmond, Yorkshire. It is the type of extremely fragrant rose which he would have appreciated, and it would have contributed nobly to his 'garden of roses, not a rose garden', as he used to say. It is extremely vigorous, with large, long-pointed, fresh green, glossy foliage and large heads of creamy white flowers, inclined to have an extra row or two of petals, with the usual glorious fragrance of the Synstylae Section. Bright yellow stamens surround the united styles. Small oval heps. Will probably achieve 25 feet. A really splendid luxuriant and prolific plant, probably related to R. *multiflora* and deserving the strongest of supports. (Fig. 6.)

'Wedding Day'. Stern, 1950. This so closely approaches the characters of the species in this Section that I think it warrants inclusion here rather than in the next chapter. It is a hybrid of R. *sinowilsonii* raised by Sir Frederick Stern at Highdown, Sussex, 1950. Green wood and scattered red thorns; rich green, glossy leaves, slightly serrated and gracefully poised. The trusses of flowers are very large; each bloom emerges from a yolk-yellow bud, opening to creamy white with vivid orange-yellow stamens around the united styles. Each petal is broadly wedge-shaped with a mucronate apex, giving a starry effect. Exceedingly fragrant of oranges. A prolific grower and flowerer, it will cover barns, hedgerows, and trees, probably achieving a maximum height or length of 35 feet, creating a billowy mass of leaves and flowers; it can also be used to cover the ground. Unfortunately the petals are inclined to 'spot' after rain, becoming blotched with pink when fading, which spoils the effect.

3

The Mystery of the Musk Rose

I saw the sweetest flower wild nature yields,
A fresh blown musk-Rose 'twas the first that threw
Its sweets upon the summer; graceful it grew
As in the wand that Queen Titania wields
And, as I feasted on its fragrance,
I thought the garden rose it much excelled.

John Keats, 1795–1821.

THE ONLY disappointment about a title such as this is that it gives too much away at the start. Few writers of detective stories would choose such a transparent title, but there *was* a mystery about the Musk Rose, and I am happy to say that part of it is now solved. The partial solution clears up several posers and will undoubtedly cause us to reassess the potentiality of the Musk Rose in the parentage of roses; it may well be that its influence was as great as that of R. *gallica* and the China Roses.

When I began to study the Synstylae Section I had no idea that there was any real mystery about the identity of the Musk Rose, R. *moschata*. I had always accepted that the great rose which used to achieve some 40 feet on the pine stems in the University Botanic Garden at Cambridge, and the old giant of the rose dell in the Royal Botanic Garden at Kew, were, both of them, R. *moschata*, THE Musk Rose, described in all the books and a well recognized and noted ancestor of the Damask and Noisette races of roses. The more I delved the more difficult the problem became. This Musk Rose of Kew and Cambridge, Bean and Willmott, is a summer-flowering rose with long narrow leaves; one great crop of bloom and all is over. The Musk Rose of the ancient herbals was an autumn-flowering rose with oval leaves. Then there was

48

the difficulty of reconciling either of these to the native Musk Rose of Shakespeare, Keats, and other poets. Lastly there was the indeterminate fragrance: What *was* musk, anyway? Why should a rose smell of it, and why should the little musk plant have lost its scent?

As so often happens in trying to unravel horticultural problems, botanical niceties—useful though they may be—were not of such value as the more outstanding characters of the various roses concerned. Let me make it clear that we are concerned in this mystery with no less than three distinct roses—one for Shakespeare, one for the herbalists, and one for the botanic gardens. Though Shakespeare's is comparatively easy to define, I doubt if we shall ever know just where and how the other two originated.

Let us start with the English Musk of the poets. I think there is no doubt that both Shakespeare and Keats described in their well-known lines (at the heads of Chapters 2 and 3) a native rose, and, bearing everything in mind and allowing a little poetic licence (not much is needed) I am sure their rose was R. *arvensis*. It is a native of this country, frequents copses and bosky hedgerows, flowers with the honeysuckle, and is deliciously fragrant. Shakespeare refers to a summer-flowering plant (not autumn-flowering), as does Bacon, mentioning specifically the month of July which is the normal time of flowering for R. *arvensis* in the south of England. To me, this trailing rose with purplish stems, neat leaves, and clusters of creamy scented flowers is even more appealing and freshly delightful than R. *canina*, the Dog Brier, which flowers rather earlier and is by comparison a coarse thorny shrub.

Turning next to the herbalists' rose, the true (foreign) R. *moschata* of Elizabethan and Jacobean days did not flower until the autumn. John Gerard, in his *Herball* of 1597, says that 'the Muske Rose flowereth in Autumn, or the fall of the leafe: the rest flower when the Damask and red Rose do'. John Parkinson, in *Paradisi in Sole Paradisus Terrestris*, 1629, describes R. *moschata simplex* and *multiplex*: 'The Muske Rose, both single and double, rise up oftentimes to a very great height, that it overgroweth any arbour in a garden, or being set by an house side, to bee ten or twelve foote high, or more, but more especially the single kinde, with many green farre spread branches, armed with a few sharpe great thornes, as the wilder sorts of roses are, whereof these are accounted to be kindes, having small darke green leaves on them, not much bigger than the leaves of Eglantine: . . . the double bearing more double flowers, as if they were once or twice more double than the single, with yellow thrummes also in the middle, both of them of a very sweete and pleasing smell, resembling Muske.' He adds that the single and double do not flower until the end of the summer and autumn.

John Ray wrote the second volume of his *Historia plantarum* in 1688 and mentions R. *moschata minor*, the Musk Rose, growing to a height of 10 or 12 feet with leaves like those of R. *alba*, glabrous above, hairy beneath; also R. *moschata major*, a bigger plant flowering in June. This, he says, on account of its flowering time can scarcely be considered the true and genuine R. *moschata* species, which flowers not before the end of summer and the beginning of autumn.

Johannes Herrmann's *Dissertatio inauguratis botanico medica de Rosa*, 1762, gives a full description in Latin of R. *moschata* and states that it flowers in autumn. Philip Miller produced the 8th edition of his *The Gardener's Dictionary* in 1768; he calls his Musk Rose R. *moschata*, with a synonym R. *moschata major*. The latter is a name used in a vague description by J. Bauhin in 1651 (*Historiae plantarum universalis*). Likewise Aiton, *Hortus Kewensis*, 1789; Jacquin, *Plantarum rariorum horti Schönbrunnensis*, 1797; we may go on, looking at Roessig, 1802–20; Andrews, 1805; Dumont de Courset, 1811; Redouté, 1817–24, and lastly at Loudon's *Hortus Britannicus*, 1830; all repeat the late season of flowering and, where such particulars are included, all state the oval leaf and the height roughly from 7 to 12 feet—sometimes not specific-ally given but compared with the Sweet Brier—and the native habitat is variously ascribed to Spain, Madeira, Barbary. Although many of the drawings are not recognizable and the descriptions are not careful in the oldest books, I think the above all amounts to a fairly clear picture of a Musk Rose imported from South-western Europe, North Africa or Madeira, grown in gardens for its sweet scent and late-flowering character and being used to cover arbours or to make a fair-sized shrub. Apart from a few Autumn Damask roses this would have been the only rose to have flowered late in the season, and as such would have been greatly treasured. To this we must add that R. *moschata* in any form was the only rose that could be called 'climbing' in those early days of gardening in Britain, for none of its Far East relatives had been introduced, and R. *phoenicea*, R. *arvensis*, and R. *sempervirens*, if cultivated, were of little value, though the second was well known in the hedgerows. It was therefore a very important garden plant, and was listed by nurserymen; W. Masters of Canterbury (1831) mentions the double form flowering in September and October, and William Paul (1848) writes 'abundant blooms, especially in the autumn'; Thomas Rivers (1843) includes R. *moschata* in his 'autumnal rose garden'. He adds some further details, stating that there was in the early days of the French Republic a rose tree at Ispahan (Persia), called 'the Chinese Rose Tree, fifteen feet high . . . seeds were sent to Paris and produced the common Musk Rose . . . large and very old plants of the Musk Rose may sometimes be seen in the gardens of old English country houses'. Other writers also mention this plant. Though it could have been a hybrid it was more likely to have been the original Musk Rose.

We cannot of course take every description as authentic; many old writers (like modern ones!) borrow from their predecessors, and there is not absolute unanimity about the time of flowering among writers of the sixteenth and seventeenth centuries. Exaggeration also played its part: thus a rose whose leaves were less rough than others would be called smooth; a deep pink rose, red (before really red roses arrived in the nineteenth century); and one which produced a few late blooms after the main crop would have this character magnified.

It is here that the mystery makes itself so greatly felt. It will be noted that up to the present there has been no mention of a gigantic climbing rose whose shoots reach 30 to 50 feet, bearing long drooping leaves and a spectacular midsummer burst of large white fragrant blossoms. Such a rose was clearly unknown unless Ray has this in mind when describing his R. *moschata major*. Yet this is the type of rose described by Bean, Willmott, and the R.H.S. Dictionary, and is commonly found in rose collections today under the name of R. *moschata*. Rehder describes the old Musk Rose—not this big summer-flowering plant—but he does not mention its flowering time.

I found a few recent writings helpful in solving the mystery. A little book by Cochet-Cochet and Mottet, 1896, claims that R. *moschata* flowers in June and July, and compares it with R. *brunonii*, which differs by its villousness. Canon Ellacombe, in *In a Gloucestershire Garden*, 1895, states that 'the Musk Rose is not a very attractive rose, and is now very seldom seen, having been supplanted by its near relation R. *brunonii* from Nepal, probably only a geographical variety of the old musk rose . . .'

In *The Shakespeare Garden*, Esther Singleton gives a conversation from Mrs Gaskell's *My Lady Ludlow*, 1859: 'That is the old Musk Rose, Shakespeare's Musk rose, which is dying out through the Kingdom now.' This is a strange statement for a character in a novel to make. Furthermore, 'the scent is unlike the scent of any other rose, or of any other flower'.

E. H. Wilson, the famous gardener, botanist, and plant collector, writes: 'The original Musk rose, R. *moschata*, appears to have been native of the Pyrenees, but has long been lost to cultivation, and its name applied to a vigorous climbing rose (R. *brunonii*) . . . whose flowers have the odor of Musk.' This I culled from his book *If I were to make a garden* (1931), prompted by Mrs F. L. Keays in her *Old Roses*. She gives us the American picture, and adds that the Musk Rose of Gerard 'may survive in some old gardens'; further, 'while R. *moschata* continues blooming until frosts cut it, after once started, R. *brunonii* is summer flowering only'. Bailey's *Cyclopedia*, also American, mentions that 'the Musk Rose of the older writers, known since the sixteenth century, seems to have at present almost disappeared from cultivation; the plant generally cultivated under this name is R. *brunonii*. . . .'

R. *brunonii* was introduced in 1812 from Nepal. It is quite obvious that under R. *moschata* Miss Willmott was describing R. *brunonii*— a native 'from Afghanistan to Kashmir, Simla, Garhwal, Kumaon, and Nepal'. From these extractions we can I think conclude that what I have called the gigantic climbing Musk Rose of the botanic gardens is a nearly glabrous form or hybrid of R. *brunonii*. Just when and where it originated and usurped the position of the Old Musk Rose is still a mystery to me. Willmott's portrait appears to be of this usurper, with its long drooping leaves.

I had looked at many gardening books in the hope of further elucidation, and also with the hope of finding a plant of this Old

Musk. Almost the last book I looked at was *My Garden in Summer*, by E. A. Bowles, 1914. Here I found: 'The true and rare old Musk Rose exists here, but in a juvenile state at present, for it is not many years since I brought it as cuttings from the splendid old specimen on The Grange at Bitton, and I must not expect its deliciously scented, late-in-the-season flowers before it has scrambled up its wall space.'

Now, whatever other opinions we might consider, I was prepared to treat Mr Bowles's with the greatest respect: He was an erudite, observant, and highly trained gardener; he had seen the canon's plant flowering late in the season, as he was a frequent visitor to that garden, and he would not have given just 'its wall space' to an enormous grower such as our present-day R. *moschata*, which would need the whole house.

All the above investigation took place during the winter of 1962–3. Many years ago, shortly after the Hitler war, E. A. Bowles had given me cuttings of several roses from his garden, and among them was one he called 'Shakespeare's Musk'. The cuttings grew well, I thought, but eventually proved to be 'Rambling Rector'. My interest in ramblers in those days was not great; the cuttings may somehow have been mixed by my then nursery staff, for conditions were not easy. I had no idea then what the plant was supposed to be, but I remembered that the cuttings were given to me off the house wall. I resolved to go and see if the plant was still growing.

Through the kindness of Mr W. G. MacKenzie, who, together with the curatorship of the Chelsea Physic Garden combines the chairmanship of the committee caring for Mr Bowles's garden, now an outlying part of London University, I visited Myddelton House in late August 1963. And there on a cold north-west facing wall of the house was a rose just coming into flower. It was without doubt the Old Musk Rose. I had walked straight to it. A pencil drawing of this plant faces page 129 (Fig. 3.) Thinking to correlate things still further, when I was in the neighbourhood of Bath during the autumn I made my way to Bitton, to Canon Ellacombe's garden. The present owners kindly gave me permission to wander round. There was the great cut-leaf beech, the fine Tulip tree and Maidenhair tree mentioned in his books, together with many another shrub and tree, *Photinia serrulata*, *Xanthoceras sorbifolia*, parrotia, sycopsis, and wistaria . . . but no Musk Rose, unfortunately.

Besides making a drawing of Bowles's Musk Rose I pressed a specimen; both were compared with Herrmann's description and Linnaeus' specimens by my old friend Dr W. T. Stearn of the Botany Department of the British Museum, who pronounced them all one and the same. Both Herrmann and also Miller, whose names are used in various books as the authority for the naming of R. *moschata*, take the species' name from prior publication by Caspar Bauhin, 1671. So far, so good.

The propagating material secured in 1963 was used partly for budding on brier stocks and partly for cuttings. The latter did not flower in their first summer under my care, but the three budded plants produced several flower heads, and judge of my surprise when every bloom turned out to be double! Here was a further puzzle: had I by chance used a twig for budding which during its year of growth had sported to the double form, or was the plant given to producing single and double blooms irregularly but constantly? Mr John Rogers, head gardener since Mr Bowles's day at Myddelton House, assures me he has seen only single flowers on the old plant; certainly the terminal flowers which I saw in the first place were simply five-petalled.

After carefully looking at portraits of double forms in old books I feel sure that my double compares exactly with the best illustration, that of Redouté. Other portraits are stylized and obviously inexact. I therefore conclude that the double form which has occurred in this unexpected way is a repetition of Parkinson's 'Coroneola'; in his *Theatrum Botanicum* of 1640 he states that 'the Coroneola that beareth in Autume is generally held by all writers to be the Double Muske Rose, which cometh only at that time and is very sweet'.

On referring again to Andrews we read that the double form 'may justly be called the prototype of the former [single]; more especially as upon the single plant double flowers have sometimes been found, but not frequent'. Miller says that the Musk Rose varies with double flowers. Only the passing years will shew how constant my double form will remain.

Its actual status is extremely important when considering the origin of the Damask and other roses (see Dr Hurst's paper in my book *The Old Shrub Roses*). Nobody has yet explained how the Autumn Damask originated; why should a union of R. *moschata* combined with R. *gallica* produce flowers again in the autumn if both parents were summer-flowering only? The rediscovery of the Old Musk Rose will undoubtedly shed light here. Hurst put forward the idea that the Autumn Damask, grown in Roman days and still in existence, owes its recurrent habit to R. *moschata*. He had little but theory to confirm this, but he recorded having in his possession a dwarf sport of R. *moschata* which was recurrent. This I have not seen. It would be a great advantage if someone could collect seeds of R. *moschata* in the wild, but I must add that the Floras I have consulted are not very encouraging. Lowe in 1868 (*A Manual Flora of Madeira*, vol. i) criticizes Professor Lindley (*Rosarum monographia*) for saying that it is found wild in Spain; 'in Madeira it is certainly not indigenous and is indeed only a rare inmate of gardens shewing no tendency whatever to become naturalized or even common. . . . It is confined to a few gardens in Funchal or Quintas'. Desfontaines in 1798 describes it as a cultivated plant in Tunisia, while Bonnet and Barratte '. . . consider it native or of sub-spontaneous origin at several points along the coast of the Mediterranean'. Jahandiez and Maire, 1931, state it to be cultivated and naturalized here and there in Morocco. Lazaro e Ibiza, in his *Compendio de la Flora Española*, 1921, does not mention it. It may well be therefore that our original old Musk Rose, described as a species, is a garden hybrid raised from that old tree in Persia; such a confusion is not without parallel in other genera. And so I must leave the matter to others with more time and resources at their disposal.

Many old books mention R. *moschata nivea*, which is none other than R. *dupontii*. It is surmised that this is R. *moschata* × R. *gallica*, and therefore is, technically speaking, an Autumn Damask, but it flowers only at midsummer. It is very downy, which might point towards R. *brunonii*, but its date of raising (1817) would seem to preclude that. Another name we find is R. *moschata damascena alba*, which appears to refer to a double white form or hybrid of R. *cinnamomea*.

It is not likely that R. *chinensis* had an influence in the old Musks if they were hybrids, for in old pictures their stems and leaf veins are distinctly shewn as pubescent, and as a general rule China Rose derivatives tend towards glabrousness, and early as well as late flowering. But we cannot altogether rule out its influence, since, through Eastern trade routes, Far East roses may have crept into Europe, married and died out long before our rose histories lead us to believe.

We are left with the description 'Musk scented'. A fact which is little known today was observed by Parkinson, mentioned above, that the Musk Rose bears its scent in its filaments—the threads that bear the anthers, or stamens: 'some there be that have avouched, that the chiefest scent of these roses [the Musk roses] consisteth not in the leaves [petals] but in the threads of the flowers' (*Paradisi in Sole*, etc.). I have found that all species of the Synstylae Section have this character; what the connection between it and their free-floating fragrance is I cannot say; one would need to test all flowers likewise to reach even a comparative conclusion. Parkinson in his *Theatrum botanicum* also has something to say about Musk: '. . . the *Moscheuton* some take to bee the Musk Rose because the stalkes are greener than in other roses, like unto a Mallow, and that the name doth the nearest concurre therewith, but this hath not Olive-like leaves, and therefore it is much doubted of by divers as *Lugdunensis* saith, and taketh that the name commeth not from Muske which was not knowne in *Pliny* his time, but hee rather thinketh it took the name from *Moxus*, because it riseth with many stemmes, or else from *Moxus malleolis pangatur*, because it was planted as well by slippes as vines are, as by rootes. . . .'

This I leave to my readers to accept or question according to their liking. If we take no notice of Parkinson we can but conclude that the name Musk was given to this one rose because of its resemblance to genuine musk. Here Dr Stearn again came to my help: the source of genuine musk is a scent gland, known in the perfumery trade as a 'pod', taken from the little antlerless male Musk Deer (*Moschus moschiferus*) of Central and Eastern Asia. This over-hunted animal is solitary and far from prolific; genuine musk is accordingly very costly. The little phial of tincture of musk which accompanied his letter was sampled and it certainly resembles very closely the delicious penetrating odour of the species of the Synstylae Section. 'Muskiness' seems nowadays to be applied to a heavy odour that one meets in Crown Imperials and 'mollis' azaleas, rather than the true refreshingly sweet musk of the deer and the rose. I was born too late to take note of the fragrance of the little Musk plant before it lost it, and so can offer no observations on this unfortunate occurrence.

4

Old and New Garden Ramblers

Jasmine is all in white and has many loves,
And the broom's betrothed to the bee;
But I will plight with the dainty rose,
For fairest of all is she.

Thomas Hood, 1799–1845.

As EXPLAINED in the previous chapter, certain species of roses, belonging to the Synstylae Section, which have been in cultivation a long time are the foundation of our garden varieties of rambling roses. A hundred years ago the only rambling roses grown were descendants of R. *arvensis*, R. *sempervirens*, and R. *moschata*, and the last named, later uniting more with Shrub and China Roses, tended to produce large-flowered climbers rather than ramblers.

Apart from the few double forms or hybrids which were growing long before, R. *arvensis* produced a little group of double ramblers, mainly white, of great hardiness and excessive vigour but unfortunately with little or no scent. One still comes across old plants of these so-called Ayrshire roses, which must be 'Bennett's Seedling' ('Thoresbyana'), 'Dundee Rambler', or some other old variety. Herr Wilhelm Kordes recently found 'Venusta pendula' and made it available again, but none of these is likely to be considered worth growing today. 'Since perfume is the soul and spirit of a flower' (Alphonse Karr), the only variety that *I* value is 'Splendens', the Myrrh-Scented Rose. Its scent is of a rare quality, and found (so far as I know) only in 'Belle Amour' and the new roses 'Constance Spry' and 'Pink Chiffon'.

There is a long account of the Ayrshire roses in the *Transactions of the Horticultural Society* for 1822, by Joseph Sabine, in which he states that seeds of R. *arvensis* were sent from eastern North America to the Earl of Loudoun at Loudoun Castle, Ayrshire, and there raised. The results were hybrids of R. *arvensis* showing a possibility of hybridity with a garden rose perhaps descended from R. *sempervirens*. He further observes that the information given in the *Botanical Magazine*, t.2054, is incorrect, and the figure refers to R. *arvensis* itself. A good picture of a double white Ayrshire rose is in *Roses et Rosiers*, Plate iii; and in a photograph of a plant in Jekyll's *Roses for English Gardens* between pages 56 and 57.

These 'Ayrshires', as they became known, apart from their hardiness, have perhaps two attributes which might still recommend them for use today. One is that they are prostrate unless given support, and would presumably make a good weed-proof ground-cover; the other is their value for climbing into trees. William Paul, as long ago as 1888, suggested them for this purpose —before wild gardening as such became a vogue—and they have an additional advantage over modern ramblers in that they will thrive and flower *in thin woodland*. R. *arvensis* itself is just as much at home *in shade* as in full exposure. New hybrids might be attempted, with better flowers but incorporating the greater hardiness and tolerance towards shade.

Whatever its influence may have been towards the Ayrshires, the Evergreen Rose, R. *sempervirens*, created another little group of superior quality, mainly at the hands of M. Jacques, who was in charge of the garden of the Duc d'Orléans at Château Neuilly in France from 1824 to 1832; 'Adélaïde d'Orléans' and 'Félicité et Perpétue' are two very beautiful varieties having some of the evergreen trait of the main parent. Their scent is delicate and reminiscent of primroses, and they have well-formed flowers. Others of this group which I have collected are 'Flora' and 'Spectabilis', the last being much less vigorous than any so far mentioned. No gardener who wants a reasonably good representation of old roses can afford to neglect the 'Myrrh-Scented' rose, 'Adélaïde d'Orléans', and 'Félicité et Perpétue'; they are unique; nothing like them has been raised since. See also page 191.

Another little group was derived from R. *setigera*, the American representative of the Synstylae Section; seeds were sown from open-pollinated flowers, and 'Baltimore Belle', 'Beauty of the Prairies', and 'Eva Corinna' resulted in the nursery of Messrs Feast in Baltimore in 1873. These are all exceptionally hardy useful ramblers and are later flowering than most, two attributes of which greater use might be made in present-day hybridizing. 'Erinnerung an Brod' was another hybrid of R. *setigera* deriving from Hungary; it is classed as a Hybrid Perpetual. In *Shrub Roses of Today*, first edition, this rose was ascribed in error to R. *rubrifolia*; not this, but R. *rubifolia* is a synonym of R. *setigera*.

'Madame d'Arblay' and 'The Garland' were, Mr Shepherd records, raised from the same hep, the result of a cross between R. *moschata* and R. *multiflora*, occurring at Tunbridge Wells, Kent. Whatever their parents, they are fragrant blush-white charmers, prolific and vigorous. With them we may group the tremendous plant that is called 'Paul's Himalyan Musk Rambler'.

We owe the ramblers of more recent raising in great part to R. *multiflora*, a Japanese species introduced in 1862, though hybrids or forms of it were introduced from Far East gardens earlier in the century—such as 'Seven Sisters' and the double pink R. *multiflora carnea*; botanically this is now R. *multiflora multiflora*, being regarded as the type species, introduced in 1804. 'Laure Davoust' is one of these early roses, but the main type is of course 'Crimson Rambler'. This is a double crimson garden hybrid of R. *multiflora* which created quite a stir, in spite of being scentless, dull in colour, and subject to mildew. It was the first of several *multiflora* ramblers to achieve considerable popularity, among which none was more free and fragrant than 'Blush Rambler'. The most important contribution of the group to gardens today is the little collection of purple ramblers, three of which are probably hybrids of R. *wichuraiana*. They are 'Veilchen-blau', well scented and early flowering; 'Rose-Marie Viaud', almost pure R. *multiflora*, scentless and late flowering; the remaining two, 'Violette' and 'Bleu Magenta', flower in between, are scentless, and are noted for their rich dark purplish-crimson colouring verging to maroon. They are invaluable for gardens of old or new roses, for they alone with one exception provide purplish colouring among ramblers to act as a contrast to all the other tints, which are mostly pale. The exception is 'Amadis', an old Boursault, which flowers before 'Veilchenblau' is really opened. With all five one can have this colour represented in the garden for five or six weeks in a normal season.

Next we have three creamy yellow varieties, 'Aglaia', the noted great-grandparent of so many Hybrid Musks, but otherwise rather pale and ineffective; and 'Goldfinch', stalwart, prolific, and full of scent, but fading rapidly in sunlight to nearly white. I have also included 'Phyllis Bide', since, though repeat-flowering and of mixed parentage, it is nevertheless a small-flowered rambler.

With the arrival of R. *wichuraiana* all was due to be changed, and its glossy leaves have contributed to the foliage of most of its descendants; its late summer-flowering propensity has also had some effect, and the true *wichuraiana* ramblers do not usually flower until the *multiflora* varieties are over. In the United States, between 1901 and 1920, a string of ramblers was raised by M. H. Walsh in Massachusetts, and several, like 'Excelsa', 'Hiawatha', 'Minnehaha', and 'Lady Gay', were to become favourites. The equally famous 'Dorothy Perkins' also appeared in 1901. None of these would take high marks for fragrance, which is their main point of difference from the *multiflora* ramblers apart from their more glossy leaves. Personally, I would grow 'Débutante' in place of 'Dorothy Perkins', extending a hand towards the latest addition—the beautiful 'Crimson Shower'—and welcoming with open arms 'Sanders' White', that most beautiful and fragrant of all the group, fit to be in any garden of roses.

A tendency is noticeable among these *multiflora* and *wichuraiana* ramblers to lack thorns or scent, or both. While R. *multiflora* certainly produces forms without thorns, and might account for the lack of these in its offspring, both this species and R. *wichuraiana* are extremely fragrant. Therefore it would seem that lack of fragrance must be the responsibility of the other parents.

While that is a general history of the development of ramblers— bearing in mind the other group of *wichuraiana* and *luciae* crosses which, to give them due importance and to keep them quite separate from the above, I have placed in Chapter 5—there are a few odd varieties which go with them, though they are not perhaps closely related. They are isolated hybrids without a real home in these pages, so I include them here. 'Francis E. Lester' and 'Kew Rambler' are both exceptionally fragrant, and that is the only thing they have in common. The second variety brings in R. *soulieana* as a parent with its greyish leaves and orange heps transmitted in part to the hybrid. 'Una' is a charming hybrid of R. *canina* and a rose of Tea derivation, and 'Russelliana', a purplish crimson, very thorny rambler, which is possibly derived from R. *setigera*. 'Rambling Rector', 'Thalia', 'Seagull' are closely related to R. *multiflora*; 'Lykkefund' and 'Helen Patricia', both hybrids of R. *helenae*, complete the selection, with 'Wedding Day' and 'Bobbie James', which were included in Chapter 2.

This little survey has been written so that the roses described in the following pages may be sorted out, but I want to stress again the overriding importance of the dark purple colouring of the few *multiflora* ramblers. If R. *multiflora* had contributed nothing else but these, it would have earned our undying gratitude. 'Dorothy Perkins' and its clan are included to complete the historical picture, although to see an arbour or pergola covered entirely with roses of this popular class is to realize that even these soulless, scentless roses must be given their due, and can look right in the right surroundings.

At the present state of rose hybridization we have to choose, when we want rambling and climbing roses, between the grace of the summer ramblers or the comparative lack of grace of those which flower recurrently. I should never allow the ramblers to be excluded, since they have a quality not provided by anything else. Fortunately a few old roses like 'Blush Noisette' and 'Alister Stella Gray', and some newer varieties like 'Mermaid' and 'New Dawn', show that grace and recurrence of bloom can be combined.

Why have I omitted 'Chaplin's Pink Climber' and 'American Pillar' from the following list? Because they are blatant, almost scentless, and would not be included in my own garden, however large, mainly owing to their growth and size of flower. I have throughout used the accepted name of R. *wichuraiana* as the parent of all these roses; my remarks in Chapter 2 will elucidate the matter of the choice of title.

'Adélaïde d'Orléans'. 1826. This appears to be synonymous with 'Léopoldine d'Orléans' (the two names commemorate the daughters of the then Duc d'Orléans); both were raised by his gardener M. Jacques. 'Adélaïde d'Orléans' is a hybrid of R. *sempervirens*, and like 'Félicité et Perpétue' is partially evergreen. It is vigorous, with long slender shoots, reddish thorns, and neat, small, dark green leaves. The flowers are borne profusely at midsummer only, opening to loosely double flowers from small shapely buds. They hang in clusters, exquisitely, like those of a double Japanese cherry, for which reason it is particularly suitable for training over arches and horizontal supports. I know of no other rose with this lovely quality. The buds are of deep, creamy rose-pink, the colour remaining on the outer petals, while those inside are blush-white. Yellow stamens. Delicate primrose scent. 15 feet. (Plate 1.)

'**Aglaia**'. Schmitt, 1896. R. *multiflora* × 'Rêve d'Or'. This was the first yellow-flowered rambler ever raised. In effect it is like any other Multiflora rambler, but is not so free-flowering as the later, paler 'Goldfinch', though it has a longer flowering season. The flowers are semi-double, cupped, pale canary-yellow with a hint of primrose and fading to lemon-white, with an intense fragrance. Young wood greenish brown; fresh bright green leaves. Occasionally seen hanging over old garden walls, but scarcely worth growing today except for its part in the ancestry of the Hybrid Musk Roses. About 12 feet.

'Aglaia' was one of the Three Graces, the others being 'Euphrosyne' and 'Thalia'. All were used as names for his roses by M. Schmitt of Lyon, France, and it is sad that all have become 'back numbers' as far as roses are concerned, but are they not immortal in all roses—as Grace, Gentleness, and Beauty?

'**Amadis**'. Laffay, 1829. In the days when there were no crimson ramblers, this was called the 'Crimson Boursault'; today, when we have several true crimson varieties, we can place this spectacular plant with the purple ramblers. It is a useful addition for its display occurs before the earliest of these opens. It is thornless, with long strong shoots, green at first becoming purplish-brown with age, smooth green leaves, and abundant flowers in small and large clusters. In some seasons it produces another crop later. The flowers are semi-double, cupped, deep crimson-purple with an occasional white streak or deformed petal, and showing stamens. It is unfortunately practically scentless, but its other characters outweigh this. A valuable shrubby rambler, ideal for contrast with 'Frühlingsgold', 'Agnes', R. *cantabrigiensis*, and other early flowering yellow roses. It is best trained upon poles or a high hedge, and then allowed to hang down in festoons. Will achieve 16 feet. (Plate III.)

The Boursault roses include 'Morlettii', which, as a shrub, I included in *Shrub Roses of Today*; 'Madame de Sancy de Parabère' occurs in this book, page 123, under which variety a note about the race is given, and 'Blush Boursault' in this chapter, below.

'Baltimore Belle'. Feast, 1843. All books acknowledge it to be a hybrid of R. *setigera* (R. *rubifolia*), but are not unanimous about its other parent. I found this many years ago at Walberswick in Suffolk under the name 'Princesse Louise', and have only recently found its correct name in Paris. It is valuable because it flowers late in the rambler season, often lasting into August, and is very hardy. Reddish buds opening to palest flesh-pink, fully double, somewhat incurved flowers, fading to ivory white, often with a 'button eye'. Drooping clusters, pretty growth, fresh green foliage. 10 feet. 'Eva Corinna' is another raised at the same time, which I acquired from the Roseraie de l'Haÿ.

'Bleu Magenta'. This rose reached me from the Roseraie de l'Haÿ near Paris, but I have been unable to trace the name anywhere. This is unfortunate, since it is the largest in flower and the richest in colour of the purplish ramblers. Fully double flowers in dense clusters, darkest violet-crimson fading to dark parma-violet and grey, with an occasional white fleck. Practically scentless. Shining dark green leaves on nearly thornless green wood. An effective garden plant. About 15 feet. The last to flower of the purple ramblers. (Plate II.)

'Blush Boursault'. Prior to 1848. 'Calypso', 'Rose de l'Isle', 'Florida'. A vigorous, thornless, early-flowering variety, similar in growth and style and size of flower to 'Mme de Sancy de Parabère', but without the large outer petals. Fully

I. Three ramblers derived from *Rosa sempervirens*, the Evergreen Rose, 'Adélaïde d'Orléans', 1826, 'Félicité et Perpétue', 1827, and 'Spectabilis', 1848.

II. Five ramblers descended from R. *multiflora* or R. *wichuraiana*. Left to right, above, 'Violette', 1921, 'Veilchenblau', 1900; below, 'Rose-Marie Viaud', 1924, 'Bleu Magenta'; and 'Goldfinch', 1907, for the delightful contrast of colour.

III. Thornless ramblers of the Boursault group: 'Madame de Sancy de Parabère', 1874, and 'Amadis', 1829.

IV. Ramblers descended from R. *luciae* or R. *wichuraiana:* 'Auguste
Gervais', 1918, and 'Alexandre Girault', 1909, noted for their glossy
leaves and delicious fragrance.

V. Noisette Roses which are constantly in flower and very fragrant:
'Alister Stella Gray', 1894; below, left, 'Blush Noisette', c.1818, and
'Céline Forestier', 1842.

VI. Graceful Climbing sports of Tea Roses: 'Mrs Herbert Stevens',
1922, and 'Lady Hillingdon', 1917, both sweetly Tea-scented.

VII. A pair of fragrant modern-style climbers: 'Lawrence
Johnston' and 'Cupid'.

VIII. An excellent modern pillar rose, 'Dream Girl',
fragrant and recurrent.

double, palest blush pink, but much deeper in the centre. An old plant grows and flowers well on the west wall of Melford Hall, a National Trust property in Suffolk. 15 to 20 feet.

'Blush Rambler'. B. R. Cant, 1903. 'Crimson Rambler' × 'The Garland'. A vigorous rambler, almost thornless, with light green leaves. Flowers cupped, semi-double, light pink, in large or small trusses and deliciously fragrant. Still occasionally found in old gardens; it appears to be of almost pure *multiflora* breed. 15 feet.
Kingsley, pp. 58, 59.

'Bobbie James'. See page 47.

'Crimson Rambler'. See 'Turner's Crimson Rambler', page 73.

'Crimson Shower'. Norman, 1951. A later flowering, richer coloured 'Excelsa'; suitable for the same positions as that variety, 'Dorothy Perkins' and the fragrant 'Sanders' White'. Small glossy leaves. Unlike most ramblers this excellent new variety does not start flowering until well past midsummer and continues into September. Almost scentless. 15 feet.

'Débutante'. Walsh, 1902. R. *wichuraiana* × 'Baroness Rothschild' (1868). At first sight similar to 'Dorothy Perkins' but infinitely more beautiful, of better colour and not subject to mildew. Dark green, rounded, neat foliage, similar to R. *wichuraiana*, and long dainty sprays of bloom set with pale green bracts. Flowers cupped at first, later reflexing with quilled petals; clear rose-pink fading to blush. A charming rambler for all purposes, and delightful for cutting. Delicate primrose fragrance. Undoubtedly the best pink rambler in its section. 15 feet.
Journal des Roses, Juin, 1908. ⎫
Strassheim, September, 1908. ⎭ Identical illustrations, poor.

'Donau'. Praskac, 1913. 'Erinnerung an Brod' × a pink hybrid of R. *wichuraiana*. This was once sent to me as a purple rambler; it is in fact cerise-pink, but with little scent, and subject to mildew.

'Dorothy Perkins'. Jackson Perkins, 1901. R. *wichuraiana* × 'Madame Gabriel Luizet' (an old pink Hybrid Perpetual which is still worth growing, raised in 1877). Too well known to need description; rather subject to mildew, and little scent. I prefer 'Débutante'. Can create an exquisite Edwardian effect, and is one of the essentials for gardens with arches and trellises where more modern roses are grown, together with 'Excelsa', 'Crimson Shower', 'Hiawatha', 'Evangeline', and the fragrant 'Sanders' White'. Well represented at Polesden Lacey, a property of the National Trust in Surrey, in the Edwardian rose garden. Small glossy leaves. 18 feet. 'Lady Godiva' is a sport of paler, more pleasing colouring, and is not so subject to mildew.

Journal des Roses, Juin 1908.
Darlington, Plate 5.

'Evangeline'. Walsh, 1906. R. *wichuraiana* × 'Crimson Rambler'. A very pretty, fragrant, single, light pink variety, sweetly scented. Richer in colour than 'Francis E. Lester'. It is to the pale pinks what 'Hiawatha' is to the crimsons. 18 feet.

'Excelsa'. Walsh, 1909. Known as the 'Red Dorothy Perkins', this rose has no recorded parentage. Except for its colour, which is clear bright crimson, it resembles 'Dorothy Perkins' and has the same uses. Small glossy leaves. Surpassed by 'Crimson Shower'. 18 feet.

Leroy, Plate 13. A good photograph in colour of a weeping standard.

'Félicité et Perpétue'. 1827, raised by M. Jacques, gardener to the Duc d'Orléans. St Felicitas and St Perpetua were Carthaginian martyrs, whose day, according to E. A. Bunyard, is 7th May, but this rose is one of the later ramblers, seldom in flower with me before the end of June. It is the most evergreen descendant of R. *sempervirens*, and will retain some leaves through a mild winter. They are small, neat, dark shining green, plum-coloured when young. It is very bushy, making masses of shoots, and is therefore best grown as a wide bush or over a stump, low wall or hedgerow; pruning is of little use, and does not promote flowering. It is completely covered at flowering time with perfect rosette-like double flowers of milk-white from crimson-touched buds, with slight button eye. Delicate primrose fragrance. A rose all on its own, and never to be forgotten when once one has seen a large plant. Very hardy, thriving in windswept Welsh and Scottish upland gardens; flowers well even in shade on north walls. 12 feet. (Plate I.) *Journal des Roses*, Avril 1884. Grossly exaggerated. *Revue de l'Horticulture, Belge et Étrangère*, 1890. Plate 18. Good. Strassheim, 1889. Poor.

'Flora'. Some authors give this as synonymous with 'William's Evergreen', which was a blush-white rose (1855). The reddish stems are best when trained up wall or fence and the subsequent growths allowed to fall forward, covering the plant with a sheet of bloom. Dark green pointed leaves. The flowers have a shape reminiscent of R. *centifolia*, being cupped, very full, of lilac-pink with dark old-rose in the centre. Delicate perfume of primroses. 12 feet. Miss Jekyll has a good photograph in *Roses for English Gardens* between pages 54 and 55.

'Francis E. Lester'. Lester Rose Gardens, 1946. Seedling from 'Kathleen', a Hybrid Musk. In the dark green leaves, neatly pointed and usually with an edging of maroon serrations, and the profuse, rather bushy growth, it has something in common with 'Félicité et Perpétue'. Reddish young shoots and flower stalks. The bunches of flowers, borne rambler-fashion, cover the plant and fill the garden with intense fragrance of oranges and bananas. The buds are clear pink, opening like apple-blossom, fading to white with good yellow stamens. Few roses give more flower and scent at midsummer. Excellent as a lax bush or supported by a stump or hedgerow. About 14 feet. Small, oval, orange heps.

'Goldfinch'. George Paul, 1907. A hybrid of 'Hélène', which was the result of a Hybrid Tea crossed with a hybrid between 'Aglaia' and 'Crimson Rambler'. Thus there are two doses of R. *multiflora* in it, and indeed it is almost pure R. *multiflora* from a garden point of view. It is practically thornless, with fresh shining green leaves; buds yolk-yellow fading to milk-white in hot sunshine after opening, with dark yellow stamens. Powerful scent of oranges and bananas. If it did not fade so much it would be the more prized, but if cut in bud and opened indoors the flowers remain full of colour. Useful as a sprawling bush or trained on stump or hedgerow. A splendid sight at Sissinghurst, Kent. (Plate II.)

'**Hiawatha**'. Walsh, 1904. 'Crimson Rambler' × 'Paul's Carmine Pillar'. On the lines of 'Evangeline', but crimson with white centre. Not fragrant. 15 feet.
Darlington, Plate 2.

'**Kew Rambler**'. Raised at Kew in 1912. R. *soulieana* × 'Hiawatha' The only pink seedling resulting from the cross; an account appears in the *Gardeners' Chronicle* for 1918, 27th July, page 32. The thorns and greyish dull leaves are reminiscent of R. *soulieana*. It is a vigorous true rambler with pointed, bright pink buds opening to beautiful single flowers, light rose pink with white zone around the yellow stamens, and thus it resembles 'Hiawatha'. Large trusses of blossom late in the season, exhaling a rich *multiflora* scent. An attractive and useful plant for many purposes, but perhaps best in a tree, where it will reach about 18 feet. Small, round-oval, orange heps. The use of R. *soulieana* apparently provides greyish foliage, and breeding along these lines might be very attractive, especially if plants bearing purple flowers could be raised, to tone with the leaves. (Photograph, Plate 4.)

'**Lady Gay**'. Walsh, 1905. R. *wichuraiana* × 'Bardou Job'. Very similar to 'Dorothy Perkins' but slightly larger in flower, deeper in colour, and not so subject to mildew.

'**Laure Davoust**'. Laffay, 1843 or 1846. Smooth stems and long-pointed mid-green leaves, with abundant flowers, leaning more towards the *sempervirens* class than the *multiflora*, with which it is usually grouped. From magenta-pink buds the flowers open almost flat, yet with cupped formation, quilled and quartered petals, and green pointel in the centre. They are soft lilac-rose fading to lilac-white. Sweetly scented. Jäger says it will grow to 15 feet or more, but my plants have not exceeded 6 feet.
Choix des Plus Belles Roses, Plate 20. Good.
Jamain and Forney, Plate 53. Poor.
Journal des Roses, Juin 1878.
Komlosy.

'**Lykkefund**'. Olsen, 1930. A 'lucky find' from Denmark. A seedling from R. *helenae* (Barbier's form); the pollen-parent is stated to be 'Zéphirine Drouhin'. I included this in *Shrub Roses of Today*, but it bids fair to make a vigorous rambler, and the raiser reports that a five-year-old plant had grown to 20 feet by 13 feet. It has one great display at midsummer, but no heps. Arching habit with small, dark green, glossy leaves and nearly single flowers in panicles of 10 to 30, creamy yellow with a salmon tinge fading nearly to white, with orange-yellow stamens and the delicious fragrance peculiar to the Synstylae Section. It is thornless, and should be admirable rambling through a tree, or making a dense arching mass.

'**Madame d'Arblay**'. Wells, 1835. R. *multiflora* × R. *moschata*, the reverse cross to 'The Garland' and by the same raiser, Mr Wells of Tunbridge Wells, who apparently has no other roses to his name. A graceful, vigorous rambler with long trailing branches, somewhat sparsely leaved and like the *sempervirens* class. Dainty, long-stalked clusters of bloom, half filled with short petals, creating open rosettes; palest blush passing to near white. Sweet fragrance. 18 to 20 feet. (Madame d'Arblay: *née* Frances Burney.)

'**Madame Sancy de Parabère**'. See page 123.

'**Marjorie W. Lester**'. I received this from the Lester Rose Gardens, California, together with 'Francis E. Lester', but it turned out to be synonymous with the old rambler 'Laure Davoust' (see page 68).

'**Minnehaha**'. Walsh, 1905. R. *wichuraiana* × 'Paul Neyron'. A deep pink, non-fading version of 'Dorothy Perkins', than which it is bolder, more effective, and flowers later. Almost scentless. Small glossy leaves. 15 feet.

'**Patricia Macoun**'. Ottawa, 1945. A hybrid of R. *helenae* made by the Central Experimental Farm in an effort to breed hardiness into rambling roses, in which they were certainly successful with this one. It is described as 'a fine white for severe climates'. In the south we should all prefer 'Sanders' White', but it is an interesting hybrid and is smothered with double, cupped flowers of snow white at midsummer. Vigorous. Glossy leaves. Fragrant. Small orange heps. 20 feet.

'Paul's Himalayan Musk Rambler'. Browsing through old books one day I came across the description of this rose, but unfortunately have no record of it. It was given to me by Mrs Ashley Slocock, of Woking, and a plant is growing on trees at the west end of Seven Acres in the Royal Horticultural Society's Garden at Wisley. It is a tremendous grower, and could therefore be linked with the vigorous species of the Synstylae Section, but as it has coloured double flowers I prefer to include it here. It will make growths 30 feet or more in length, thin and trailing, and is admirable to grow into trees, when its dainty sprays will hang down in festoons of bloom at midsummer. Each flower, on thread-like stem, is a little rosette of blush-lilac-pink, exhaling a sweet *multiflora* scent. Narrow pointed leaves. Dark wood and thorns. It is possible that this is a hybrid of R. *filipes* on account of its thread-like flower stalks; many flowers have united styles. Its vigour and thorns enable it to creep from one tree to another, enveloping all in a mantle of beauty. Very small oval heps.

'Phyllis Bide'. Bide, 1923. The parentage is stated to be 'Perle d'Or' × 'Gloire de Dijon', but Mr Gordon Rowley tells me that the number of chromosomes (fourteen) would preclude the possibility of this cross. This interesting parentage has produced good results, though R. *multiflora*, through 'Perle d'Or', is most in evidence. Small leaves and small rambler-type flowers in constant succession until autumn. Double, clear yellow flushed with salmon pink, in clusters. Sweet scent. 12 feet.

'Rambling Rector'. Almost pure R. *multiflora* but semi-double, and bears a superficial resemblance to 'The Garland', but is coarser in all its parts; its flowers are creamy on opening, and the flower stalks do not grow perpendicularly as in that variety. The leaves are long with lacy stipules and downy beneath, the flower stalks densely glandular-hairy; the flowers open cream and fade to white, borne in large heads with yellow stamens which quickly turn dark on maturity—its only fault. It is dense-growing, mounding itself rapidly into a large bush, or will scramble over hedges or into trees, and is thorny and impenetrable and un-prunable; quite overpowering in flower, both from the quantity of blossom and the delicious *multiflora* fragrance. It was included in the Daisy Hill Nursery catalogue for 1912. Small oval heps.

'**Rose-Marie Viaud**'. Igoult, 1924. A seedling from 'Veilchenblau' and like that variety almost thornless, except for a few bristles at the bottom of strong basal shoots. The stems are stout enough for it to make a large arching shrub, but are also of sufficient vigour to climb 15 feet into trees and to hang down in festoons. Its lack of thorns makes it easy to manage. The leaves are broad, beautifully shaped, and coarsely toothed. Flowers in typical large bunches, fully double like little rosettes; they are from vivid cerise to lilac on opening, turning to pure parma-violet and fading still paler, giving an exquisite range of cool tones. This is one of the last purplish ramblers to flower, and coincides with the flowering of 'Kew Rambler'; they look very beautiful when growing together. Unfortunately it is scentless and prone to mildew on the flower stalks—but it is worth it!—and the mildew is seldom noticed owing to the colour of the flowers. (Plate II.) Gault and Synge, Plate 222.

'**Russelliana**'. 1840. An old rose which is generally classed with R. *multiflora* varieties, but possibly it is more nearly related to R. *setigera* or R. *rugosa*. It was variously known as 'Russell's Cottage Rose', 'Scarlet Grevillea', 'Old Spanish Rose', and more recently 'Souvenir de la Bataille de Marengo' has been added to this list of synonyms. Its name 'Scarlet Grevillea' points to its having perhaps been brought from the Far East by Sir Charles Greville (together with R. *multiflora platyphylla*), and I suppose by comparison with that pale rose its intense colouring might in those days be called 'scarlet'. In these days it certainly would not, being of intense cerise-crimson flushed crimson-purple, fading to magenta; flowers very double, small, in clusters. Dark green obovate leaves. Stems densely covered with small thorns. A hardy floriferous rose making a good colour effect at midsummer, but rather coarse. Will reach to 20 feet and appears to be imperturbably hardy. Old rose scent.

Possibly related to 'de la Grifferaie', a shrub rose frequently used as an understock.

'Sanders' White Rambler'. Sanders, 1912. A beautiful white rose similar to 'Dorothy Perkins' and its group except for colour. Small glossy leaves. Assorts well with varieties like 'Dorothy', but as it has no upsetting colour it can be used with any class of rose, especially as it has a delicious fruity fragrance. Flowers late in the rambler season. 18 feet.

'Seagull'. Pritchard, 1907. A wonderful sight in flower, this may be likened to a large-flowered version of R. *multiflora*, possessing many characteristics of that species, including its amazing perfume. Semi-double white flowers borne profusely in large trusses with bright yellow stamens. See also under 'Thalia'.

'Spectabilis'. Prior to 1848. 'Noisette Ayez'. A *sempervirens* hybrid which flowers after the others of its class are over. Greeny-brown wood and dark thorns; leaves slim, pointed. Globular buds opening to regular, incurved, fully double rose-pink flowers, with a lilac tint, reflexing into a perfect rosette. A dainty little rose of similar perfection in flower to 'Félicité et Perpétue' but not so vigorous. Will reach 6 or 7 feet. There are few roses of any class with such exquisite buds and blooms, reminiscent of the most perfect of rosettes; the whole plant is refined and delightful. Sweet primrose fragrance. (Plate I.)

'Splendens'. 'Ayrshire Splendens' or 'Myrrh-Scented Rose'. A R. *arvensis* hybrid with small dark green, pointed leaves borne on long trailing shoots, freely branching and making a thicket. The buds show reddish plum colour, but open to loosely double, cupped flowers of creamy colouring, with yellow-orange stamens, borne singly or in small clusters. This rose has a delicious and pronounced fragrance of myrrh and is, therefore, worth retaining. 15 feet.

'Thalia'. Schmitt, 1895. Known as 'White Rambler', this and 'Seagull' were for many years the best fragrant white ramblers, until the coming of the later flowering 'Sanders' White'. 'Thalia' was a hybrid between R. *multiflora* and 'Paquerette', one of the earliest Poly-poms or Dwarf Polyanthas. Small double white flowers in big clusters on a vigorous plant achieving 12 feet or more. Very fragrant.

'The Garland'. Wells, 1835. R. *moschata* × R. *multiflora*. A renowned old rambler which once again proves how scent can be paramount in our affection for roses. One of its characteristics is the green wood with dark purplish-brown thorns; another is that at whatever angle the flower trusses grow, the actual flower stalks grow erect, resulting in all the flowers being held in an upright position. This is clearly shown in the photograph facing page 21 in Miss Jekyll's *Roses for English Gardens*. Vast multitudes of flowers are produced in large and small clusters; buds creamy salmon opening to cream with a faint blush and quickly fading to creamy white, flat, with quilled petals giving a daisy-like effect, with some yellow stamens. Dark green smallish leaves. Rich orange perfume, carrying well in the air. An ideal rose for new or old gardens, where its bushy vigour will suit it for a number of uses, even as a loose shrub. Small oval red heps. 15 feet. (Fig. 7.)

'Thelma'. Easlea, 1927. R. *wichuraiana* × 'Paul's Scarlet Climber'. The soft colouring, luxurious flowering, and fragrance all commend this pale pink rambler for continued cultivation. Less vigorous than most others in this chapter, and suitable for a pillar. Nearly thornless. 10 feet.

'Turner's Crimson Rambler'. Introduced to Western gardens in 1893. Affectionately known as 'Crimson Rambler', 'The Engineer', 'Shi-Tz-Mei', or 'Ten Sisters', this was once a popular plant but is very subject to mildew, scentless, and should be discarded in favour of 'Crimson Shower'. Dusky dark red. It was imported from Japan, and is probably a hybrid of R. *multiflora* × R. *wichuraiana*. A landmark in the development of rambling roses, having a profound influence on rose breeding, but otherwise not worth growing today.
Revue Horticole, 1894, p. 156.
Hoffmann, Plate 12. Very good.
Journal des Roses, 1886.

'Una'. George Paul, 1900. A Tea Rose, perhaps 'Gloire de Dijon' × R. *canina*. Hooked thorns and dull green leaves sharply serrated, inherited from R. *canina*; young foliage bronzy. The flowers are borne in small clusters and are nearly single—with two or three extra petals—creamy white opening from creamy buff buds about 3 inches across; delicious primrose scent. One crop of flowers only. Usually grows to 12 feet or so, but can achieve 18 feet on a wall. Large round heps which usually remain green.

'Universal Favourite'. Horvath, 1898. R. *wichuraiana* × 'Paquerette'. Minute, double, dusky pink flowers in 'Dorothy Perkins' sprays. May have some value for cutting. No fragrance.

'Veilchenblau'. Schmidt, Erfurt, 1909. 'Crimson Rambler' × 'Erinnerung an Brod'. Almost thornless green wood bearing smooth, fresh green leaves, long and pointed. It is of typical rambler growth with flowers in generous clusters. Buds crimson-purple, petals opening violet, streaked with white (not variegated, but seemingly a character connected with the central vein in each petal); semi-double, incurved, with a few small petals around the yellow stamens. White centre. The colour verges to maroon later and fades on the third day to lilac-grey. Sweetly fragrant of green apples. Excellent on a shady wall, where the colour remains fairly uniform. It flowers early in the rambler season, and achieves 12 feet. (Plate II.)

'Venusta pendula'. An old R. *arvensis* form or hybrid, redis-covered by Herr Kordes. A complete smother of blossom, but practically scentless. Pink buds, opening blush white, fading to creamy white, with yellow stamens. 15 feet.

'Violette'. Turbat, 1921. This flowers just after 'Veilchenblau' opens, early in the rambler season. Thornless and vigorous with green wood and dark green leaves, rather recurved and bluntly serrate. Large trusses of flowers with buds and freshly open flowers of intense crimson-purple, and occasionally a white streak, intensifying to maroon-purple and fading to maroon-grey, with subtle brownish tints; yellow stamens; very slight scent of apples. Will attain 15 feet on good soils.

I first saw this rambler at Nymans, interlaced with the large pink single flowers of 'Lady Curzon'; the contrast of size and colour was admirable. 'Complicata' and other large pink varieties would do equally well; another favourite companion is 'Goldfinch'. (Plate II.)

'Wedding Day'. See page 47.

'White Dorothy'. Inferior to the excellent 'Sanders' White'.

'Wichmoss'. Barbier, 1911. R. *wichuraiana* × 'Salet', a pink moss rose. This effort to produce a rambling rose with mossy buds is only partially successful, for it lacks decisive colour and the mossy buds are invariably covered with mildew. However, it is a true rambler with fairly glossy leaves and double small blooms of blush white. Fragrant. 15 feet. I include this as evidence that we could have mossy buds on ramblers, and hope that it may be raised again and be free from mildew.

'Wickwar'. A seedling of R. *soulieana*, recently raised and introduced by Mr Keith Steadman of Wickwar, Gloucestershire. It retains the vigour, greyish leaves and delicious fragrance of R. *soulieana*, but has clear pink single flowers and a more tractable climbing habit.

PART 2

Ramblers and Climbers Derived from the Musk Rose or Synstylae Section Intermarried with the Offspring of the China and Tea Roses

5

*The Luciae Group of Ramblers**

All that's bright must fade,
The brightest still the fleetest;
All that's sweet was made
But to be lost when sweetest.

Thomas Moore, 1779–1852.

THIS RACE of roses is, I consider, in the top rank of beautiful, fragrant, graceful ramblers, and further hybridization, along the same lines but using more modern parents, might give splendid results. No ramblers or climbers raised before or since surpass their prodigality of bloom, extreme fragrance, and beautiful foliage, coupled with ease of training.

As the most popular of this group is 'Albéric Barbier', and as so many of the varieties were raised by Messieurs Barbier et Cie, of Orléans, France, using R. *luciae* rather than R. *wichuraiana*, I think we may justly give the title of 'Luciae Ramblers' to these roses. They need a special title because they are usually classed together with 'Dorothy Perkins' and others related to R. *multiflora* and R. *wichuraiana*, but with these varieties our present roses have nothing in common. They are as different as Hybrid Teas from Floribundas.

They do not produce long straight canes bearing in the next season stiff heads of small flowers as do the varieties in the previous chapter. Rather do they produce, with their free-branching and luxuriant glossy dark greenery, a mantle of richness following the contours of whatever they cover in a free and continuous way, further encouraged by the fact that they do not depend on annual summer pruning to give of their best. The flowers are borne

* See also page 191.

singly or in graceful small clusters, and are anything from two to four inches across, mostly fully double in the old floral style, extremely sweetly scented with the 'fresh green-apple' fragrance which is their own contribution to this addition to the visual delight of roses. They flower mainly at midsummer, but most of them produce odd blooms until the autumn, especially if not parched or starved; in fact a thorough soak after flowering will often start them into bud again.

In this group for the first time we are dealing with roses in modern colouring. Only 'Alexandre Girault' and 'May Queen' have a touch of the soft mauve tone of the Old Roses, with 'Gerbe Rose' and 'Mary Wallace' a neutral pink; all the others verge towards salmon and copper or creamy yellow. Some are therefore hardly suitable for growing with the Old Shrub Roses, but their old-style quartered blooms and fragrance endear them to lovers of the Old Roses, while their somewhat recurrent flowering habit and more modern colouring give them pride of place among graceful ramblers for the modern rose garden; the creamy white varieties will of course blend with anything.

The group really starts, as far as we are concerned—by which I mean the varieties I have collected together—with hybridizing by W. A. Manda of New Jersey in the United States. We cannot be certain whether he used R. *wichuraiana* or R. *luciae*. In 1898 and the year following he launched 'May Queen', 'Gardenia', and 'Jersey Beauty', lilac-pink and double and single creamy yellow respectively. These are seldom recurrent, but create a wonderful display at midsummer and are extremely fragrant. The Barbier firm produced 'Albéric Barbier', 'Paul Transon', 'René André', 'Léontine Gervais', 'François Juranville', 'Alexandre Girault', and 'Auguste Gervais', in that order from 1900 to 1908, and the species used was R. *luciae*, which is sometimes considered a form of R. *wichuraiana*, or vice versa. The two species are very near. Meanwhile Fauque et Fils, also of Orléans, introduced 'Gerbe Rose', 'La Perle', and the little charmer 'Madame Alice Garnier'. 'Gerbe Rose' is not quite so graceful as the rest of them, while 'La Perle' equals any in vigour. The Barbier and the Fauque seedlings are all somewhat recurrent. H. A. Hesse of Ems, Germany, brought out 'Fräulein Oktavia Hesse' in 1909, which is very similar to 'Albéric Barbier'. In 1918 Benjamin Cant introduced 'Emily Gray', which with 'Albéric Barbier' has remained very popular in public esteem; and the last of the group, 'Mary Wallace' and 'Breeze Hill', came from Van Fleet in the United States in 1924 and 1926 respectively. These have less glossy foliage than the bulk of earlier varieties.

There is no doubt that they make a most attractive group, and the recurrent habit of the two French groups indicates possibly that R. *luciae* makes a better parent than R. *wichuraiana*. All those with salmon or yellow tints have as their other parent a China × Tea hybrid, and the others go back to Bourbons or Hybrid Perpetuals. None is connected with R. *multiflora*.

It is unfortunate that these lovely ramblers are not so hardy as many of the *wichuraiana* and *multiflora* types, and it is understandable when we read that R. *luciae* is less hardy than R. *wichuraiana*. This precludes their use in very cold countries except on sheltered walls, a use for which they are well suited. Unlike many of the other ramblers they are not prone to mildew, they thrive excellently in all manner of positions, and are hardy throughout England.

Although the varieties in this chapter make a homogeneous group I have included two well-known varieties, 'Albertine' and 'Mary Wallace', which would in some ways be better left until Chapter 9. To save unnecessary repetition I have used the accepted name of R. *wichuraiana* as the parent of all these roses in the following pages; my remarks above will elucidate the confusion with R. *luciae*. (See page 46.)

'Albéric Barbier'. Barbier, 1900. R. *wichuraiana* × 'Shirley Hibberd' (a small yellow Tea Rose). Right in the forefront of beautiful rambling roses and a splendid sample for its relatives in this section. The flowers are large, opening from pretty, pointed buds to starry flowers of soft yellow expanding to creamy white, many-petalled and quartered. Extremely sweet green-apple scent. Almost dense enough for ground-cover, and constantly produces scattered late flowers until the autumn. 20 feet or more.

'Albertine'. Barbier, 1921. R. *wichuraiana* × 'Mrs A. R. Waddell', a coppery Hybrid Tea. Not uniform with the other roses in this chapter. This is a shrubby climber or a lax bush, for while it is usually made to climb or ramble, it creates such a thicket of stems that it is far nobler when allowed to do as it likes among shrubs. Glossy leaves. Coppery pink, two-toned, loosely double, but too well known to need description. Creating an unforgettable midsummer display, with or without pruning; the rich fragrance carries well in the air. 18 feet on a wall or 6 feet high by 15 feet across if unsupported.

'**Alexandre Girault**'. Barbier, 1909. R. *wichuraiana* × 'Papa Gontier' (a pink Tea Rose). Dark glossy leaves, very vigorous growth. Pretty buds of deeper colour open to almost scarlet flowers, nearly filled with rather quilled petals but shewing white centre, green eye, and yellow stamens; the colour deepens to lilac-carmine, but remains paler on the reverse of the petals. This strange mixture of colours blends into a deep coppery carmine at a distance and is very satisfying, so much so that it has been given an important position at the Roseraie de l'Haÿ near Paris, where it covers a long high trellis around the formal pool. Rich green-apple scent. Few thorns. 20 feet. (Plate IV.)

'**Auguste Gervais**'. Barbier, 1918. R. *wichuraiana* × 'Le Progrès', a yellow Hybrid Tea. First-class foliage and large flowers for this Section; coppery flame-pink on the reverse which makes a splendid contrast to the bland creamy-apricot on the inside of the petals. Considerably paler but always beautiful in hot weather, and, as usual with these varieties, deliciously fragrant. Has a long flowering season and odd blooms later. 20 feet. (Plate IV.)

'**Breeze Hill**'. Van Fleet, 1926. R. *wichuraiana* × 'Beauté de Lyon', a coral red Hybrid Tea. This variety has not such glossy foliage as the others in this class, and G. A. Stevens suggests that it may be a 'lost' seeding of 'Dr Van Fleet' which had R. *soulieana* as one parent. The rounded foliage could certainly have come from such a hybrid; otherwise the large flowers conform to the normal and are a warm creamy apricot-rose, fading to buff-cream. Good scent of green apples. Perhaps achieving 12 feet, but can be grown as an arching bush.
McFarland, 1937, p. 27. Rather dull.
Stevens, p. 106. The same plate as above.
American *Rose Annual*, 1927. Plate 1.

'City of York'. Tantau, 1945. A hybrid between 'Dorothy Perkins' and a Hybrid Tea 'Professor Gnau'. Though of rather more involved parentage than most, the R. *wichuraiana* in 'Dorothy Perkins' accounts for the general appearance, and this glossy-leaved vigorous rose may be likened to 'Albéric Barbier', but has larger, semi-double, cupped flowers of creamy white. So far it has had no later crop with me. Also known as 'Direktor Benschop'. Fragrant.

'Emily Gray'. Williams, 1918. 'Jersey Beauty' × 'Comtesse de Cayla'. A favourite for many years, to which the beautiful glossy foliage, richly tinted while young, contributes greatly. Clusters of warm buff-yellow nearly single flowers with good stamens and fragrance. Seldom flowers after midsummer. Strong grower, reaching 20 feet.

'François Juranville'. Barbier, 1906. R. *wichuraiana* × 'Mme Laurette Messimy', a salmon-pink China Rose. The next in popularity to 'Albéric Barbier' and 'Emily Gray', with slightly less glossy, smaller leaves and slightly smaller flowers, but equal vigour and charm. Flat double flowers filled with quilled and quartered petals, opening rich coral rose fading to light rose, base of petals yellow. Sweet fresh-apple scent. Adds grace and beauty to whatever it grows upon. Inclined to be 'leggy' at the base. Not suitable for walls, where it sometimes gets mildew. 25 feet.

'Fräulein Oktavia Hesse'. Hesse, 1909. R. *wichuraiana* × 'Kaiserin Augusta Viktoria'. Similar to 'Albéric Barbier', which is a superior rose. This variety is nearer to white and less fragrant, but has well-formed flowers at first cupped and creamy, later reflexing flat and passing to white. Sweet apple scent.
Strassheim, December 1909.

'Gardenia'. Manda, 1899. R. *wichuraiana* × 'Perle des Jardins', a yellow Tea Rose. Similar to 'Albéric Barbier' with small dark green glossy leaves. The flowers are very double, quartered, rather cupped, of creamy white deepening to yolk-yellow in the centre, fading to nearly white in hot sun. True apple scent. 18 feet.

'**Gerbe Rose**'. Fauque, 1904. Of the same parentage as 'Débutante', but further removed from R. *wichuraiana*; in fact it approaches the 'Albéric Barbier' group, with its larger, glossy dark leaves. It is not a vigorous rambler, but rather a robust pillar rose, with almost thornless reddish shoots. The flowers are large, loosely double, petals cupped, quartered and crinkled, soft pink with a hint of lilac and cream, with a delicious fragrance of white peonies particularly noticeable in the evening. Apart from its main crop it is seldom without flowers until the autumn. 12 feet.

'**Jersey Beauty**'. Manda, 1899. R. *wichuraiana* × 'Perle des Jardins'. A luxuriant plant which will densely cover its support with excellent glossy foliage. Single creamy yellow flowers with deep yellow stamens at midsummer. Very fragrant. Kingsley, p. 62.

'**La Perle**'. Fauque, 1904. R. *wichuraiana* × 'Mme Hoste', a pale yellow Tea Rose. Similar to 'Albéric Barbier', but more vigorous, and with less glossy leaves; the young foliage has a red-brown tinge. The buds are also brown-touched, opening to a cupped globular bloom of greenish creamy white with a lemon-yellow centre; later becoming flat with some quilled petals. Deliciously intense fragrance of green apples, lemon and tea. Extremely vigorous, reaching 30 feet.

'**Léontine Gervais**'. Barbier, 1903. R. *wichuraiana* × 'Souvenir de Catherine Guillot'. In all respects very similar to 'François Juranville' except the colour, which inclines towards copper and orange. As 'Paul Transon' (*q.v.*) has a much longer flowering season I prefer it. 25 feet.

'**Little Compton Creeper**'. Brownell, 1938. Though the parentage is not recorded, this is obviously related to the others in this chapter with highly polished dark green leaves. The flowers are single, reminiscent of 'Emily Gray', but of warm coppery flesh-pink, with cluster of stamens. Orange-red fruit. *Multiflora* scent; short flowering period and does not repeat, but is an attractive plant at all times. Medium to large red heps. 18 feet.

'**Madame Alice Garnier**'. Fauque, 1906. R. *wichuraiana* × 'Madame Charles', a yellow Tea Rose. A miniature in growth, leaf, and flower, making a sprawling bush or a short climber, set with neat dark leaves. The flowers are flat rosettes of quilled and quartered petals, bright rose with yellow centre, passing to light pink giving a creamy-apricot effect. Extremely fragrant of green apples. Perhaps 10 feet.

'**Mary Wallace**'. Van Fleet, 1924. R. *wichuraiana* × a pink Hybrid Tea. A lovely graceful plant, less full of foliage than the others, and less glossy. Large, loose, semi-double, rose-pink flowers, sweetly fragrant. Seldom repeats. 20 feet.

'**May Queen**'. There were two roses of this name raised in the United States in 1898, and that introduced by W. A. Manda of New Jersey is R. *wichuraiana* × 'Champion of the World'; the Van Fleet hybrid is R. *wichuraiana* × 'Madame de Graw'; in both the second parent is a Bourbon. Our plant could be either; it has green wood with a few reddish thorns and fresh green leaves somewhat glossy, bluntly serrate. The flowers are clear rose-pink on opening, taking on a delicate flush of lilac similar to 'Champion of the World'; slightly cupped on opening, they become flat and reflex, filled with quartered petals and often a button eye. Few roses create such a sheet of blossom; I have seen it equally good on south, east, and north walls. It can also be grown as a dense arching bush, since it is not so prone to make long shoots as the other varieties, but creates more of a mass of interlacing twigs. Delicious green-apple scent. 15 feet. (Photograph, Plate 5.)

'**Paul Transon**'. Barbier, 1901. R. *wichuraiana* × 'l'Idéal', a coral-red Tea Rose. Purplish shoots and thorns, shining small leaves with acute serrations, richly tinted when young. The little buds are coppery-orange opening to salmon-coral, fading to creamy salmon with yellow tints in the centre. Semi-double to double, flat, with pleated petals. Well scented of green apples. A very charming free-flowering variety which produces so many late flowers that it might be called recurrent; in fact I find it as free with later blooms as 'Albéric Barbier'. 15 feet. (Photograph, Plate 6.)

'**Réné André**'. Barbier, 1901. R. *wichuraiana* × 'l'Idéal'. Exceptionally lax, and will climb into trees to 20 feet or more, hanging down in slender festoons, with small flowers of soft yellowish apricot flushed with pink, loosely double and somewhat cupped. Sweet apple scent.

Journal des Roses, Octobre 1903. Very large and of too brilliant colouring.

As a result of a visit to the Paris rose gardens I noted the following worthy varieties:

'Élisa Robichon'. Barbier, 1901. Salmon pink.
'François Foucard'. Barbier, 1900. Lemon yellow.

(The above two are the result of R. *wichuraiana* × 'l'Idéal'.)

'Valentin Beaulieu'. Barbier, 1902. Lilac pink with darker centre.
'Madame Constans'. L'Haÿ, 1902. Soft pink.

6

The Noisette and Tea Roses

I have loved flowers that fade,
Within whose magic tents
Rich hues have marriage made
With sweet unmemoried scents.

Robert Bridges, 1844–1930.

IN *Shrub Roses of Today* I explained the derivation of the Hybrid Musk Roses, how they probably owed their fragrance to R. *multiflora* and how successfully they had retained the power of floating their fragrance in the air—a propensity very noticeable in R. *multiflora* and others of the Synstylae Section. What we know as the original group of Noisettes is believed to be of practically the same parentage; they may be crosses between China × Tea hybrids and R. *moschata*. Such a hybrid was the double pink 'Champneys' Pink Cluster', whose full story can be read in Dr C. C. Hurst's dissertation in my book *The Old Shrub Roses*. This rose I have not seen, but it is comparable in parentage to several others of the China Rose hybrids with members of the Synstylae Section.

I have never been quite happy about the rose figured in Bean's *Trees and Shrubs* as R. *noisettiana*. It would appear to be very near to R. *moschata*. However, there is a photograph of the same plant, presumably, in *The Garden*, vol. lxxi, page 335, shewing a rounded bush some 10 feet across and 6 feet high, bearing single white flowers. The contributor, W.D[allimore], states that it is beautiful for about a fortnight, and that its glossy leaves shew affinity to the China Rose; this plant still grows at Kew but there is no record of its origin.

In the second generation the plants are apt to be perpetual or recurrent flowering. A friend of John Champneys in Charleston, South Carolina, was Philippe Noisette, a nurseryman, who sowed seeds of the Champneys' rose, and raised a plant perpetually in flower through the summer and autumn. He sent it to his brother in Paris, Louis Noisette; it was figured by Redouté in 1821 under the name of R. *noisettiana*, and was distributed in France and no doubt sent to England in due course.

My first acquaintance with what I believe to be this rose was at Nymans, Sussex, now a National Trust garden, but then the home of Lieut.-Colonel Leonard Messel; his gardener James Comber had a plant of considerable age on his cottage and it still grows there. Roses, particularly the old varieties, were especially treasured at Nymans by Mrs Messel, and hours were spent turning the pages of Redouté's great volumes trying to identify some of those which had reached the garden from various sources. Comber's eye picked on Plate 77 in vol. ii as the original portrait of his rose, and when I visited the garden before the Hitler war I was shewn the 'Blush Noisette'. Though I have seen this rose here and there in old gardens through the south of England, I have never met anyone before or since who has had an inkling of its name and history.

Considering its original importance, its continued long life in the face of neglect, its floriferousness and scent, it is most extraordinary that this rose has escaped the notice of all the writers of rose books during the last fifty years or so.

Also at Nymans were 'Aimée Vibert' and 'Fellemberg', both comparable varieties combining the vigour and small clustered flowers of the Musk Rose group with perpetual flowering habit of the China Rose. 'Aimée Vibert' is recorded variously as a sport from the Noisette 'Repens' and also as a hybrid between 'Champneys' Pink Cluster' and R. *sempervirens*. If the latter be true then this may account for its being poorly scented. These small-flowered cluster roses were the originals of the Noisette group, and were 'much improved by the Tea Rose' (William Paul). Others are reported to have derived purplish colouring from R. *multiflora*, but up to the present I have traced none of these.

There is an interesting account in the *Florist and Pomologist* for September 1878 about hedges of the Noisette Roses 'Aimée

Vibert' and 'Fellemberg', with a few 'Gloire de Dijon' and 'Duchesse de Cazes' to give variety of colour. They were grown from cuttings and provided delicious scent in the evening.

It will be seen that so far the Tea Rose had had little influence in Noisettes, in spite of its possible presence to a small degree in the parentage. But around 1830 the 'Blush Noisette' was crossed with 'Parks's Yellow Tea-Scented China', and the first yellow garden roses were raised, starting two new races, the dwarf or shrubby Tea Roses and the yellow Tea-scented climbing Noisettes. The latter soon disappeared as a race, and became Climbing Tea Roses, owing no doubt to the constant crossing with yellow Tea Roses—and one can well understand the enthusiasm for this, in gardens stocked almost entirely with roses of white, pink, mauve, and allied shades.

With the appearance of the first yellowish Noisettes, 'Lamarque' and 'Jaune Desprez' in 1830, a new standard had been reached, and these together with their descendants 'Céline Forestier' (1842) and 'Gloire de Dijon' (1853) provide us still with great beauty. I would go further and say that 'Jaune Desprez' and 'Gloire de Dijon' are among the most free-flowering climbing roses which are grown today, and this and their scent will surely make them treasured for ever. It is rather remarkable, considering the un-doubted excellence of these and similar roses, that some breeding has not been done among them more recently. It would be more profitable than with many yellow roses that have been raised since, and fortunately these old yellow Tea hybrids are still available.

It is manifest that the Noisette Roses formed a very mixed group about which there can be little generalization. In cultiva-tion they grow best on sunny walls in warm districts, as one would expect from their ancestry. 'Lamarque' indeed is best grown under glass in cold districts.

Although it departs from a normal alphabetical progression, I think it best to arrange the roses in this chapter in four groups. First, the original Noisette and closely allied varieties, derived probably from R. *moschata* and China Roses or Bourbons. (Full details of R. *chinensis* and its hybrids will be found in my two earlier books on roses.) Next comes R. *gigantea* itself, followed by the Tea-Noisettes with yellow colouring in them, derived from the

Tea Roses. These are followed by a few comparatively new, large-flowered climbers derived from R. *gigantea* and modern roses, and a selection of Tea Roses which, while they are not all actually climbers, deserve the shelter of a wall.

ORIGINAL NOISETTE ROSES

'Blush Noisette'. Philippe Noisette, prior to 1817. In my previous writings this has been given in error the name of 'Champneys' Pink Cluster', which was the original cross between the Musk and the China, and from which seeds were taken giving rise to the first Noisette, called 'Blush'. It is a beautiful lax shrub covered with copious leaves of mid-green, rather dull, borne on nearly thorn-free green wood. The flowers are borne in small or large clusters from midsummer onwards on smooth plum-coloured shoots; they are small, cupped with several rows of petals—about three-quarters double—and show yellow stamens. In bud they are deep old-rose, fading to creamy lilac-pink, and have a rich clove fragrance.

It may be grown as a bush, and one sees it frequently so, peeping over a garden wall, or sometimes it is grown up a house wall to 15 feet. It is often referred to in disparaging terms, but is never discarded, on account of its scent and freedom of flower. It was grown by Mr T. Smith of Newry as 'Blush Cluster', and Mrs Gore called it 'Flesh-coloured Noisette'. Miss Willmott adds greatly to the confusion over this rose; her plate does not conform to the text, although it may well be a portrait of a cross between the two species. Her specimen may have been taken from the Kew plant referred to earlier (see page 87).

As this pretty rose is found so freely up and down the country in old gardens, and 'Blush Noisette' would have been so popular in old days owing to its recurrent habit, I feel there is no doubt now about the identification of this fragrant plant, and illustrations add corroboration. (Plate V.)

Redouté, vol. ii, Plate 77. 'Le Rosier de Philippe Noisette.' Exquisite.

Drapiez, vol. iv, p. 260.

Andrews, Plate 106.

Andrews, Plate 95. Very similar and of the same derivation.

Willmott, Plate 93. This is possibly a portrait of the original hybrid, but not of 'Champneys' Pink Cluster' or of 'Blush Noisette'.

'Aimée Vibert'. Vibert, 1828. 'Bouquet de la Mariée.' As this is derived from China, Tea, Musk, and Evergreen Rose parentage it is a little difficult to place it, but it was raised from a Noisette crossed with R. *sempervirens* about the time when Noisettes were creating a stir, being the first perpetual-flowering climbing roses, and so I feel it should occur here. It is a climber to 15 feet, when trained on wall or shrub, but can well remain as an arching loose bush, covered with some of the most beautiful of all rose foliage, dark green, deeply veined, glossy, long-pointed and serrated, and gracefully poised. Great, branching, nearly thornless, brownish shoots are thrown out during the summer, bearing a truss of blooms at the end, and clothed well in leaves. The buds are pink-tipped, opening to fairly full white flowers, showing yellow stamens, with a peculiar 'faded' scent, rather like that of 'Souvenir de la Malmaison'. Superb for cutting; a clean white; and the flowers are produced from about mid-July on bushes in the open, until autumn. This late flowering is partly because it is slightly tender, losing many of its flowering shoots in hard winters. On a sheltered wall a much earlier crop is given, in June or late May, on well-ripened shoots; the big late crops of flowers are no doubt an inheritance from the original R. *moschata*. There is a remarkable photograph between pages 36 and 37 in Miss Jekyll's *Roses for English Gardens*, and another facing page 55. A glance at these will make us all want to grow it; it is, after all, the only perpetual flowering white rambler of any quality.

Jamain and Forney, Plate 59.

Roses et Rosiers, Plate 15.

Willmott, Plate 94. Flowers not full enough.

Journal des Roses, Février 1881. Rather gross.

Journal des Roses, Mai 1905. 'À fleur jaune'. I have not seen this form, probably a sport, raised 1900, introduced 1904. Salmon-orange in colour.

Komlosy.

Choix des Plus Belles Roses, Plate 5. Very good.

'**Fellemberg**'. Fellemberg, 1857. 'La Belle Marseillaise.' Sometimes classed as a China Rose, this rather obscure but well-
known rose is, according to Miss Willmott, a hybrid between
R. *chinensis* and R. *multiflora*. I think this is doubtful, for it
would not then be recurrent. It does, however, conform reasonably closely to the larger growing China Roses and the 'Blush
Noisette', and thus I place it here. It is far removed from the
dwarf original Chinas.

'Fellemberg' makes a large open angular-branching bush
up to 8 feet high and wide on any soil. It takes some time to
build itself up, and is never dense. The young shoots are of
glaucous green or purplish and bear reddish thorns; the young
leaves have much the same colour, maturing to dark green,
and are small and pointed. Small and large clusters of flowers
appear, emerging from crimson buds, and opening to rich
warm pink or light lilac-crimson, fading to lighter pink as they
age, semi-double, cupped, showing stamens, with sweet-pea
fragrance. Sometimes the central petals remain balled, some are
quilled, and the flowers seldom exceed 2 inches in width.

It is one of the few shrubby roses which have been given the
Award of Garden Merit by the Royal Horticultural Society, an
honour it richly deserves, for flowers are produced so long as
the weather is mild, right into the autumn. It assorts well with
the Hybrid Musk Roses, or can be used with white Rugosas
and other flowering shrubs, but (as a shrub) should never be
placed near the front of the border on account of its somewhat
leggy habit. Two yards back, enhanced perhaps by *Caryopteris
clandonensis* or lavenders, or ceanothuses of the 'Topaze' persuasion in the foreground, it comes into its own as a very
beautiful and useful shrub. Alternatively, it is a constant
flowerer if pruned as a bedding rose, achieving about 3 feet
annually.

Choix des Plus Belles Roses, Plate 33. 'La Marseillaise': rather
light in colour.

Willmott, Plate 97. Seldom have I seen it in such magnificent
form.

'**Madame Legras de St Germain**', 1846, and '**Madame
Plantier**', 1835. The parentage of these two roses is obscure,

but they could be called non-recurrent hybrids of Noisette derivation. (See *The Old Shrub Roses*, pages 168 and 204.)

'Manettii'. Raised in Italy at Manza Botanic Garden by Dr Manetti; brought to England by Rivers, the Sawbridgeworth nurseryman, in 1835. A bush with reddish erect shoots and smooth pointed leaves. Semi-double, light pink flowers about 2 inches in diameter produced singly and in small clusters. No particular garden value, but included here in view of its supposed parentage; much used for an understock, and as a consequence it lingers in gardens long after its scions have died. Susceptible to 'black spot'.
Bailey, vol. iii, Fig. 3441. Pen drawing.

ROSA GIGANTEA AND ITS INFLUENCE ON THE NOISETTES

R. *gigantea*, 'the giant rose'—we might say the queen, the empress of wild roses—ascends in nature to a height of 40 feet or more by means of its strong shoots and hooked prickles, with large elegant drooping leaves and great lemon-white silky flowers 5 inches across. They have lent their poise and length of petal, their texture and their fragrance, to the old Tea Roses of the last century, which became merged with the Hybrid Teas and are now seldom seen. It is scarcely surprising that this luxuriant inhabitant of South-west China and Upper Burma, where the monsoon spends itself in the mountains, should not take kindly to the British climate. We can perhaps give it the rain it needs, but not the sun's ripening power, and in consequence its sappy stems get cut by autumn frosts, and really cold winters will raze it to the ground or kill it outright. In greenhouses and on the Riviera the tale is different, and superb blooms have been picked under glass. For some years Mrs Nigel Law grew large plants in the open in her garden at Chalfont St Peter, Buckinghamshire, but they were killed in a cold winter; they flowered well in warm summers. There are records in the 1939 *Annual* of the National Rose Society, page 177, of its growing and flowering well in such varied districts as Chepstow, Monmouthshire; Hinckley, Leicestershire; Hayward's Heath, Sussex, and in Suffolk. It grows and flowers well on the pergola at Mount Stewart, Northern Ireland, a property of the National Trust.

This regal rose was introduced from the Far East in 1888; there appears to be more than one form in cultivation in this country: a white-flowered plant with rather small leaves and flowers and a much larger plant with large leaves and large lemon-white flowers. The former grows well on a sunny wall at the John Innes Institute, Hertfordshire; the latter was my first introduction to this species when it flowered in the corridor of the greenhouse range at the University Botanic Garden, Cambridge, in 1929. An account of this particular form is in *The New Flora and Silva*, vol. i. The smaller type would appear to be more hardy, but could certainly not be called 'regal'. It is possible that the larger type may be that which Collet called 'macrocarpa'.

We must, I am afraid, write this rose off as a garden plant for general use in England. But if what Dr Hurst called his 'Four Stud Chinas'—or at least two of them—were descended from the China Rose and this species, it has had a profound influence on modern rose-breeding. 'Parks's Yellow Tea-Scented China' in particular, and 'Hume's Blush Tea-Scented China' are both looked upon as of *gigantea* derivation, if only on account of their scent. They were, presumably, old roses in China before being brought over here. These China hybrids produced flowers throughout summer and autumn, and R. *gigantea* gave them what yellow colouring they had, together with long petals and a silky texture.

All this and more is fully explained in my two earlier books on roses. Here we are concerned with climbing roses, and fortunately these two 'Stud Chinas' became linked with a species of the Musk Rose Section, and gave several roses of diverse characters which later became known as Tea-Noisettes or Climbing Teas.

It has been stated that the fragrance of the Tea Roses resembles that of crushed leaves of the Tea plant (*Thea sinensis*), but I have not found this so. On the other hand, several of them smell exactly like a freshly opened packet of gentle China tea—not the fully 'tarry' quality but 'slightly tarry'. This delicate and delicious aroma is found in several roses, one of the best known being 'Lady Hillingdon' and another 'Paul Lédé'. The source of this delicate fragrance is R. *gigantea* itself.

THE PARENTAL SPECIES OF THE TEA ROSES

GIGANTEA. South-west China, Burma. Introduced in 1889. Discovered by Sir Henry Collet in the Shan Hills in Northern Burma, and subsequently found in neighbouring states. Sometimes called R. *odorata gigantea*, but I prefer to consider it a species, whereas R. *odorata* correctly refers to garden hybrids introduced from China and called 'Tea Roses'. Like the China Rose it belongs to the Indicae Section. A pink form or hybrid is called R. *gigantea erubescens*.
Willmott, Plate 99. Splendid portrait.
Botanical Magazine, t.7972. Poor.

'Cooper's Burmese Rose' or **'Cooperi'**. Raised about 1931. A plant was received by Mr Courtney Page at the National Rose Society's Trial Ground, then at Hayward's Heath, Sussex, from an unrecorded source, and no other plants were traced at Kew or Edinburgh where Mr Cooper's seeds, collected in the wild in Burma, were being grown. It grew well on a pillar at Hayward's Heath, but used to suffer in cold winters. The leaves are extremely glossy, the flowers single, pure white, and the plant somewhat resembles R. *laevigata*. An interesting undetermined rose suitable for a sheltered wall.

CLIMBING TEA-NOISETTES

'Alister Stella Gray'. Raised by Gray, introduced by George Paul, 1894. Synonym 'Golden Rambler' in the United States. For the back of the border, where it will make an open shrub up to about 8 feet, or for a wall with any aspect where it will climb to 15 feet or more, this is one of the most perpetual of roses. Perhaps because I have known it since a child I look upon it with over-fond appreciation, but there was seldom a day from July to October when my father could not pick one of those perfect scented buds for his buttonhole; and who, with this memory and the vigour and fragrance of the plant before him, could neglect to grow it?

At midsummer all the short zigzag shoots, with their horizontally poised glossy leaves and few thorns, produce one or several flowers at their extremity; opening, a day or two later, from the tightly scrolled, yolk-yellow bud, to a silky, double, flat flower about 3 inches across, quartered and with button centre. These small sprays are excellent for cutting. Later on the plants throw up great thorny shoots which, no matter how woody or strong, produce huge branching heads of bloom, even into the autumn. Then they have less colour, but just as much scent. It is ideal behind Hybrid Musk Roses or at the back of flower and shrub borders. On a wall with a sunless aspect it has not much colour. It received an Award of Merit from the Royal Horticultural Society in 1893 when exhibited by the raiser. Delicious sweet scent, with a suspicion of tea. (Plate V.)

Journal des Roses, Août 1903. ⎫
Strassheim, June 1903.   ⎬ Identical plates. Fanciful.
                    ⎭

'Cécile Brunner, Climbing'. Hosp, 1894. This occurred as a sport from the original bush form in California. It is a vigorous, handsome, leafy plant, somewhat larger in leaf and flower than the bush, and will reach 20 feet in height on wall or tree. (The original bush form is described in *Shrub Roses of Today*, Chapter 12.) A fine plant in the University Botanic Garden at Oxford annually covers itself with hundreds of flowers of the same exquisite shape as the original, but rather richer in colouring. Each bloom is like a miniature Hybrid Tea Rose, of a size to go in a thimble, of clear pink, deeper in the fully double centre. Unfortunately the climbing form flowers only very sparsely after midsummer. Sweetly fragrant.

It is worth recording that a plant of this was sent to the Royal Horticultural Society's garden at Wisley some years ago; the plant came from Malta, where it is prized commercially and is known as 'Fiteni's Rose'. It has also been distributed as 'Climbing Bloomfield Abundance'.

I never lose an opportunity for extolling the qualities of 'Cécile Brunner'; my sole excuse for including it in this chapter is that it does not fit the others any better, and bears some resemblance to 'Alister Stella Gray'. It is not a Noisette. (Photograph, Plate 7.)

'Céline Forestier'. Trouillard, 1842. Although this is the result

of 'selfing' one of the earlier yellowish Noisettes, its Tea ancestry has come considerably to the fore, particularly in its colouring and scent. In view of its parentage and its flat Old Rose shape, I prefer to retain it among the Noisettes. It is a tough old variety, happy when settled, but slow in building up. The thorny wood and light green, limp leaves are pleasing, but no particular asset to the flowers, which are of especially high quality. Tight buds borne singly or in small clusters open out to a perfect circle of flat petals, with quartering and pronounced button eye, silky, and of refreshing creamy pale yellow with peach tones in the centre on opening. Spicy Tea-fragrance, powerful, delicious, and intense; always in flower. This is a rose to treasure on a warm wall. 8 to 10 feet. (Plate V.)
Journal des Roses, Octobre 1880. A splendid portrait.
Floral Magazine, 1861, Plate 64. Rather exaggerated.

'Claire Jacquier'. Bernaix, 1888. 'Mademoiselle Claire Jacquier.' Although its parentage is not recorded, it is no doubt of similar derivation to 'Alister Stella Gray', which it resembles closely in its flowers. It is, however, more hardy and much more vigorous, achieving 25 to 30 feet on a wall. This it has done as far north as at St Nicholas, Richmond, Yorkshire, and covers the east end of the exposed house with luxuriant greenery, bearing a copious crop of flowers at midsummer and a few later. It is not so continuous as 'Alister Stella Gray', but its vigour brings us a *tall* yellow climber, neat double yolk-yellow blooms like those of 'Alister Stella Gray', and delicious perfume. Its leaves are more pointed with coarser toothing. (Photograph, Plate 8.) Gault and Synge, Plate 200.

'Desprez à fleur Jaune'. Desprez, 1830. 'Jaune Desprez.' A hybrid between the 'Blush Noisette' and 'Parks's Yellow Tea-scented China'. The name indicates that it may have been a yellow sport from 'Desprez', but I have been unable to trace any information about it. We could not, however, wish for anything more beautiful; and I think it is wonderful that this rose, raised so long ago and without probably any idea in the raiser's mind as to what might materialize, should remain one of the most perpetual of all roses. I received this treasure from the late W. B. Hopkins of Hapton House, near Norwich; on the sunny front of his house was a luxuriant old plant reaching to some 15 feet, its strong branches trained up and all subsequent growth allowed to arch and fall outwards and downwards. It has few prickles, and is well clothed in rather light green leaves. The shoots, both small and large, have a zigzag turn at every node. One or a few flowers are borne at the end of every shoot, and the display is kept up unceasingly. They are silky, about 2 inches across, double, showing a few stamens, of creamy-tinted apricot-pink, with peach and yellow flushes, quite indescribable, and with an amazingly delicious, powerful fruity scent of equal charm. The only other rose really like it is a plant I have known for years as R. *moschata* 'Autumnalis', and until these have been seen no satisfactory image can be conjured up. If these roses could be bred again, and given more colour, they would take the world by storm. Prince, in his *Manual of Roses*, 1846, wrote: 'It is so powerfully fragrant that one plant will perfume a large garden in the cool weather of autumn.'

Choix des Plus Belles Roses, Plate 35. Very good portrait.

Jamain and Forney, Plate 51. A very poor copy of the above in reverse.

'Duchesse d'Auerstädt'. Bernaix, 1888. Jäger says this is a hybrid of 'Rêve d'Or'; McFarland, 1952, (V) claims it to be a sport from the same. I found it growing and flowering well at the Roseraie de l'Haÿ, producing large blooms, full of petals in the 'Gloire de Dijon' persuasion, and of similar colouring. Handsome foliage. This appears to be a valuable variety and I have it on trial.

'Gloire de Dijon'. Jacotot, 1853. Far removed from the original Noisettes, and as near to a Tea Rose as 'Lamarque', but included here as it seems to be of the hardy class of climbers and not what one associates with the delicate Teas. It was the result of crossing a vigorous Tea Rose with the Bourbon 'Souvenir de la Malmaison'. It would certainly seem to have derived some vigour and fullness from the Old Roses. It is the most popular and satisfactory of all old climbing roses; in constant flower in sun or shade, and admirable for wall training, and the giver of a rich fragrance from its deep buff-yellow flowers suffused in warm weather with pink and apricot. It is rather leggy in growth, but this can be cured by planting with it a small-growing clematis, or growing it between two shrubs on the wall, for it certainly needs support. With its many assets it was indeed an epoch-making rose, at a time when yellow roses were tender, or drooping, or pale. 15 feet.

Dean Hole, in *A Book about Roses*, ranked it as his favourite and most successful climbing rose. With so much competition from climbing Hybrid Teas, Luciae Ramblers and many newcomers, we cannot quite place it as No. 1 climber today, taking all things into consideration, but it is certainly no back number, and is in many respects the best yellow climber still. In my experience it still retains its vigour. 'Bouquet d'Or', raised in 1872 and a descendant of 'Gloire de Dijon', is of similar colouring to its parent. This I have recently acquired again. There is a good plate of it in *La Belgique Horticole*, 1879. Jamain and Forney, Plate 28. Poor.

Roses et Rosiers, Plate 17.

Hariot, Plate 4. Very full-coloured.

L'Horticulteur Français, 1856, Plate 10.

Komlosy. Very good.

Flore des Serres, vol. ix, Plate 39. Too pink.

Hoffmann, Plate 5. Good.

'Jaune Desprez'. See 'Desprez à fleur Jaune', page 97.

'Lamarque'. Maréchal, 1830. Originally known as 'Thé Maréchal', having been raised by M. Maréchal and grown as a window plant, subsequently named in honour of Général Lamarque. This, with 'Desprez à fleur Jaune', was one of the first yellowish Noisettes raised. It is of the same parentage as the Desprez rose, but leans more towards the Tea Rose. It is a plant only for the warmer west outdoors, but is a success under glass. At Dartington Hall, Devon, it grows on a sunny wall to perfection; its few limp light green leaves and large lemon-white flowers against the varied pattern of stone and moss and lichen provide a picture that could not be improved upon. The flowers are nodding—a well-known trait of the Tea Roses— very double, flat, with quilled and quartered petals, and pass from fresh lemon-white to nearly white, with a most exquisite tea-scent. A great treasure. 10 feet in our cool climate. (Photograph, Plate 9.)

In *The Floral World*, 1874, page 118, occurs the following amazing description:

The mammoth rose-tree of Santa Rosa is, we think, of sufficient importance to justify its being noticed in these pages. This immense rose-tree, now clothing the cottage of a Mr Rendall, of Santa Rosa, is an example of our old friend Lamarque, one of the finest of Noisette roses. It covers an area of four hundred superficial feet, and in due season is fairly loaded with flowers. Indeed, so profusely does it bloom, that it has had no less than four thousand fully expanded roses and twenty thousand buds at one time. It appears to have been planted fifteen years since, and so vigorous has been the growth from the first, that it now extends over the roof of the house, and when in bloom it presents a magnificent sight.

How I long for a warm climate!

Choix des Plus Belles Roses, Plate 30. Excellent portrait.
Jamain and Forney, Plate 17. 'Général Lamarque'. Poor.
Journal des Roses, Juillet 1905. A good but flattering portrait.
Jekyll. Facing p. 80 (photograph).

'Madame Alfred Carrière'. Schwartz, 1879. Very far removed from our original Noisettes, but a wonderful plant and as perpetual as any. It can be treated as a large shrub, some 10 feet high and wide, like the old plant that grew at Kiftsgate Court, or as a climber reaching 20 feet, as at Sissinghurst. It remains one of the more popular old climbing roses to this day, and can compete on equal terms with modern roses in every respect, if we do not cavil at its pale colouring. The leaves are of light fresh green on green stems. The flowers are large, fully double, rather globular when opened from the pretty scrolled buds, creamy blush fading to blush-white, sometimes quartered or with muddled centres. The scent is more like that of a modern rose than an old Noisette. (Photograph, Plate 10.)
Journal des Roses, Avril 1886. Excellent portrait.
Strassheim, 1907. February–May.

'Maréchal Niel'. Pradel, 1864. Said to be a seedling of 'Cloth of Gold'. What exciting days they were, when 'Gloire de

Dijon', that robust, coppery yellow garden rose, was followed eleven years later by the wonderful 'Maréchal Niel'! Nothing so yellow, so voluptuous, so fragrant of Tea had been seen before, and it has more good portraits in colour than any other rose of its kind, some so flattering that one might think it was sunflower-yellow rather than its own softer buttery tone. Unfortunately it has a weak flower stalk, and a loose nodding bloom, of long Tea-shape, and does not last well in wet weather. Its growth and foliage are excellent. Whether it has deteriorated I do not know; I have grown it in the sunny angle created by two sheds facing south-west, and it grew well to 10 feet, and flowered fairly freely. Decidedly a specialist's rose, but one that we cannot afford to lose. It is in effect a climbing Tea Rose, but for the sake of convenience I follow most authorities and include it here, as it has R. *moschata* in its parentage, though rather far back.

There is no doubt that in warmer climates it could be a glorious rose; sunny positions in South Devon might suit it. Abroad it should still be grown; anyone who has read C. M. Villiers-Stuart's *Gardens of the Great Mughals* will remember the passage in her description of the Shalimar Bagh in Kashmir on page 175: 'But the loveliest roses in the garden are the Maréchal Niels which climb the grey green walls of the Hall of Public Audience and hang their soft yellow globes head downward in clusters from the carved cedar cornice.'

It is excellent for greenhouse culture, so long as its root is in the open soil, outside like that of a vine, with its branches on a framework under the sloping glass. (See *The Rose Annual*, 1931, page 166—The National Rose Society.) When in stale borders in the house or in pots or tubs it does not thrive for long. There are some wonderful pictures of it in various books, thriving under glass, and I cannot think of any species of any genus for which I would be more ready to give wall space under glass.

Paul, 9th Edition, Plate 1.
Jamain and Forney, Plate 22.
Roses et Rosiers, Plate 6.
Niedtner, p. 144. Good.
Hariot, Plate 8.

Journal des Roses, Mars 1877.
L'Horticulteur Français, 1864, Plate 20.
Nestel's Rosengarten, 1866. Very good.
Komlosy. Too dark a colour.
The Garden, 1883, p. 426. Excellent portrait.
Floral Magazine, 1865. Plate 237.
Hoffmann, Plate 8. Excellent.

'Paul Lédé, Climbing'. Low, 1913. A sport from the bush original, bred by Pernet-Ducher and introduced in 1902. It is surprising how rare this rose is. One would expect its delicious tea-scent to have warranted its more general use. It is a vigorous plant with good foliage and is satisfactory in every way, producing a big initial crop and subsequent blooms until the autumn; full-petalled, yellowish buff with deep carmine flush in the centre; like a deeper coloured even more fragrant 'Gloire de Dijon'. And this must be my excuse for its inclusion here; none of the normal check-lists even mentions it. 15 feet.

'Rêve d'Or'. Ducher, 1869. 'Golden Chain' in the United States. A seedling from 'Madame Schultz'. A vigorous plant for warm sunny gardens; beautiful rich green glossy leaves, coppery tinted while young, and loose semi-double flowers of deep buff yellow suffused with salmon fading to butter-yellow, with dark yellow stamens; the petals are often quilled. An excellent rose constantly in flower until the autumn, but best on a warm wall. Slight tea-fragrance.
Journal des Roses, Décembre 1882. Exaggerated.

'William Allen Richardson'. Ducher, 1878. A sport from 'Rêve d'Or'; richer in colour, but of less vigorous and graceful growth. I doubt whether this rose could have remained in cultivation apart from its vivid orange colouring, as rare then as it was until recently. The young shoots and foliage are richly coloured with a dark mahogany tone; prickly on strong growth, but almost thornless on small twigs. The flowers are borne singly or two or three together, rather shapeless, double, of intense orange/yolk-yellow colouring, quickly fading to near white in sunny weather. Slight tea-scent. An awkward angular plant for sunny walls, where its extraordinary colour, arising from unattractive buds, can be tolerated, but more of an historic piece than one of great beauty unless exceptionally well grown. 12 feet.

Hariot, Plate 14. Exaggerated.

Journal des Roses, Mars 1886. Poor.

Florist and Pomologist, 1883. Rather flattering.

Kingsley, Plate 71. Poor.

Garten-Zeitung, Berlin, 1883. Exaggerated.

Hoffmann, Plate 13. Good.

The following Tea Rose hybrids are tender except in favoured parts of England, but are popular in California and the South of France. In districts suited to them they are a great success and very strong-growing. A number of similar hybrids have been raised in Australia by Alister Clark, and I have grown 'Flying Colours', 'Kitty Kininmouth', 'Lorraine Lee', 'Nancy Hayward', and 'Pennant', but our summers do not ripen their wood sufficiently to make them flower. I hear of 'Lorraine Lee' as a spectacular hedge-plant in Australia.

'Belle Portugaise'. Raised in the Lisbon Botanic Garden by Henri Cayeux, 1903. R. *gigantea* × 'Reine Marie-Henriette', a pink Hybrid Tea. A fine old plant of this vigorous rose grows on the Lutyens building in the Royal Horticultural Society's gardens at Wisley. It has large elegant drooping leaves and large gracious flowers emerging from long pointed buds—in the true Tea fashion, in fact. The loosely double flower is composed of silky quilled petals, rolled at the edges, creamy salmon with deeper reverse. Delicious tea-scent. One magnificent season of flower. Requires a warm wall and does best in sheltered districts; it is obvious from the Wisley plant that it is vigorous enough to thrive on sand. 20 feet. A hybrid of this, 'Susan Louise', is a prolific large bush in California.

'La Follette'. Raised at Cannes by Lord Brougham's gardener, Busby, about 1910. It resembles 'Belle Portugaise', but is much richer in colour, rose pink with cream, but dark coppery salmon-pink to crimson on the reverse. A beautiful flower of loose, long-pointed shape. A plant used to grow and flower well in the walled garden at Nymans, Sussex. In an article in *The Rose*, vol. x, No. 3, Mr Peter Harkness describes a stupendous plant growing in a greenhouse at Southill Park, Bedfordshire, producing annually between fifteen hundred and two thousand flowers during the early months of the year. It has stems about 18 feet high and then spreads out horizontally aloft covering an area about 48 feet by 30 feet. Out of doors in England it may achieve 18 feet on a warm wall; it is vigorous but needs a warm sunny wall in England; on the Riviera it flourishes.

'Sénateur Amic'. Nabonnand, 1824. R. *gigantea* × 'General MacArthur'. Vivid cerise-crimson, nearly single flowers from long pointed buds. This is a satisfactory wall plant in sandy soil at Wisley, and annually provides a brilliant display in June. 15 feet.

TEA ROSES

Notes on a few varieties

There remain the Tea Roses, and I wish my cultivation of them were more successful so that I could hand on plenty of first-hand experience. They do not thrive in our bleak part of Surrey. One has to go to sheltered rich gardens in the heart of Sussex or in the West, or in Ireland—or to France—to see them really thriving. And yet every now and again one comes across a grand old plant making a great show in the most unexpected places. While the old Tea Roses were not climbers—at least most of them—they are best when given the protection of a wall, and hence their inclusion here. They should be encouraged to build up slowly, with light pruning, and should be given protection in winter with mats or evergreen branches and a good deep mulch.

I think we can claim that all the China Roses of flame or yellowish colouring are really hybrids of the original Tea Roses, which are presumed to be old Chinese garden hybrids between R. *chinensis* and R. *gigantea*, and known botanically as R. × *odorata*. I include some true climbers and also the climbing forms of 'Lady Hillingdon' and 'Mrs Herbert Stevens'; the former is a true Tea, the latter has one parent a Hybrid Tea. They give us the loose

Tea-Rose shape, unfolding from long shapely buds, and delicious perfume of the Tea Roses coupled with a reasonable hardiness.

Writing in the Royal Horticultural Society's *Journal*, in the account of the Society's Rose Conference in 1889, the Rev. C. Wilks, a noted rosarian of that time, gave a list of what he considered the hardiest Tea Roses: 'Madame Lambard', 'Marie van Houtte', 'Anna Olivier', 'Souvenir d'un Ami', 'Gloire de Dijon', 'Rubens', 'Franzisca Kruger', 'Homère', 'The Hon. Edith Gifford' 'Jean Ducher', 'Caroline Kuster', 'Catherine Mermet' 'Madame Willermoz', 'Madame Bravy', 'Madame Berard'. Most of these I have seen or grown and they are very free-flowering. It would seem worth while for someone to try to collect these together and grow them in a sheltered garden. In those days they found *Rosa canina* the best understock. I wish I had a large, slightly heated greenhouse to accommodate them. They are too good to lose forever; the gentle elegance of bygone days is preserved in them.

'Devoniensis, Climbing'. Introduced in 1858, while the original bush form was introduced in 1841, by Lucombe, a nurseryman at Exeter, famous for the hybrid oak bearing his name. Known as the 'Magnolia Rose'. Large double well-shaped flowers of creamy white, tinged with carmine on the bud, and with a warm flush of apricot in the centre on opening. Richly tea-scented and recurrent. Perhaps 12 feet on a warm wall. (Photograph, Plate 12.)
Paxton, t.169.
Curtis, vol. i, Plate 1.
Hibberd, p. 167. Poor.

'E. Veyrat Hermanos'. Bernaix, 1895. Also known as 'Pillar of Gold'. Long and shapely but opening to coppery apricot-pink.

'Fortune's Double Yellow'. R. *odorata pseudindica* or 'Beauty of Glazenwood'; 'Gold of Ophir'. Introduced by Robert Fortune from China in 1845. This was the most brilliant rose of its time, and will make people blink even today. It is not a strong grower except in favoured climates such as that at Mount Usher in Ireland, where it covers a wall some 9 feet high. The loose semi-double flowers are bright coppery yellow, heavily flushed with coppery scarlet, borne singly or in small clusters at midsummer. It was already an old garden plant when Fortune discovered it in a 'rich Mandarin's garden at Ningpo', and for five or six years after its introduction its pruning was so misunderstood that growers everywhere cut away its flowering wood. Eventually beautiful plants were grown and flowered without pruning—except after flowering—by Messrs Standish and Noble, the then proprietors of Sunningdale Nurseries. This is recorded in *The Botanical Magazine*, t.4679.

Komlosy.
Willmott, Plate 85. Good.
Flore des Serres, vol. 8, p. 53.
Nestel's Rosengarten, 1866.
Le Jardin Fleuriste, vol. 4, Plate 361. Poor colour.
Botanical Magazine, t.4679. Pale.
Journal des Roses, Mai 1877. Exaggerated colour.

'**Général Schablikine**'. Nabonnand, 1878. A thrifty, hardy, vigorous plant with beautiful plum-coloured shoots and elegant leaves. Produces three big flushes of bloom, but is seldom out of flower. Flowers borne on a characteristic somewhat nodding but firm stalk, each one scrolled and shapely; deep coppery carmine-pink, opening well and fading but little. Delicate fragrance. A bush, 5 feet or so, but higher on a wall.

'**Lady Hillingdon, Climbing**'. 'Papa Gontier' × 'Madame Hoste', both Tea Roses. The original was raised by Lowe and Shawyer in 1910, but the climbing sport did not occur until 1917. This and the climbing form of 'Mrs Herbert Stevens' are precious, hardy, vigorous climbing roses in the Tea tradition. A most beautiful plant, with plum-coloured young wood and prickles, darkest green leaves, plum-tinted when young, and gracious flowers, loosely double, from long shapely buds of softest apricot yellow. Delicious fragrance of a freshly opened packet of tea with a hint of apricots. Is in constant production from midsummer until the frosts stop it, and a wonderful plant for sunny walls, where it will reach some 20 feet, its blooms nodding down at one and shedding its rich scent. It is vigorous, and will thrive even on poor sandy soils.

Wing-Commander Young, in the American Rose Annual for 1956, placed this and 'Zéphirine Drouhin' right in the top rank for continuous production. (Plate VI.)

'Madame Antoine Mari'. Mari, 1901. Quilled petals, creamy blush with reverse of rosy lilac to carmine; deep pink buds; large and full-petalled. Plum-coloured wood and prickles. A bush of some 4 feet; satisfactory in reasonably sheltered districts, but considerably stronger when trained on a warm wall. Delicate perfume.
Journal des Roses, Février 1904. Good.

'Madame Falcot'. Guillot Fils, 1858. Rich nankeen-yellow, fading paler, with somewhat quilled petals. Large double flowers. A bush, perhaps 5 feet on a wall. Jäger calls this a 'subspecies' of 'Safrano'.
Roses et Rosiers, Plate 46. Pale.
Niedtner, facing p. 48. Good.
Journal des Roses, Juin 1880.
Jamain and Forney, Plate 49.

'Mademoiselle Franziska Krüger'. Nabonnand, 1880. 'Catherine Mermet' × 'Général Schablikine'. Long treasured by the late James Comber at Nymans. A fairly tough Tea Rose, pale yellow and pink, very double. Rather weak stem. A bush, perhaps 7 feet on a wall.
Journal des Roses, Février 1888. Good.
Hoffmann, Plate 15. Too yellow.

'Marie van Houtte'. 'Mademoiselle Marie van Houtte.' Ducher, 1871. 'Madame de Tartas' × 'Madame Falcot'—distinguished parents which have produced many a good rose. This is no exception, and it is perhaps the most satisfactory of all Tea Roses. Beautiful, shapely, high-centred, full blooms of deep creamy yellow, intensifying in the centre, and tinged with rose around the perimeter. Handsome foliage. This grows well to 4 to 5 feet, in the lee of an old wall at Oxford Botanic Garden. Delicious tea-fragrance.
Hariot, Plate 9. All the grace is captured.

Journal des Roses, Avril 1880. Good.

The Garden, 1879, vol. xvi, Plate 221.

Brougham, 1898. In an account of roses growing at the Château Éléonore, Lord Brougham and Vaux shows a photograph of a bush some 10 feet high by 70 feet circumference, densely bushy and flowering freely.

Paul, 9th Edition, Plate 14. Might be mistaken for a portrait of 'Peace'!

Hoffmann, Plate 10. Very good.

'Mrs Herbert Stevens, Climbing'. 'Frau Karl Druschki' × 'Niphetos'. The climbing sport of this famous 1910 McGredy rose occurred with Pernet-Ducher in 1922. It is a rose all on its own today, when so few Tea Roses remain to us. Vigorous stems and good foliage always producing exquisite tea-scented blooms of creamy lemon-white with long bud and scrolled petals. The thin quality of the petals suffers occasionally in wet weather. Even so, it is well worth growing, giving flowers singly and in clusters. Some of the delicacy of the old Tea Rose 'Niphetos' is preserved in this hardy hybrid, but it is infinitely more fragrant. A splendid vigorous plant which grows well even in poor sandy soil, and is recurrent. 20 feet. (Plate VI.)

'Niphetos'. Bougère, 1843. The climbing form was introduced in 1889. Lemon-white, drooping flowers closely resembling 'Maréchal Niel' except in colour. A delicate beauty needing a cool greenhouse and there worthy of every attention. Delicate tea-scent. A beautiful photograph is in *Favourite Flowers* by Constance Spry, page 52 (Dent, 1959).

Hariot, Plate 11. Excellent portrait.

'Papa Gontier'. Nabonnand, 1883. The climbing form was introduced in 1904, and is reputedly of better substance. Semi-double, bright coppery pink, deeper reverse.

'Reine Marie-Henriette'. Levet, 1878. 'Madame Bérard' × 'Général Jacqueminot'. Two famous ancestors, bringing in 'Madame Falcot' and 'Gloire de Dijon', and there is indeed plenty of Tea-quality in the colour, shape, and fragrance. Large cupped flowers of deep cerise-crimson on a vigorous plant with plenty of foliage. Classed correctly in works of reference as a Hybrid Tea, but just suitable for inclusion here. 15 feet.

'Solfaterre'. Boyau, 1843. A seedling from 'Lamarque' and resembling it in habit. Large double flowers, light sulphur yellow, full, graceful; free-flowering. Very fragrant. Comparatively hardy and a rose to keep. Vigorous in warm climates. Curtis, vol. ii, Plate 1.

'Sombreuil, Climbing'. The bush form was raised in 1850 and introduced by Robert, and was a hybrid of 'Gigantesque', a pink Hybrid Perpetual. I have not grown the climbing form for long, but it produces good flowers of wonderful beauty, somewhat reminiscent of the flat quartered character of 'Souvenir de la Malmaison', but infinitely more refined, of creamy white with flesh tint in the centre. Delicious tea-scent. To be treasured for all time. Perhaps 12 feet on a warm wall, and repeatedly in flower. (Photograph, Plate 11.)
Hariot, Plate 12.
Nestel's Rosengarten. 'Madame de Sombreuil.' Claimed to be very hardy.

'Souvenir de Madame Léonie Viennot'. Bernaix, 1898. Beautiful shapely buds of coral-red opening to blooms shewing clear yellow colouring, heavily flushed with clear coppery-pink and coppery-red, the whole losing colour with age, but always pleasant. Loosely double, silky petals; delicious tea-scent. Recurrent flowering. Good foliage. Will probably achieve 15 to 20 feet on a warm wall.

'Souvenir d'un Ami'. Bélot-Defougère, 1846. A delicate beauty worth all the care we gardeners can bestow upon it in the way of a sheltered wall, good soil, and protection in winter—or to be grown under glass. Incurved petals of warm, light coppery-pink enfold yellow stamens; a large cupped flower, semi-double. A fragrance to which one returns again and again. A bush, perhaps 5 feet on a warm wall. Preserved by Mrs Ruby Fleischmann for many years.
Choix des Plus Belles Roses, Plate 18. 'The most beautiful bright flesh that it is possible to see.' Excellent portrait.

Curtis, vol. ii, No. 13. Poor.
Jamain and Forney, Plate 44. Poor.
Hariot, Plate 13. Poor colour.
Nestel's Rosengarten, 1868. Exquisite.

'Vicomtesse Pierre de Fou'. Sauvageot, 1923. 'L'Idéal' ×
'Joseph Hill' (a yellowish-red Noisette and a yellowish-orange
Hybrid Tea respectively). A magnificent, strong-growing
climbing rose with broad glossy leaves and two good crops of
flowers. They are large, full, dusky coppery-orange passing to
deep coppery-pink, quite unusual, the rolled, quartered, and
somewhat quilled petals making an elegant flower, nodding
always at the admirer underneath. Delicious tea-fragrance. Will
achieve 20 feet even in poor soil. An extraordinarily good rose
which has been unaccountably neglected. (Fig. 8.)

7

Large-flowered Climbers of Hybrid Tea Style

See how the flowers, as at parade,
Under their colours stand display'd:
Each regiment in order grows,
That of the tulip, pink, and rose.

Andrew Marvell, 1621–78.

SO FAR this book has proceeded with only botanical and historical difficulties; enough, certainly, in a genus so involved in hybridity as *Rosa* to daunt us all, but nothing compared with the difficulty we must all experience in making a selection from among countless favourites. The whole book is, however, a selection—*my* selection—and it so happens that in horticulture, and maybe in other walks of life too, the odd variety which does not conform to the general style becomes neglected. Our more favourite genera are littered with these individuals: good varieties on their own which have been unaccountably passed by. The catalogues seem to like to offer to the public solid groups of varieties which vary in colour but not in other particulars. I have always championed the odd varieties because I like individuality, and if Mr A grows 'Garnette', his neighbour 'Pink Garnette' and Mrs B down the road buys 'White Garnette', I certainly would not choose a 'Yellow Garnette'; I would have the unique 'Cécile Brunner'—otherwise we shall all be levelled down to the least common denominator and our gardens will all be the same.

Among climbing roses there are many isolated varieties which do not conform to the main stream of varieties. This is because very little attention has been given by hybridists to the raising of climbing roses, and because there are few available compared with the thousands of bush varieties. The good new varieties of ramblers raised since the Hitler war are less in number than the fingers on one hand, and if we put the number of good, equally new, strong-growing, perpetual-flowering climbers at two handsful, we shall not be far wrong. But the bushes are counted in hundreds over the same period. If it were not for the climbing sports of Hybrid Teas we should indeed be suffering from a scarcity of climbers—and yet they are just the roses which can give the greatest display of all. There is much research needed and much has to be done to bring our climbing roses up to the standard of the Hybrid Teas and Floribundas.

Many climbing sports of Hybrid Teas have arisen but have not become popular, since they were not sufficiently prolific of blooms later in the season. Sometimes a more recurrent sport arises after the original, but it is manifest that climbing sports are only likely to be selected from the more modern varieties in commerce today, though it is equally true that some of the oldest are among the very best. Miss Wylie describes in the Royal Horticultural Society's *Journal* for January 1955 how it is possible, following observation by D. Morey, that these climbing mutants or sports are similar in origin to certain graft hybrids (periclinal chimeras) like *Laburnocytisus adamii*. If so, this would account for the readiness of some of the less stable to revert to the original bush form when propagated from root cuttings.

This chapter, then, contains my selection of Climbing Hybrid Teas, together with a number of similar quality and a few isolated gems which are not recurrent but which we cannot afford to lose.

To help intending planters we will discuss the collection, and can at once dispose of a few which need not be referred to again in these pages, since they have had their due in my two previous books. They are the extra-strong-growing varieties of Bourbons and Hybrid Perpetuals, which will reach anything up to 8 feet without support or even more if trained on wall or fence. As their colours are all soft, being on the blue side of red in the spectrum, they are valuable with many of the old ramblers for providing climbing roses to decorate a garden or border devoted to Old Roses. They include some really excellent fragrant plants

1. The fine form of *Rosa brunonii* known as 'La Mortola'.

2. *Rose longicuspis*, a reliable and prolific species of the Synstylae Section for growing into trees. Extremely fragrant.

3. *Rosa moschata*, the original Autumn-flowering Musk Rose, together with semi-double blooms from the same plant. Very fragrant.

4. 'Autumnalis', closely related to *Rosa moschata*, flowering from August onwards. Very fragrant.

5. *Rosa wichuraiana*, practically evergreen and a
splendid ground-coverer. Delicious scent
from the flowers which appear in August.

6. 'Bobbie James'. A seedling of one of the Synstylae roses, of great
vigour and fragrance.

7. 'The Garland', a sweetly scented and prolific rambler raised in 1835.

8. 'Vicomtesse Pierre de Fou', 1923, a vigorous climbing Tea-scented rose
shewing the typical 'quartering' of old-style varieties.

such as 'Blairi No. 2', the perpetual-flowering 'Zéphirine Drou-hin' and its sport 'Kathleen Harrop' and 'Climbing Souvenir de la Malmaison'. The climbing China Roses were described in *Shrub Roses of Today*. Lists of these and others will be found on pages 182–6.

These are a few descendants of R. *wichuraiana* for this chapter. With some hesitation I included 'Albertine' and 'Mary Wallace' in Chapter 5, for they do not conform to the fairly uniform Luciae Ramblers, but they would not really have fitted here, though 'Mary Wallace' might be considered as a step towards 'New Dawn'. Equally they link with 'Dream Girl' and 'Purity' in the next chapter, where 'Albertine' might have been included. All of these roses have the glossy leaves and some of the fragrance of R. *wichuraiana* and R. *luciae*. I have omitted 'Dr Van Fleet',[1] since though it makes a superlative contribution annually in flower and fragrance, it is not recurrent, and I therefore prefer the other-wise identical though rather less vigorous 'New Dawn'. 'Éten-dard' or 'New Dawn Rouge' comes into the same category.

Next we have a few really splendid climbing roses, not sports of Hybrid Teas, and not recurrent. Oldest is 'Madame de Sancy de Parabère', one of the Boursault Roses, thornless and very early-flowering. It has a shape unlike any other double rose, but little fragrance. Even so, I would retain it for the wonderful early display. 'Cupid' is a pretty, large-flowering single with large heps in autumn. The three most magnificent varieties in this little set are 'Easlea's Golden', yellow; 'Paul's Lemon Pillar', lemon-white; and 'Madame Grégoire Staechelin', rich pink. All are exceptionally fragrant, large-flowered, but not recurrent. They are indispensable.

There are two recurrent varieties alike only in name: 'Gruss an Aachen' and 'Gruss an Teplitz', both full-petalled in the old style, creamy pink and crimson respectively.

Now we can look at the sports of Hybrid Teas, and roses similarly shaped and recurrent. As suggested earlier (page 22), even these are not without disadvantages. While I like a rose of the Hybrid Tea persuasion to be erect and carry its flower well aloft

[1] 'Dr Van Fleet' and 'Mary Wallace' are some of the principal descendants of R. *wichuraiana* used by Dr and Mrs Brownell in the United States to help to produce hardy roses of the Hybrid Tea class for the colder States. This is set forth by Miss Wylie in the Royal Horticultural Society's *Journal* for December 1954.

on a good stem so long as it is a bush, I am certain that this is a disadvantage when a climbing sport occurs. We train the shoots along and up the wall, or, if they will bend, over an arch—and what happens? The flowers are produced on side shoots mostly erect with their flowers at the top, and as a rule most of the flowers will be well up the wall or over the top of the arch. The result is that, unless one looks out of an upstairs window, the flowers cannot really be appreciated, except for their show of colour. This applies to the bulk of the Hybrid Tea climbing sports. In other words, I do not like my climbing roses to be without grace even when the flowers are large and recurrent. The great joy of a climbing rose is when its flowers nod down or at least are poised outwardly from the wall or support. There are just a few modern-type, large-flowered, recurrent-flowering climbers that do this, and among them I would cite 'Souvenir de Claudius Denoyel', 'Crimson Glory', 'Madame Édouard Herriot', 'Shot Silk', and 'Ena Harkness'.

Let us look at pure pink varieties first. Few of superlative worth have been raised recently; my first choice, historically, would be 'La France', nearly one hundred years old, with 'Madame Abel Chatenay' and 'Madame Caroline Testout' both raised in the last century, followed by one of the 'Ophelia' breed—'Ophelia' itself, 'Madame Butterfly' or 'Lady Sylvia', dating back to the original in 1912—with the addition of 'Shot Silk'. The 'Ophelia' breed are very stiff but extra recurrent and probably produce more flowers in a season than any of the other climbing Hybrid Tea sports. It is astonishing how all these grand old varieties still stand unrivalled, but it is partly because breeders have been interested in extraneous colours like red and yellow and their intermediates. 'Michèle Meilland', 'Picture', 'Souvenir de la Malmaison', and 'Lady Waterlow' might also be chosen, with the pretty single 'Dainty Bess'.

Of tones approaching copper and flame are the old 'Madame Édouard Herriot' ('Daily Mail') and 'President Hoover'; 'Flaming Sunset', 'Madame Henri Guillot', splendid 'Mrs Sam McGredy', and the new 'Soraya'. 'Independence' is all on its own for colour. Other strong claimants for inclusion here are some of the Tea Roses in Chapter 6.

Among the true reds and crimsons are two very dark-coloured

roses, 'Château de Clos Vougeot', 1908, containing all the oldest wine, and 'Guinée', 1938, made of the darkest port-wine-coloured velvet. The first to flower is generally the bright crimson 'Souvenir de Claudius Denoyel' followed by the two stalwarts 'Étoile de Hollande' and 'Crimson Glory', and 'Ena Harkness', if a third be wanted. Of equal value for effect is 'Allen Chandler'.

The yellows are comparatively new. I should plead for 'Golden Dawn' to take first place on account of its beauty and fragrance (but it is not very recurrent), likewise 'Lady Forteviot' in warm yellow; 'Apeles Mestres' foremost in shape and quality, with 'Spek's Yellow', 'Ellinor LeGrice', 'Christine', and 'Elegance' of similar quality, all rather stiff in growth. 'Mrs Arthur Curtiss James' has never found the favour in Britain that it has beyond the Atlantic, and should be tried more frequently. Helen Van Pelt Wilson, in her book *Climbing Roses*, ranks it 'absolutely tops'. 'High Noon' probably produces more flowers during the year than other yellows, apart from 'Mermaid' (see Chapter 9) but is gaunt in growth and sparse in foliage; it has a healthy rival in 'Golden Showers' (Chapter 8). The Tea Noisettes (Chapter 6) must be considered when selecting yellows.

There are practically no white varieties; for this colour we must turn to the ramblers and 'Purity', 'Mrs Herbert Stevens', 1910, a Tea to be found in Chapter 6, and 'McGredy's Ivory', 1930, hold the field still among large-flowered climbers; the climbing form of 'Frau Karl Druschki' seems to have died out, only the bush remaining in cultivation.

The dates I have given above indicate when the original bush form was raised, and it is interesting to see how well these climbing sports—for most of them are such—hold their own through the decades.

Lovely and appreciated as are the best climbing Hybrid Teas and these few others, this type of rose cannot be considered as the ultimate goal. Already surpassing them in freedom of flowering are a few new climbers of bright modern colours. These are to be found in the next chapter. If it is the aim of the breeders to produce strong-growing climbers of graceful growth and good foliage giving Hybrid Tea type of fragrant flowers at midsummer and with later crops, then one of the few varieties which approach this ideal is 'New Dawn'. When a race of these superlative roses is

available there will be no need to cherish the ungainly sports of
Hybrid Teas, unless like 'Ophelia' and its breed they are really
recurrent. One reservation should be made here: a climbing rose
can often be given a suitable position in a garden, fitting in with
any design, whereas bush Hybrid Teas, needing individual cultivation, generally in isolated beds, may be felt out of place. Therefore we should retain the best Hybrid Tea climbers, because there
is no substitute for the perfection of their blooms.

I have found it difficult to describe the scents of the roses in
this chapter and the next. The Hybrid Tea is of such mixed
parentage that its fragrance is also often composed of different
characters, and frequently their smell in the evening is quite
different from that in the morning.

POSTSCRIPT. One is never up to date with modern roses; the
new varieties come so fast. Since writing the above, several good
new climbing sports of Hybrid Teas have arrived, and among
them are some which will be highly desirable if they produce a
good second crop. Varieties to be watched are 'Climbing Gail
Borden', 'Grand'mère Jenny', 'Bettina', 'Josephine Bruce',
and 'Perfecta'. There is also a 'Climbing Queen Elizabeth'; this
should be a real giant as the original is so strong.

'Allen Chandler'. Prince, 1923. A hybrid from 'Hugh Dickson'
and a really excellent red rose, with greater brilliance, better
texture and shape—though nearly single—and larger flowers
than 'Paul's Scarlet', shewing golden stamens. It is a sturdy
climber with good foliage, and is seldom without flower after
the main crop. Produces a copious and lasting display of large
orange-red heps; valuable as these may be in late autumn, if
they are removed as they develop more flowers are the result.
15 feet.

'Allen's Fragrant Pillar'. Allen, 1931. 'Paul's Lemon Pillar' ×
'Souvenir de Claudius Denoyel'. With two such distinguished
parents this is justly good. Large loose blooms, cerise pink

with yellow base giving a touch of brilliance. Delicious scent, glossy foliage, and very vigorous. Recurrent. 8 to 10 feet.

'Apeles Mestres'. Pedro Dot, 1925. 'Frau Karl Druschki' × 'Souvenir de Claudius Pernet'. A beautiful rose, owing its long shapely bud to 'Druschki'; pale clear yellow, sweet-scented. A good strong grower producing flowers mostly at midsummer. 12 feet.

'Château de Clos Vougeot, Climbing'. Morse, 1920. A sport from the bush form, 1908. Open, short-petalled flowers of darkest red with maroon and black shadings, fully double. No purple tints. Normal Hybrid Tea foliage. A vigorous plant, will thrive on light soils, and gives blooms after the main display. Fragrance as deep and powerful as the colouring. 15 feet.
Journal des Roses, Août 1908.
Strassheim, February 1909.

'Christine, Climbing'. The McGredy variety, a famous yellow of the '20s, gave rise to the climber in 1936. This beautiful, fragrant, clear yellow variety flowers freely at midsummer and intermittently later. Well worth growing. It has comparatively small but shapely flowers. 15 feet.

'Crimson Glory, Climbing'. Kordes, 1935. 'Catherine Kordes' seedling × 'W. E. Chaplin'. The climbing sport was intro-duced in 1946. This magnificent, very fragrant, deepest crimson rose gives a number of later blooms after the main crop. Those who object to purplish tints should place this variety where it is protected from the hottest sun. 10 to 12 feet.
Leroy, Plate 8.
Baird, p. 48.

'Cupid'. Cant, 1915. Strong thorny shoots with brownish tinted foliage when young, turning to dark green. The flowers are light peach pink, very large and nearly single, with crinkled petals, shewing good stamens. One season of flowering, but the heps are large, rounded, orange-red with persistent calyces and last in beauty well into the winter. I like it best when planted among other shrubs, so that it can grow through and over them, as it is never overpowering; it grows like this at St Paul's Waldenbury, Hertfordshire. Sweet raspberry scent. Probably 15 feet. (Plate VII.)

'Dainty Bess, Climbing'. Introduced in 1935, from the original bush raised in 1925 by Archer. 'Ophelia' × 'K. of K.'. The exquisite single pink variety, deeper on the reverse, and with lovely red-brown stamens. The petals are often divided or fringed, but not so much as in 'Ellen Willmott', a descendant of 'Dainty Bess'. Fragrant. 8 to 12 feet.

'Doubloons'. Horvath, 1934. R. *setigera* hybrid × R. *foetida bicolor* hybrid. An interesting rose of rich buff yellow; large flowers opening somewhat cupped, and borne in long-lasting clusters. Good foliage. A few later blooms. Some fragrance and fairly graceful. 10 to 12 feet.
American *Rose Annual*, 1937, p. 266.

'Easlea's Golden Rambler'. Easlea, 1932. The best known rose raised by Walter Easlea, who was a keen rosarian and appreciated the rose in all its forms. It is a pity this was called a Rambler, since this conjures up a small-flowered rose. It does certainly ramble, but would be better described as a once-flowering climber. The foliage distinguishes it from all other roses—rich green and glossy, broader at the end than at the middle, and distinctly corrugated by the deep veins. Large, lovely flowers filled with petals of rich butter-yellow touched with red in the bud, borne singly and in clusters early in the season. Glorious fragrance. 12 to 15 feet.
McFarland, 1937, p. 166.
American *Rose Annual*, 1934, p. 40.

'Eden Rose, Climbing'. I hear of a sport of this bright, deep, pure-rose variety. The original was 'Peace' × 'Signora' (Meilland, 1953). Among the many flame-coloured roses this is a welcome change.

'Elegance'. Brownell, 1937. A beautiful, large, full Hybrid Tea bloom opening from shapely buds, pale clear yellow fading to white except in the centre. Fine dark glossy foliage. Seldom flowers after the main crop; fragrant. 15 feet.

'Ellinor LeGrice, Climbing'. Bide, 1959, from the original by LeGrice 1950. 'Lilian' × 'Golden Dawn'. Clear yellow, a well-formed full Hybrid Tea, with fruity fragrance. Repeat-flowering. 10 to 12 feet.

'Ena Harkness, Climbing'. The original was raised by Norman and introduced in 1946. 'Crimson Glory' × 'Southport'. The climbing sport occurred in 1954. I have never been very fond of this rose, but its crimson blooms are large and somewhat fragrant, and have the advantage of nodding down at one. 15 feet.

'Étoile de Hollande, Climbing'. Verschuren, 1919. 'General McArthur' × 'Hadley'. The climbing sport was introduced in 1931. A superlative old crimson rose with amazing rich fragrance. Vigorous, 18 feet, and recurrent. Splendid under glass, but quite hardy.

'Flaming Sunset, Climbing'. This deep orange sport of 'McGredy's Sunset' (1936) occurred in 1948 in Canada, and this climbing sport cropped up with Mattock in 1954. Glossy, bronzy foliage. Deliciously fragrant, orange, reverse lighter. Some repeat blooms. 12 feet.

'Golden Dawn, Climbing'. Grant, 1929. 'Élégante' × 'Ethel Somerset'. The best climbing sport is that introduced by LeGrice in 1947. A delicious tea-scented, full double, light yellow rose of power and persuasion. Some later blooms. Good foliage. 12 feet.

'Gruss an Aachen, Climbing'. A sport from the bush form, which occurred at Sangerhausen and was introduced by Kordes in 1937. (The parentage is reputedly 'Frau Karl Druschki' × 'Franz Deegen', but chromosome numbers suggest otherwise. Both of these are Hybrid Teas, so that it is strange that 'Gruss an Aachen' should be cluster-flowered and classed as a Floribunda, in spite of its having been raised in 1909, long before the term was invented! It is described on page 150 of *Shrub Roses of Today*.)

The climbing form is a good grower and is recurrent-flowering, but is not as free after the main display as the bush form. Its delicate ivory-white tone enriched with apricot-pink and its rich fragrance and full-petalled shape make it too good to neglect. Probably 12 feet.

'Gruss an Teplitz'. Described in my book *Shrub Roses of Today*, (page 179) since it is more of a shrub than a climber, though it can be trained up to some 8 or 10 feet. Gorgeous crimson without purple, recurrent and fragrant. This has much of the true dark crimson of the 'Slater's Crimson China' which I guess is in its pedigree. A climbing sport was named 'Catalunya'. Hoffmann, Plate 19.
Strassheim, 1899.
Journal des Roses, Septembre 1899. 'Salut à Teplitz.' Poor.

'Guinée'. Mallerin, 1938. Owing its dark colour to 'Château de Clos Vougeot', this rose is of mixed modern parentage, but its colour resembles the most dusky of Hybrid Perpetuals, such as 'Souvenir du Docteur Jamain': deepest maroon with crimson centre, pure, unfading, without purple; beautiful shapely flowers and intense red-rose fragrance. A vigorous satisfactory plant which has no peer in its colour class among old or new roses. Foliage good. 18 feet. Needs a light background and does not shew up against greenery. A good first crop and many odd blooms later.

'High Noon'. Lammerts, 1946. A lanky plant with sparse foliage, suitable for pillar or wall-training to about 12 feet. Clear bright canary-yellow flowers freely produced at midsummer and fairly constantly afterwards. Fragrant. A highly productive rose, but it is essential to place it behind other shrubs and plants as it is so lanky; on a wall a *Clematis alpina* variety would furnish the lower stems.
American *Rose Annual*, 1948, p. 104. Too dark.

'Independence, Climbing'. 'Climbing Kordes' Sondermeldung'. 'Baby Château' × 'Crimson Glory' were the parents of the original raised by Kordes; the sport occurred in 1960 in

Italy. Though the colouring might be classed with all the other modern orange-reds it would be careless to do so; the vivid vermilion tones are softened by subtle coppery and metallic tints, even mauve and orange in some lights: it is at times infinite in its shades and indescribably rich for blending in a bowl with other flowers. Slightly fragrant, fully double, shapely flowers; 9 to 10 feet.

'Independence Day, Climbing'. For many years this was one of the most popular climbers of yellowish colouring. Originated in 1930, at Murrell's Nursery, from the 1919 Hybrid Tea 'Madame Édouard Herriot' × 'Souvenir de Gustave Prat'. It thus has two doses of Pernetiana race in it. Vigorous with some repeat bloom, loosely double, golden yellow flushed flame and apricot. Sweetly scented. 15 feet.

'La France, Climbing'. Henderson, 1893. Presumed to be 'Madame Victor Verdier' × 'Madame Bravy'. While the climbing sport (Guillot Fils, 1867) is not nearly so free-flowering as the original bush form, it does give me an opportunity to mention this exquisite hardy fragrant rose, one of the first Hybrid Teas raised. Grow the bush by all means, but do not let us lose this delightful charmer. The climber will reach 12 feet or more.

'Lady Forteviot, Climbing'. Cant, 1928. The climbing sport occurred in 1935. Its rich scent and soft orange-apricot suffusion over the yellow of the petals warrant its inclusion, though it is not very recurrent, but vigorous and with good foliage.

'Lady Sylvia, Climbing'. Stevens, 1926; a sport from 'Madame Butterfly'; produced climbing sport in 1933. The deeper of the two well-known and exquisite descendants of 'Ophelia'. 20 feet.

'Lady Waterlow'. Nabonnand, 1903. 'La France de '89' × 'Madame Marie Lavalley'. Full blooms of very clear pink, with salmon shadings; beautifully veined petals. Some later blooms. Clean, sweet fragrance. 12 feet.

'Madame Abel Chatenay, Climbing'. The climbing sport originated in 1917 from the original raised by Pernet-Ducher in

1895. 'Dr Grill' (Tea) × 'Victor Verdier' (Hybrid Tea). The bush form is extremely good and there is no need to grow the climber, but like 'La France' it does allow me to include this outstandingly beautiful and highly productive rose also in this book. The flowers are very full with quilled petals, light pink deepening towards the centre, and with deeper reverse. A poor description for an exquisite flower, unsurpassed for its neat fullness and its revivifying, penetrating, delicious fragrance. 15 feet.
Journal des Roses, Juin 1913. A poor portrait.
Revue Horticole, 1906, p. 64. Fair.
Hoffmann, Plate 9.

'Madame Butterfly, Climbing'. E. G. Hill Co., 1918. 'Ophelia' sport, from which the climbing sport was introduced in 1926. Delightful pale pink. Regularly recurrent. See also 'Ophelia'. 20 feet.

'Madame Caroline Testout, Climbing'. Pernet-Ducher, 1890. 'Madame de Tartas' × 'Lady Mary Fitzwilliam'. The sport was introduced in 1901. Little fragrance, and the flowers are apt to 'ball'. Even so it is, after all these years, one of the most prolific and recurrent of climbing sports. Clear silvery pink with rolled petals. Mid-green leaves. It has had an immense influence on the breeding of roses. 20 feet.
Kingsley, p. 97.

'Madame Édouard Herriot, Climbing'. Pernet-Ducher, 1913. 'Madame Caroline Testout' ×. a Hybrid Tea, from which the climbing sport was introduced in 1921. '*Daily Mail* Rose'. A noted favourite; nothing quite like it in colour has been raised since. Buds deep flame-pink, opening coral pink, loosely double, starry. Early-flowering, with a few blooms later. Fragrant. 15 feet.

'Madame Grégoire Staechelin'. Dot, 1927. 'Spanish Beauty.' 'Frau Karl Druschki' × 'Château de Clos Vougeot'. It is unfortunate that this handsome rose flowers only once, but what a flowering it is! Early in the season with 'Easlea's Golden', 'Blairi No. 2' and others, it coincides with the flowering of the Bearded Irises and makes a most glorious display, with delicious sweet-pea fragrance. Large generous flowers, semi-double, glowing flesh pink with much deeper reverse. Dark glossy leaves. An indispensable rose which will thrive on a north wall, as at Tintinhull House, Somerset, a property of the National Trust. 20 feet.

McFarland, 1937, p. 172 } The same picture.
Stevens, p. 154

'Madame Henri Guillot, Climbing'. 1942, a sport from the original by Mallerin, 1938; 'Rochefort' × unnamed R. *foetida bicolor* seedling. Very much a Pernetiana; vivid coral-scarlet with orange flush. Large and vigorous. Fragrant. Good foliage. 12 feet.

'Madame Pierre S. du Pont, Climbing'. An involved parentage includes 'Ophelia', 'Rayon d'Or' and others; Mallerin, 1929. The climbing sport dates to 1933. Scented, golden yellow, fading paler; reddish buds. 7 feet.

'Madame de Sancy de Parabère', prior to 1845. The largest flowered and most beautiful of all the old Boursault Roses. Clear, soft pink flowers of large size, 5 inches across; as a rule the outer petals are far larger than those in the middle, which are inclined to make a central rosette. Gentle scent. Free-flowering very early in the season on long shoots which are completely thornless. 15 feet. (Plate III.)

I think the floral style of this rose is unique, and coupled with its early season and thornlessness makes it well worth growing. The smaller-flowered crimson-purple Boursault 'Amadis' is also sometimes seen, as at Sissinghurst, but is included in Chapter 4.

In my earlier books I have followed the usual authorities describing the Boursault roses as hybrids between R. *pendulina* and R. *chinensis*. Mr Gordon Rowley tells me the chromosome count of R. *pendulina* renders this improbable and that it is likely that some other diploid thornless species was concerned, such as R. *blanda*. The three varieties I have found are only slightly fragrant, but this and the others, the shrubby 'Morlettii' and 'Amadis', are worth retaining for their other attributes.

Redouté, vol. iii, Plates 79 (R. *reclinata*) and 80 (R. *reclinata sub multiplici*). These plates shew thorny roses which cannot be reconciled with any Boursault known today.
Redouté, vol. iii, Plate 21. R. *lheritierana*. Also thorny!

'McGredy's Ivory, Climbing'. McGredy, 1930. 'Mrs Charles Lamplough' × 'Mabel Morse'. Climbing sport introduced 1939. A vigorous plant, ivory-white flowers of good shape and fragrant. A few later blooms. 12 feet.

'Michèle Meilland, Climbing'. Meilland, 1945. 'Joanna Hill' × 'Peace'. Two vigorous growers produced this lovely rose. The climber occurred in 1951. A symphony of delicate warm pinks, with lilac and salmon undertones. Fragrant, shapely. 12 feet.

'Mrs Arthur Curtiss James'. 'Golden Climber.' Brownell, 1933. 'Mary Wallace' × seedling. One of the most popular yellow-flowered climbers in the United States. Brilliant sunflower-yellow, semi-double, shapely blooms borne singly. Sweet tea-fragrance. Glossy dark leaves. Recurrent. 12 feet.
American *Rose Annual*, 1933, Plate 1.
American *Rose Annual*, 1934, p. 72.

'Mrs Sam McGredy, Climbing'. McGredy, 1929. 'Donald MacDonald' × 'Golden Emblem', crossed with a hybrid of the 'Queen Alexandra Rose'. A valuable sport (1938) from the bush form; magnificent deep salmon-pink with coppery-red shadings. Mahogany-tinted foliage. Fragrant. Recurrent. 15 feet.

'New Dawn'. A perpetual-flowering sport of 'Dr Van Fleet' which occurred in the United States (1930). Justly famous for its glossy foliage and deliciously fragrant, light silvery pink small flowers, of exquisite shape in bud and when open; they are produced freely in clusters, just past midsummer usually, for many weeks, and later crops occur. Lovely with old or new roses. Will achieve 20 feet on a wall, but is superb when allowed to grow as a lax bush, or trained loosely over a stump or hedge, with *Lonicera americana*. Less vigorous than its once-flowering parent, 'Dr Van Fleet'.
Stevens, p. 208.

'New Dawn Rouge'. See 'Étendard', page 135.

'Ophelia, Climbing'. W. Paul, 1912. Parentage unknown. The climbing sport was introduced in 1920. This exquisite blush-pink rose, of beautiful scrolled shape in bud and ideal for cutting on strong stems, has produced two equally valuable darker sports, 'Madame Butterfly' and 'Lady Sylvia'. All are first rate and very recurrent and fragrant. Good under glass but quite hardy. 20 feet.

An interesting account by Miss Wylie of sports and hybrids from this prolific parental rose will be found in the *Journal* of the Royal Horticultural Society for January 1955.

'Paul's Lemon Pillar'. William Paul, 1915. 'Frau Karl Druschki' × 'Maréchal Niel'. Distinguished parents have produced a unique once-flowering rose, and its crop of huge scented blooms in early midsummer will excuse it from its failure later. The flowers are extra large, filled with petals rolled at the edges, and of sumptuous quality and fragrance, clear lemon-white with a slight primrose-green tint in the centre. In spite of its Tea parentage, it has not suffered from cold in the open with me, but should be given a warm wall in cold districts, where it may reach 20 feet. There is nothing like it.

'Peace, Climbing'. 'Madame A. Meilland', 'Gioia', 'Gloria Dei'. Meilland, 1945; the climbing sport, 1950. The old 'George Dickson' united with 'Souvenir de Claudius Pernet', and the seedling was crossed with a hybrid between 'Joanna Hill' (of tremendous vigour) and 'Charles P. Kilham'. The climber needs a huge wall, 20 feet by 20 feet, which it will cover with splendid foliage; a big crop of flowers may occur in the fullness of time. Light yellow, flushed clear pink, in varying tones, according to the season. Some fragrance.

'Picture, Climbing'. McGredy, 1932. Parentage unknown. The climbing sport was introduced ten years later. In the 'Ophelia' tradition, but smaller in flower. Dusky deep pink. Fragrant. Recurrent. 15 feet.

'President Herbert Hoover, Climbing'. Coddington, 1930. 'Sensation' × 'Souvenir de Claudius Pernet', the climber occurred with B. R. Cant in 1937. Red, orange, and rose in the bud opening to warm yellow; the colours are paler in autumn but at all times lovely. Fragrant. 15 feet.

I have sometimes wondered whether my bush 'Hoover' was intended to be a climber, for it is not unusual to see it 8 feet high! The bush form is the most noticeable Hybrid Tea in July as one goes through towns, because it is tall enough to shew up over every fence and hedge.

'Royal Gold'. Morey, 1957. Excellent brilliant golden yellow pillar rose, with large, shapely full blooms, well scented, borne singly and in clusters. A pillar rose or suitable as a loose shrub. Good dark foliage. A little fragrance. For sheltered walls. 9 feet.

'Shot Silk, Climbing'. Dickson, 1924. 'Hugh Dickson' seedling × 'Sunstar', from which the sport was introduced in 1931. Beautiful, rounded, deep warm salmon-pink blooms with yellow base. Fragrant. Recurrent. 12 feet.

'Soraya, Climbing'. Meilland, 1955. Sumptuous blooms of strange blends of flame, blood, cerise, and copper, adding up to an unusual richness. Fragrant. Vigorous.

'Souvenir de Claudius Denoyel'. Chambard, 1920. A hybrid of 'Château de Clos Vougeot', and possessing its informal, somewhat cupped, flowers. Vigorous, with large mid-green leaves. A great crop of flowers is borne at midsummer, early in the flowering season of Hybrid Teas, the whole plant becoming a sheet of bright crimson, of unfading quality; repeats in less quantity in later months. Lovely loose flowers of old style; intense sweet fragrance. Very fine at St Paul's Waldenbury. 18 feet.

'Souvenir de la Malmaison, Climbing'. Bennett (the raiser of 'Mrs John Laing'; Shepperton, Surrey), 1893. A climbing sport of the original bush form, described in the 1961 (fourth) edition of *The Old Shrub Roses*. Vigorous, with good foliage, and two crops of flowers, of which those in September are always best. A flat, double, blush rose of great size in the old tradition. Useful for sunny or shady walls. 12 feet.

'Spek's Yellow, Climbing'. Spek, 1950. A seedling from 'Golden Rapture'; the sport was introduced in 1956. Known as 'Golden Scepter' in the United States. Brilliant yellow medium-sized blooms singly and in clusters. Fragrant. Glossy leaves. Erect growth. Somewhat recurrent. 15 feet.

8

The New Climbers

Oh, how much more doth beauty beauteous seem
By that sweet ornament which truth doth give!
The rose looks fair, but fairer we it deem
For that sweet odour which doth in it live.

Shakespeare, Sonnet LIV.

IF THE ROSES in the last chapter may be called 'Hybrid Tea climbers', denoting a large formal style of flower, those in this chapter might well be dubbed 'Floribunda climbers'. There is a lot of variation in size and shape among them, but in the main they are loosely double or semi-double and of informal shape. Some are actually climbing sports of Floribundas and, with the vast quantities of these roses in current cultivation today, we can expect to see their numbers increased every year.

As we have found in earlier chapters, there are some outlying varieties, some quite old, which have to be included simply because they do not fit elsewhere.

First there are a few derived from descendants of R. *foetida*, the Austrian Briar: 'Star of Persia' (1919) and 'Réveil Dijonnais' (1931); the former inherits the peculiar scent of R. *foetida*, and seldom is recurrent, while the brilliant 'Réveil' is more recurrent, with a sweet fragrance. Many class these both as shrubs, but they are the better for some support. 'Lawrence Johnston' and 'Le Rêve' were raised in 1923, and the former is one of our most brilliant, somewhat recurrent yellow climbers with medium-sized flowers, as might be said of 'Paul's Scarlet Climber' (1916) among those of that colour.

A rose raised by George Paul, 'Paul's Single White', is seldom seen today, but for those who prefer quietness and charm to brilliance and splendour it is worth growing, and is always in flower.

R. *wichuraiana* intrudes through 'Purity'—an excellent pure white—'Dream Girl' and several others. The last is of salmon-pink tone, and I regard it as one of the best and most fragrant of recurrent pillar roses in this colour, while 'Dr W. van Fleet', and its perpetual sport 'New Dawn' (see page 124) might well be included in this category.

One of the best of perpetual-flowering shrub roses, R. *rugosa* has produced a lot of hybrids but, owing to its character of being unable to transmit fertility to succeeding generations, it has never entered into the main stream of garden roses. However, a remarkable thing has happened. The hybrid 'Max Graf', raised in 1919 between R. *rugosa* and R. *wichuraiana*, was never really appreciated, because at that time nobody was looking for ground-covering roses, among which this hybrid is one of the best. Now we look for them, but apart from that, in the care of Herr Wilhelm Kordes, seeds of 'Max Graf' ripened in the early 1940's with spontaneously doubled chromosomes and produced tetraploid seedlings. One of these has been named R. *kordesii*, and is in effect a new fertile species, combining great hardiness and disease resistance, and has been used as a parent with various roses, resulting in many new perpetual-flowering climbing roses, including 'Dortmund', 'Hamburger Phoenix', 'Leverkusen' and 'Parkdirektor Riggers'. These and the bulk of new varieties are red, flame, or yellow in tone.

With these introductory remarks we may now cursorily go through the roses in this chapter; taking the yellows first, 'Leverkusen' is a delightful creamy lemon colour, 'Casino', soft yellow, and 'Magic Carpet' is brighter, with the distinction of having extremely attractive well-filled flowers with petals quilled and quartered in the old style. 'Golden Showers', 'Alchymist', and 'Royal Gold' are clear bright yellows of varying tones. 'Climbing Allgold' is a vivid deep yellow—and, judging how well the parent Floribunda does in the wetter west, this rose should be a reliable grower where rain and 'black spot' abound. It appears to be resistant to both!—but the climbing sport is at present rather shy flowering, unfortunately. 'Maigold' is a very deep and lovely buff yellow, nearly single with splendid dark foliage, a character in which practically all these modern roses excel. I place 'Dreaming Spires' high among the soft orange-yellows.

Next we have one rather on its own, the nearly single 'Meg' in rich peach and apricot tones, and the double 'Schoolgirl' and 'Compassion' of similar warm colouring.

Really flaming scarlet is found in 'Soldier Boy'—comparable with 'Scarlet Fire' among the shrubs—and 'Kassel', which has a coppery sheen. 'Danse du Feu' and 'Danse des Sylphes' I have omitted from this chapter of personal choices; the former dies off with contrasting tones of purplish red against the orange-red of the freshly open flowers.

Darker reds are 'Dortmund', 'Hamburger Phoenix', 'Sweet Sultan', 'Raymond Chenault' and 'Sympathie'; 'Sweet Sultan' verges towards maroon. Less intense, with a good deal more crimson or carmine in it is 'Étendard', descended direct from 'New Dawn' while the splendid 'Parade' in light crimson brings us to the pinks. My favourite is 'Dream Girl', mentioned above; 'Nymphenburg' I deal with in *Shrub Roses of Today*, though it could be grown as a climber equally well. This leaves us several good pinks: 'Ritter von Barmstede', 'Climbing Ballet', 'Bantry Bay', 'Handel', 'Coral Dawn' and 'Pink Perpétue'. These are in the forefront of modern climbing roses and it is to be regretted that, while in cool weather they are so delightful, several of them —and others mentioned above—fade disagreeably.

All on its own is 'Ash Wednesday', or 'Aschermittwoch'; its light lilac-grey fades on expansion to grey-white, and the flower is in the old style well filled with petals and quartered. This and 'Leverkusen' are good varieties for cooling down the welter of orange-red varieties.

None of these varieties is likely to exceed greatly 12 feet in height. It is misleading in books and catalogues today to read of their being 'rampant growers'; this term is best reserved for such enormous plants as the 'Kiftsgate' R. *filipes*, R. *rubus*, 'Mermaid', 'Albéric Barbier', and 'Madame d'Arblay', to name but a few. It is disconcerting to find the term 'rampant grower' immediately followed by recommendation of the variety being described for growing on a pillar. Really rampant growers are quite unsuited for such a use, as very hard pruning results in fewer flowers, and the average pillar (usually of wood) in our gardens does not exceed 8 feet in height. I should like to grow all these modern varieties—and all the Climbing sports of Hybrid Teas—in one field, with identical cultivation. Then it would be possible to assess their relative merits, vigour, fragrance, and most particularly their proclivities towards perpetual flowering. Only then can we make a choice with any degree of accuracy. Unfortunately I have been unable to grow all these roses, and neither the Royal National Rose Society nor the Royal Horticultural Society are able to institute so space-taking a trial; only a few have been given any really studied reports from a disinterested body. One therefore has to rely on raisers' original descriptions coupled with one's observations on seeing odd varieties in various gardens. My descriptions must therefore be taken as an indication only of the values of each variety.

First let us look at four older varieties which still have their values and were derived from R. *foetida* in early days and the unique 'Single White' of George Paul.

'Lawrence Johnston'. Raised in 1923 by Pernet-Ducher, this rose was out of the same cross as 'Le Rêve' ('Madame Eugène Verdier' × R. *foetida persiana*). For some reason it did not appeal to the raiser, while 'Le Rêve' was put on the market. It languished unappreciated until Major Lawrence Johnston saw it, bought the original and only plant, and transferred it to his garden at Hidcote Bartrim, Gloucestershire, some time between the wars. There it was christened 'Hidcote Yellow' (but distinct from 'Hidcote Gold', which is a hybrid of R. *sericea pteracantha*), and was distributed to a few favoured gardeners, eventually finding its way into my hands. I thought so highly of it that I asked Major Johnston if I could exhibit it; he assented and asked that his name should be put on it. It received the Royal Horticultural Society's Award of Merit, 1948. It outclasses 'Le Rêve'; the growth is stronger, the foliage equally good, the yellow warmer and richer and the flowers are better formed, with larger petals. The scent is just as rich and powerful. Fortunately it flowers with equal abandon in June and also goes on producing flowers intermittently through the summer. Shoots may grow to 30 feet. The original plant still grows at Hidcote and young ones have been planted there. (Plate VII.)

'Le Rêve'. Pernet-Ducher, 1923. 'Madame Eugène Verdier' × R. *foetida persiana*. A vigorous climbing rose with good, rich green, glossy leaves and a great display of light canary-yellow, loose, semi-double or nearly single flowers, usually produced before midsummer. Deliciously fragrant. From the same cross as 'Lawrence Johnston'. 20 to 25 feet.

Strassheim, 1927. Poor.

'Réveil Dijonnais'. Buatois, 1931. This spectacular rose owes its brilliant colour to 'Constance', a Pernet-Ducher rose with 'Rayon d'Or' in its parentage; the other parent was 'Eugène Fürst', a splendid dark red Hybrid Perpetual. The result is a vigorous plant with good, light green foliage richly tinted when young, producing semi-double or nearly single flowers at midsummer and a few later through the growing season; brilliant cerise-scarlet with wide yellow centres and yellowish reverse, obviously inherited far back from 'Austrian Copper'. Useful for 'hot' colour schemes. Branches achieve about 12 feet, but it is best used as an open shrub; not so suitable for pillars or confined wall spaces, since it is bushy. Pleasant sweet scent, without trace of R. *foetida*.

McFarland, 1937, p. 223.

American *Rose Annual*, 1935, p. 201.

'Star of Persia'. Pemberton, 1919. R. *foetida* × 'Trier'. No doubt this was an attempt to get a really yellow Hybrid Musk, but the result is too near to R. *foetida* in foliage and wood; lanky in growth and without the Hybrid Musk scent, leaning more towards that of R. *foetida*. Semi-double, brilliant yellow. Hardly worth growing, but included here because it has never entirely lost favour. 8 to 10 feet.

Stevens, p. 149.

'Paul's Single White'. George Paul, 1883. Seldom seen today, George Paul's rose does not compare with William Paul's 'Paul's Scarlet'. It is a plant achieving 6 to 8 feet with good foliage and a constant production (a few at a time) of single, blush-white flowers in clusters. Sweetly scented. Makes a pleasing foil to larger double blooms. There is a good mono-chrome photograph of this in Miss Jekyll's *Roses for English Gardens*, facing page 11. In the days when ramblers flowered only at midsummer this must have been greatly prized; today it is unique and that is all one can say, though a range of colours on plants like this would be acceptable. At least it is perpetual, which is a rare attribute. A close relative of R. *moschata*. It still grows at Blickling Hall, Norfolk.

The Garden, 1886, vol. xxix, Plate 526, facing p. 28.

MODERN FLORIBUNDA CLIMBERS

I have omitted all references to coloured illustrations from the descriptions of these newer roses. There is a wealth of coloured illustrations today, some good, some bad, in catalogues and books, but very few shew more than a bloom or two, omitting all details of growth, foliage and armature, and so their citing loses point.

'**Alchymist**'. Kordes, 1956. 'Golden Glow' × R. *rubiginosa* hybrid. Though not recurrent this is well worth a place in the garden for the sake of its very full-petalled, old-style, double, fragrant flowers, of clear light yellow warmed by orange in the centre. Excellent bronzy foliage. Fragrant. 12 feet.

'**Allgold, Climbing**'. Gandy, 1961. Rather shy flowering until well established. Clear yellow, double. Some fragrance. Glossy foliage. About 12 feet.

'**Aloha**'. Boerner, 1949. 'Mercédès Gallart' × 'New Dawn'. From famous antecedents in the previous generation 'Aloha' gives a lot of the quality of the big, full roses of the past. Clear rose pink with much deeper reverse to the petals. Not really a climber, but suitable for a pillar or for use as a shrub. Delicious Tea-fragrance. Possibly 8 feet.

Park, Plate 48. Gault and Synge, Plate 230.

'**Altissimo**'. Delbard-Chabert, 1967. Though often classed as a climber it is equally suited to be grown as a large bush, when its brilliant red, single blooms and matt foliage create a wonderful picture. Little scent.

Gault and Synge, Plate 231.

'**Aschermittwoch**'. See 'Ash Wednesday'.

'**Ash Wednesday**'. ('Aschermittwoch'.) Kordes, 1955. R. *rubiginosa* hybrid. Grey-lilac buds develop into large, full, grey-white flowers borne in bunches. Abundant bloom at mid-summer. 12 to 18 feet.

'**Ballet, Climbing**'. Kordes, 1962. 'Florex' × 'Karl Herbst'. The fully double flowers are beautifully coiled in the bud, opening with rolled petals. A very good warm pink; fragrant. Matt foliage. This does well on sandy soil at Wisley and is recurrent. 10 feet.

'**Bantry Bay**'. McGredy, 1967. Semi-double flowers, opening flat, of rich deep flesh pink, produced recurrently. Good glossy foliage. Sweet brier scent. 10 feet.

'**Blossomtime**'. O'Neal, 1951. 'New Dawn' is one parent, the other being an unnamed Hybrid Tea. It has derived good from both parents, being a lax shrub or low climber with good foliage and bearing Hybrid Tea-style flowers of clear pink, deeper on the reverse, in clusters. The first crop is followed by numerous later flowers. It has much of the beauty of the old 'La France'. Very fragrant. 6 to 8 feet.

'**Casino**'. McGredy, 1963. 'Coral Dawn' × 'Buccaneer'. The large double flowers are of soft yellow, paling with age, fragrant, with dark green, glossy, abundant foliage. 12 feet. Frequent later blooms. 10 feet.

'**Compassion**'. Harkness, 1974. 'White Cockade' × 'Prima Ballerina'. Beautifully scrolled buds, of warm apricot orange, opening to soft salmon-pink. Splendid dark glossy foliage and vigorous growth to 8 feet. Very fragrant and continuous.

'**Coral Dawn**'. Boerner, 1952. A 'New Dawn' seedling × unnamed yellow Hybrid Tea, crossed with unnamed orange-red Polyantha; anything might happen!—but a very charming rose is the result. Large blooms, cupped, of rich coral pink. Leathery foliage. Fragrant. 7 to 9 feet. Gault and Synge, Plate 238.

'**Dortmund**'. Kordes, 1955. Seedling × R. *kordesii*. Very large single blooms, crimson red with white eye, in large clusters. Dark glossy foliage. Recurrent. A good pillar rose. 7 to 8 feet. Gault and Synge. Plate 241.

'**Dream Girl**'. Jacobus, 1944. A seedling of 'Dr Van Fleet'. Lambertus C. Bobbink sent me this rose with very high recommendations which it has upheld to the full. Seldom reaching more than 10 feet, it is suitable for fence or pillar, and would, I believe, with suitable pruning make a shrub. It flowers after midsummer; large, fully double, warm coral-pink flowers, fading paler, in branching clusters, with delicious penetrating aroma. The flowers resemble those of the old shrub roses and are often quartered; and it has dark glossy leaves. (Plate VIII; photograph, Plate 13.)

'**Dreaming Spires**'. Mattock, 1977. 'Buccaneer' × 'Arthur Bell'. A welcome addition to the warm deep yellows, with orange flush, fading paler, well contrasted by dark stamens. Handsome dark foliage, neatly veined. Constantly in flower. Fragrant. Perhaps 12 feet.

'**Étendard**'. Robichon, 1956. Also known as 'New Dawn Rouge', this was produced by crossing 'New Dawn' with a seedling and the result is very successful. Dark, leaden green, glossy leaves and clusters of deep carmine flowers in the 'New Dawn' tradition. Fragrant. Very free-flowering in summer and through till autumn. Perhaps 12 feet.

'**Golden Showers**'. Lammerts, 1956. 'Charlotte Armstrong' × 'Captain Thomas'. Good glossy foliage and erect growth, making with a little support almost a shrub, but probably best as a pillar or wall rose. The flowers are large, loosely semi-double, emerging from shapely buds, bright clear yellow, fragrant. This rose bids fair to be as floriferous as any throughout the summer and autumn. 8 to 10 feet.

'**Hamburger Phoenix**'. Kordes, 1954. R. *kordesii* × seedling. Clusters of cupped, semi-double, medium-sized blooms of dark crimson, followed by red fruits unless picked off, when more flowers mature. Constantly in production; some fragrance. Glossy dark leaves. 8 to 10 feet.

'**Handel**'. McGredy, 1965. Exquisite buds and scrolled half-open blooms of creamy white with pink picotee edge. In hot weather the picotee increases in area over the expanding petals, and deepens in colour. Lovely in autumn, it is constantly in flower after the main crop. 8 feet. Some fragrance.

'**Iceberg, Climbing**'. Cant, 1968. This Kordes rose, raised in 1958 sported ten years later to give us this excellent white fragrant climber, which when well established is constantly in flower. 10 feet.

'**Karlsruhe**'. Kordes, 1957. Of *kordesii* derivation, and a vigorous glossy-leaved rose with fully double old-type flowers of deep rose-pink. Very free at midsummer and intermittently until autumn. Some fragrance. 10 to 12 feet.

'**Kassel**'. Kordes, 1957. 'Obergärtner Wiebicke' × 'Independence'. This brilliant shrubby rose, with recurrent crops of loosely double flowers of cinnabar and cherry-red tints, is mentioned in *Shrub Roses of Today*, but is lax enough to be used as a pillar or climbing rose. The colour is decidedly modern but rich and not blatant. Some fragrance. 10 to 12 feet on a wall, less as a shrub.

'**Leverkusen**'. Kordes, 1854. R. *kordesii* × 'Golden Glow'. Glossy light green leaves blend well with the light yellow blooms, large and double. Its grace, glittering foliage, pleasing colour, and lemony fragrance, a main crop and frequent later sprays of blooms, add up to a fine rose. Freely branching, can be used as a shrub or hedge with suitable training and pruning. Will achieve 10 feet or more on a wall.

'**Magic Carpet**'. Brownell, 1941. 'Coral Creeper' × 'Stargold'. Starry, full-petalled, well-formed flowers of bright yellow flushed pink round the edges of the petals. Glossy dark leaves borne on reddish wood. Attractive plant. Not recurrent. Very sweet scent. 12 feet.

'**Maigold**'. Kordes, 1953. 'McGredy's Wonder' × 'Frühlingsgold'. From its parentage this is obviously a shrub, but I omitted it from *Shrub Roses of Today* as it appeared to incline towards climbing. Like 'Nymphenburg' and 'Kassel' it lies between the two classes, and is perhaps best treated as a sprawl-ing shrub, or used to cover low hedges or supports, as is so excellent for 'Albertine'. This rose has really excellent foliage, rich and glossy and profuse. The flowers appear early in the season, and are of deep buff yellow, reddish in the bud, semi-double, shewing a bunch of golden stamens. Powerful, delicious fragrance. Repeats occasionally through the summer. 12 feet.

'Masquerade, Climbing'. For those that like this sort of thing . . . personally I would rather have R. *chinensis mutabilis*, which is *always* in flower, and exquisite (see *Shrub Roses of Today*, page 120).

'Meg'. Gosset, 1954. Probably 'Paul's Lemon Pillar' × 'Madame Butterfly'. These two classic parents have produced an un-classical but beautiful child. It is almost single—about ten petals—with large blooms of apricot-pink with yellow base and dark stamens; borne in clusters. Fragrant. A vigorous climber to 10 feet with good foliage. Occasional later blooms after the main crop. 10 feet. Gault and Synge. Plate 250.

'New Dawn', see page 124.

'Nymphenburg'. Kordes, 1954. 'Sangerhausen' × 'Sunmist'. This splendid rose is described in *Shrub Roses of Today* (page 188), and there illustrated in colour. Being a lax grower with long, strong shoots it would make an admirable climber, probably achieving 18 feet with support, but ideal for covering a shed or tree stump or hedgerow. Clear salmon-pink, shaded cerise-pink and orange with yellow base. As perpetual as any.

'Parade'. Boerner, 1953. 'New Dawn' seedling × 'Climbing World's Fair'. A brilliant and free-flowering rose bearing two big crops of bloom and odd blooms in between. A deep rich crimson-pink, cupped, on good stems. Good fragrance. Helen Van Pelt Wilson claims that it will grow well in shade. 12 feet.

'Parkdirektor Riggers'. Kordes, 1957. R. *kordesii* × 'Our Princess'. Velvety crimson, semi-double, in clusters; slightly fragrant. I have reports that this is constantly in flower. Foliage good. 12 to 15 feet. Gault and Synge, Plate 256.

'Paul's Scarlet Climber'. William Paul, 1916. The most popular of all climbing roses, though 'Chaplin's Pink' and 'Albertine' run it close. The three together usher in the summer rose season on countless garden walls throughout the country. The bright crimson-scarlet of Paul's splendid rose together with its unsophisticated shape make it suitable for association with the older roses as well as the new. Slightly fragrant. Later blooms are most plentiful when it is not pruned after the first crop. 20 feet.
The Garden, 1897, vol. ii, p. 464.

'Pink Perpétue'. Gregory, 1965. 'Danse du Feu' × 'New Dawn'. The most popular pink, repeat blooming, climber. Rich warm pink, double flowers, in clusters, well set off by glossy foliage. Fragrance of green apples, derived from R. *wichuraiana* far back in its parentage. 10 feet.

'Purity'. Hoopes, 1917. The unnamed seedling which was crossed with 'Madame Caroline Testout' must have been of *wichuraiana* parentage, judging by its offspring's glossy leaves, reminiscent of 'New Dawn' and the *Luciae* ramblers. Pure white flowers, loosely double, shewing a yellow stamen. Delicious fragrance. A vigorous, thorny plant. Seldom repeats. 12 feet.

'Raymond Chenault'. Kordes, 1960. R. *kordesii* × 'Montezuma'. Large rich red flowers, loosely semi-double, like 'Golden Showers' in general character. A brilliant rose, constantly in flower but not fragrant. 9 feet.

'Ritter von Barmstede'. Kordes, 1959. Shiny excellent foliage, vigorous growth, suitable for a pillar or as a sprawling shrub. Repeat flowering, producing deep rose-pink flowers, fully double, in large clusters. 10 feet.

'Rosy Mantle'. Cocker, 1968. 'New Dawn' × 'Prima Ballerina'. A good repeat-flowerer with dark glossy foliage, and considerable fragrance. Rich silvery pink, flushed cerise on opening, fairly full flowers with quilled petals. 9 feet.

'Santa Catalina'. McGredy, 1970. 'Paddy McGredy' × 'Heidelburg'. Soft creamy salmon pink; shapely buds open to shew dark brown stamens. Leaves profuse, rich green. Very free flowering until autumn. Fragrant. 9 feet.

'Schoolgirl'. McGredy, 1964. 'Coral Dawn' × 'Belle Blonde'. Shapely double blooms of soft apricot-orange, produced recurrently. Glossy dark foliage, vigorous growth to 10 feet, usually rather bare at the base, but a useful colour.

'Soldier Boy'. LeGrice, 1953. Seedling × 'Guinée'. Blazing scarlet, single shapely blooms with yellow stamens. For brilliance this pillar rose would be hard to beat. The main crop is succeeded by frequent later blooms. 8 to 10 feet. Gault and Synge, Plate 260.

'Swan Lake'. McGredy, 1968. 'Memoriam' × 'Heidelburg'. A beautiful white rose, with rosy flush in the centre. Full, large flowers, shapely, borne singly and in clusters through the season. Glossy leaves. No fragrance. 10 feet.

'Sweet Sultan'. Eacott, 1958. This is a splendid infusion of Hybrid Tea, *wichuraiana*, and all sorts of roses, a direct seedling of 'Independence' × 'Honour Bright'. Large single blooms in large and small clusters, crimson-scarlet, shaded maroon, with prominent yellow stamens. Coppery-coloured foliage. Altogether a dusky beauty, and recurrent. 10 to 12 feet.

'Sympathie'. Kordes, 1964. Velvety, shapely, double, dark red blooms borne repeatedly among glossy foliage. Some fragrance. 10 feet.

In spite of a tendency towards strident colouring and lack of scent I find many of these newer 'Floribunda climbers' of real value when designing mixed borders for colour effect. They assort well with shrubs and plants, and, either as a background trained on a wall, or allowed to hang over a big evergreen shrub or otherwise to be enjoyed as informal loose shrubs themselves, they are in the main an asset to present-day horticulture. Very few would be suitable in a garden of the older roses, but I think we could include 'Aloha', 'Étendard', 'Dream Girl', and 'Parade'; 'Leverkusen' and 'Magic Carpet' if yellows are wanted; while the white 'Purity' and 'Paul's Single White' and grey 'Ash Wednesday' would have right of entry on account of colour.

It has been extremely difficult to try to divide all these Hybrid Tea- and Floribunda-types of climbers into two chapters, and every now and again I have felt the shrubby character was so much to the fore that they might well have been included in my earlier book. Today there are no clear-cut races of roses, except the three main divisions: BEDDING ROSES, SHRUB ROSES, and CLIMBERS (including ramblers). Breeding proceeds apace and roses of every conceivable variation in growth, shape of flower, style, and colour are being raised, mainly among bedding and shrub varieties, and it is inevitable that the old group-names should become unsuitable to cover all this variety. The range of varieties will increase with every fresh species that is pressed into service for hybridizing.

While it should not be necessary to abandon the old group names of roses (such as the Old Shrub Roses, the Noisettes, the Hybrid Musks, and others) for *roses already raised*, it cannot be pretended that new varieties will necessarily fit into these groups, which are genealogical rather than functional. I very much hope that some may be raised along the old lines, for these old groups give us something which we can ill afford to lose. Taking the roses in this book alone, perpetual production, fragrance and vigour are at their best in some of the old Noisettes; grace and vigour and Edwardian charm in some of the old ramblers; foliage, fragrance, vigour, and old-style flowers in what I have called the *Luciae* ramblers.

But today, with an ever more complex race evolving, the term Bedding Roses should cover all those bush varieties suitable for pruning low, to make a pattern of colour, up to say 3 feet in height, in formal or informal bedding: these would include as subdivisions the small-flowered Poly-poms (at one time classed Dwarf Polyanthas), the Hybrid Teas, and the intermediates, the Floribundas. It would be quite right to retain these group names for roses which have been raised and conform to one group or another. As gradually bush roses are bred infusing all these types, which seems the obvious and inevitable trend, they can be termed simple Bedding Roses.

With the shrubs, in which might be included certain Bedding Roses which make good bushy plants of 4 feet or over, once again the old group names should be retained for such distinct strains as the true Rugosas, the Old Shrub Roses, and the Hybrid Musks, and, as for the Bedding Roses, when new perpetual- or recurrent-flowering varieties of mixed parentage are raised, they could simply be termed Shrub Roses, recurrent.

And so with climbers—retaining old terms like Ramblers, Tea Noisettes and Climbing sports of Hybrid Teas, and using simply a term such as Climber for all the new kinds.

These terms would be all-embracing, or as nearly so as possible, and would make for ease of reference and selection in the future, until some species of untold potentiality is pressed into service. None of the groups above specifically makes provision for ground-covering varieties, but these are, of course, ramblers which are used without supports.

It may well be that, in addition to the three big group names, the need will be felt for some new terms for new groups, when raised. For instance, supposing recurrent flowering ramblers are produced, where would they be classed? While obviously still coming into the category of Climbing Roses they would not fit the modern Floribunda-climbers any better than the once-flowering ramblers. A new group name would have to be coined. It is quite possible that, using 'Aimée Vibert', the Old Musk, 'Paul's Single White', R. *setigera*, 'Crimson Shower', and a few more, hybridizing might result in a race of ramblers flowering *from July onwards*.

Several paragraphs in *Shrub Roses of Today* were devoted to roses of the future, and I venture to suggest once again some lines of breeding which would greatly increase the breadth of rose-appreciation. Not being a breeder myself, this may seem presumptuous, but my reiterated thought is that until one delves deeply into roses—all kinds of roses—one cannot realize the almost limitless array of characters that are available; breeding along stereotyped lines is quite unnecessary. Breeders today generally know what they want. As a rule it is size and brilliance, coupled with stout stalks, hard shiny foliage, and vigour. Fragrance, grace, and charm are not qualities which are given so much thought. A few breeders, such as the late E. B. LeGrice, saw beauty in single roses as originally contrived by nature. As the fragrance in the Synstylae species is in their stamens, there is no need in rambling roses to increase the petals to provide more fragrance. In short, I should like to see breeders bringing in the stamen-borne fragrance of the Synstylae species, the superb foliage of 'Albéric Barbier' and 'Mermaid', the Tea fragrance and pale and apricot yellows—coupled with their perpetual habit— of the best Noisettes; uniting the purple colouring of the main ramblers of that colour with good characters of other groups; creating late-flowering ramblers and re-creating our favourite ramblers so that they are all fragrant.

As I have said earlier in this book, compared with the effort that has gone into the production of bedding roses, little has been done for climbers and ramblers, and I like to think that one day breeders will turn their attention to a greater variety of colour, fragrance, and charm than is apparent today in the ceaseless stream of red, scarlet, and flame.

PART 3

Some Rare Species
and their Hybrids
together with a Chapter on
The Botany
of
Climbing Roses

9

The Banksian, Macartney, and Cherokee Roses; their Forms and Hybrids

Oh love (the more my wo) to it thow art
Yeven as the moysture in each plant that growes
Yeven as the soonn unto the frosen ground
Yeven as the sweetness to th'incarnate rose
Yeven as the Centre in each perfait rounde.

Sir Walter Raleigh, ?1552–1618.

THE BANKSIAN ROSES

There is no doubt that where they can be grown the forms of the Banksian Rose give unique beauty. They are exceedingly vigorous ramblers producing their small flowers in clusters in *spring,* and figures have been quoted in gardening journals giving the number of flowers on large plants as fifty thousand. I can well believe it, after looking at some of the pictures in these old books. In the list of Roses at the Château Éléonore, Cannes, compiled by Lord Brougham and Vaux in 1898, there is a photograph of a plant of the double yellow form covering an olive tree with countless trails and branches, creating a mound of blossom some 30 feet high. An article in *Arizona Highways* for January 1956, kindly sent to me by Mr W. L. Hunt of North Carolina, describes a tree, in Tombstone, Arizona, of the double white form supported as a canopy and covering 4,620 square feet; it produces hundreds of thousands of blooms. To be there at flowering time and to smell the fragrance of violets floating from it must be among the greatest floral experiences of the world.

In England this exuberance is not achieved. They are roses that need lots of sunshine to ripen their wood, and a corresponding absence of severe frost. There is no doubt that the proper ripening of the wood enables it to resist winter cold, and on sunny walls in the south of England the double yellow form may be expected to thrive and flower freely.

The various forms flowered first in Europe during the nineteenth century and just into the present century, and their discovery provides an interesting sequence of events.

A celebrated gardener at the turn of the century, E. H. Woodall, whose name is remembered best perhaps in the fine form of *Carpenteria californica* that bears his name, must have been very delighted and even thrilled in 1909 when he first saw flowers on an unknown rose in his garden. He had obtained cuttings from Megginch Castle, Strathtay, Scotland, where it had grown for many years, having been brought from China, so the story goes, by one Robert Drummond, with various other plants in 1796. He had cruised to the Far East with his brother the Admiral. This intriguing rose had lived at Megginch for all those years without a flower, having been cut back annually by the severe winter weather. It was thornless, with neat small leaves. Its flowers, produced at Nice for the first time, were small, single, white, with a pronounced fragrance, and I think we can say that this was the first time this wild form of R. *banksiae*, known as *normalis*, had flowered in Europe.

Meanwhile, in 1803, William Kerr was sent to China by the Royal Society to look for good garden plants to bring home, and among others he found in a Canton garden the double white form of the species, which arrived in England in 1807 and flowered at Isleworth, being named after Lady Banks, the wife of the then director at Kew. This is now known botanically as R. *banksiae banksiae*, the type-species, though most usually called R. *banksiae albo-plena*; it also is deliciously scented.

A little later, the Royal Horticultural Society sent J. D. Parks (the introducer of 'Parks's Yellow Tea-Scented China Rose') on a trip to Asia, and his instructions included the obtaining of the double yellow Banksian rose which had been reported at

Calcutta Botanic Garden. It had been brought from China; it was collected successfully and flowered here in 1824, and is now known as R. *banksiae lutea*. It is delicately fragrant.

In 1870 plants of the single yellow form were introduced to England by Sir Thomas Hanbury from his famous garden at La Mortola, Menton, though I cannot find out whence he obtained it. It is called R. *banksiae lutescens* and is as sweetly scented as the single and double white forms. This rose and its varieties had presumably been favourites in Chinese gardens for a long while; most of the Europeans collecting in China had not penetrated far into the mainland, but had found many plants in gardens around the coastal towns. In the wild state it occurs mainly in Western China, in the mountain ranges between Yunnan and Shensi and as far east as Hupeh. In these areas the wild forms are found at altitudes of around five thousand feet.

This rose and its forms have no immediate relatives among other species of *Rosa* except R. *cymosa*, which I have not seen. In cultivation they are practically thornless, with long green flexible canes bearing the small pointed smooth leaves with usually five leaflets, and the stipules fall away very early in the season. When the plants get old the bark becomes flaky and brown, and very thick trunks are produced. It is important to retain all the young wood, up to six or seven years old if possible, as the flowers are produced in greatest quality and quantity on the two- to three-year-old side-shoots growing off the long trails. Consequently pruning should consist of removing occasionally very old wood. This is always difficult because usually there are strong young shoots coming from it which should be allowed to arch gracefully from the wall. But if a percentage of, say, five-year-old shoots is removed each year there will usually be plenty left to produce flowers. When the plant is young no pruning is required, but hampered as we are by having to give the rose wall-space, some limit will be reached and some pruning must be done from time to time. I would much prefer to see it covering a tree in its loose and graceful way, but this could be successful only in really warm sunny gardens, where little or no frost occurs.

The double yellow is a splendid free-flowering plant, and it is unfortunate that this most popular Banksian variety has less scent than the others. Contrary to the statements in many books, and to the usual opinion, I find it is not scentless by any means. The other three forms do not flower so freely in England in my experience, though they grow and flower at Leonardslee and at Highdown, Sussex, and also at Powis Castle, Montgomeryshire, a property of the National Trust. At Kiftsgate Court the soft buttery yellow of R. *banksiae lutea* creates a lovely picture with *Clematis montana rubens*. Both colours are particularly tender in quality and assort well together against the stone wall.

It grows and flowers freely in the South of France and other Mediterranean districts where the climate is congenial. It is easy to grow from cuttings and has been used as an understock. In severe winters in Surrey, I have known the young wood to be killed.

BANKSIAE. The single forms are considered to be variants from the wild. All will achieve 20 feet or more in good conditions.

BANKSIAE BANKSIAE (ALBO-PLENA). Double flowers densely packed with small petals, making a neat rosette, very fragrant; 'having a sweet perfume as though it had just returned on a visit from the Violet' (Dean Hole).
Redouté, vol. ii, Plate 43.
Botanical Register, vol. v, t.397. R. *banksiae flore pleno*.
Andrews, Plate 76.
Drapiez, vol. i, p. 71. R. *banksiana*, double white.
Roses et Rosiers, Plate 21. 'Le Rosier Banks épineux.' Perhaps R. *fortuneana*.
Botanical Magazine, t.1954. Poor.

BANKSIAE LUTEA. Small, double, yellow; fragrant.
Paul, 9th Edition, Plate 9. Too bright.
Roses et Rosiers, Plate 8. 'Le Rosier Banks à fleurs jaunes.' Good.
Botanical Register, vol. xiii, t.1105.
Willmott, Plate 35. Excellent portrait.
Florist and Pomologist, Plate 28. Very good.
Reeves, vol. ii, Plate 33.

BANKSIAE LUTESCENS. Small, single, yellow, very fragrant.
Botanical Magazine, t.7171.
Botanical Cabinet, t.1960.

BANKSIAE NORMALIS. Small, single, white. Very fragrant.

William Paul records several varieties or hybrids which are no longer grown in this country, including a large double yellow (*lutescens spinosa*—presumably thorny and a hybrid), 'Jaune Sérin'; and *rosea*, with vivid pink cupped flowers. It would be interesting to know if these are still grown in Europe or elsewhere.

ANEMONEFLORA. (R. *triphylla*). A double-flowered garden rose, introduced from Eastern China in 1844, about whose origin we cannot be certain. It has been variously described as a hybrid between R. *banksiae*, R. *laevigata*, and R. *multiflora*; it bears considerable resemblance to the first, has the hispid pedicels and three leaflets of the second, while the styles are united in a column like those of all Synstylae Section roses, of which R. *multiflora* is a member. It suffers in cold winters, but breaks forth from the old wood as Miss Willmott's illustration shows. Leaves slender and pointed, neatly serrate, glaucous beneath. Flowers small, fully double, in small clusters pink in the bud fading to nearly white, central petals narrow and often with frayed edges. Pretty, but not in the first flight of ramblers; a connoisseur's plant, to be grown on a sheltered wall.
Willmott, Plate 67. Very good.
Revue Horticole, 1849, p. 15.

FORTUNEANA. A hybrid, presumed with R. *laevigata*, introduced from Chinese gardens by Robert Fortune about 1845. It should not be confused with 'Fortune's Double Yellow' (R. *odorata pseudindica*) (see page 105). It does not flower very freely in England, but I hear of it as a success in warmer climates. The growth and foliage resemble the Banksian roses, but it is larger in all parts, while the flowers are fully double, creamy white, somewhat like 'Albéric Barbier' but less well formed. The flower stalk inherits the glandular hairs of R. *laevigata*. Apart from ornamentation it is also used in southern Europe as an understock, for which purpose it is said to be admirable and to transmit its vigour to the scion.
Flore des Serres, vol. vii, p. 256. Line drawing.
Willmott, Plate 36.
Roses et Rosiers, Plate 21. Possibly this is R. *fortuneana*.

THE MACARTNEY ROSE, R. BRACTEATA

This aristocratic and altogether splendid rose was introduced from China by Lord Macartney in 1793. Not being very hardy, it has remained a rare rose in England, but has so many admirable qualities that it should be attempted more often. It is usually a success against a sunny wall in the more favoured parts of the country. As an evergreen wall shrub with a long flowering period it has few peers. The sturdy twigs are covered with brown-grey down and bear pairs of stout hooked prickles as well as scattered smaller ones. The leaves raise it to a very high level among shrubs, being glossy, of darkest green and divided into 5 to 9 leaflets, which are often blunt at the apex—most unusual in a rose. The name 'bracteata' refers to the leafy bracts surrounding the flowers, which are usually about 3 inches across, pure white—lustrous and of silky appearance like those of a cistus—with bright orange-yellow stamens. They appear on exceedingly stout shoots before midsummer and until autumn, singly or in clusters, and have a rich scent of lemons.

When growing well it may reach to 15 feet in height but is always dense and more like a shrub than a climber. It has become naturalized in the Southern States of North America, and roots readily in the ground as it grows and can even be considered a nuisance in some districts. It grows well at Trelissick, a National Trust garden in Cornwall, and I remember a splendid plant at Wormley Bury, Hertfordshire, the home of the late Major Albert Pam. It has proved particularly resistant to 'black spot' fungoid disease, but this character has not been transmitted to its noted hybrid 'Mermaid'.

BRACTEATA.

Botanical Magazine, t.1377.
Willmott, Plate 125.
Duhamel, vol. vii, Plate 13.
Andrews, Plate 78. R. *lucida*.
Lawrance, Plate 84. R. *lucida*, Single White China Rose.
Redouté, vol. i, Plate 35. Very good.
Braam, Plate 10. Chinese painting, excellent.

Hu, t.78. A pen drawing.

Paul, 9th Edition, p. 77. Excellent line-engraving.

Kingdon Ward describes how in Burma, forty miles from Myitkyina, 'the botanist gets his first thrill. Here the long ribs of slate rock, which in March are exposed in the river bed, are covered with wild Roses (R. *bracteata*) and crimson Azalea (*Rhododendron indicum*)'. (*Plant Hunting on the Edge of the World*.)

As is understandable with a rose that has been in cultivation for so many years, this species has produced some hybrids, and Miss Willmott recalls several of rich colouring which apparently have died out, at least in England. A double white is still grown, sometimes called *alba odorata* and sometimes 'Marie Leonida', but according to the latest ruling is now R. × *leonida*. It is unfortunately not a success in England, since its flowers seldom open properly, although they are freely produced on a vigorous plant. It tries hard on a sunny wall at the John Innes Institute, Hertford. In warmer climates it is splendid. Miss Willmott's Plate 127, a semi-double flowered hybrid between R. *bracteata* and R. *laevigata*, does not appear to be this double variety. Other doubles have also been recorded and various raisers have tried to make hybrids, but with little success apart from the splendid climber 'Mermaid', a hybrid with a yellow Tea Rose. See also page 190.

'**Mermaid**'. William Paul, 1918. This grows best in England on sunny walls, but flowers very freely even on north walls. In less sheltered districts it is liable to be killed to the ground in severe winters. It may be evergreen or deciduous, according to climate and situation. The leaves and flowers and freedom of growth are all greater than in R. *bracteata*, and the colour is a warm soft canary-yellow. After the petals have fallen the stamens remain in beauty for some days. In really sheltered districts on sunny banks it may be allowed to make a great sprawling bush, but however it may be grown it remains an outstandingly beautiful plant. In frost-free sunny climates it develops a strength and magnificence far surpassing anything we see in Britain. 25 feet.

McFarland, 1937, p. 159.

American *Rose Annual*, 1931, Plate 12.

Park, Plate 217. Flowers only.

Another hybrid, supposedly of R. *bracteata* × R. *rugosa*, is the shrub 'Schneezwerg', for which see *Shrub Roses of Today*, page 193.

CLINOPHYLLA. A tender rose, native to Bengal, Nepal, and China, introduced from India in 1917; synonymous with R. *lyellii*, R. *involucrata*, and R. *lindleyana*. I have not seen this rose, but it is a close relative to R. *bracteata*, and is figured in the *Botanical Register*, t.739. William Paul, in his ninth edition, shews a superb double form or hybrid, which he calls R. *lucida duplex*. The large full flowers are pure white with a rosy flush in the centre. Even though this may not be hardy everywhere, it should be retrieved.

THE CHEROKEE ROSE, R. LAEVIGATA

It is quite an achievement, I think, for a wild rose of China to become so established and naturalized in the United States that it has acquired the name of 'Cherokee Rose', and has, moreover, been accepted as the State flower of Georgia, U.S.A. Yet such is the fortune of R. *laevigata*. Nobody knows when it arrived in America.

Known also as R. *sinica*, R. *cherokeensis*, and R. *camellia*, it is a strong-growing rambling species for mild climates; when grown on a warm wall or district it is nearly evergreen, with only three leaflets, glossy and coarsely toothed, of dark shining green. It is a beautiful plant even when out of flower. The green stems are set with red-brown prickles, large and small, which diminish into mere bristles below the flower and all over the receptacle and calyx. The large single well-formed flowers are creamy white with broad rounded petals and beautiful yellow stamens. Deliciously scented. The flowers appear in late May and June. I fear that few of us would give it the 25 feet square of space that it needs on a warm wall owing to its short flowering period, and for this reason it remains uncommon.

LAEVIGATA.
Botanical Magazine, t.2847.
Botanical Register, t.1922. Very good.
Willmott, Plate 117. Very good.

Stevens, p. 186. R. *laevigata*, 'Anemone', and 'Ramona'; the portraits give very little idea of the beauty of these three.
Braam, Plate 19. Chinese painting, very good.
Reeves, vol. ii, Plate 39.

Two very beautiful coloured descendants of R. *laevigata* are in cultivation, and it is presumed that the other parent was a Tea Rose; however, as they very closely resemble R. *laevigata*, I think it best to include them here.

ANEMONOIDES. R. *sinica* 'Anemone'. Schmidt, Erfurt, 1895. Known as the 'Anemone Rose', though I can see no reason for this descriptive name. Usually the term 'anemone-flowered' refers to a double flower with petaloid stamens, but there is no suggestion of anything like this in the shapely, wide, single blooms of this rose, so very much like R. *laevigata* except in colour. Presumably it is thought to resemble a Japanese anemone. The soft clear pink is veined with a deeper shade, but paler on the reverse. The growth, buds, and foliage all resemble those of R. *laevigata*, but it is by no means such a luxuriant rambler. R. *anemonoides* is hardy in all but the most severe winter (I have seldom known it hurt on a wall) and is rather angular, sparsely leaved, and open-growing. Starting early in the season the flowers appear over many weeks, and are some 4 inches across. *Revue Horticole*, 1901, t.548. Poor.
Willmott, Plate 121.

'Ramona'. A deeply coloured sport of R. *anemonoides* which originated in California in the nursery of Dietrich and Turner in 1913. Exactly resembles its parent except that its colour is an intense glowing cerise-crimson, with effective greyish tint on the reverse. Again, it has an early and long flowering season, and sometimes a few blooms appear in September.

'Silver Moon'. Van Fleet, 1910. R. *wichuraiana* × *laevigata* is usually given as the parentage, but it is highly likely that a hybrid rose also was used, and the latest supposition is that it was 'Devoniensis'. A very vigorous, noble rose, creating a curtain of handsome dark glossy leaves, and bearing clusters of large creamy white semi-double flowers at midsummer,

opening from butter-yellow buds, and with yellow stamens. Rich fragrance of green apples. Glaucous stems set with a few purplish prickles. An unforgettable sight at Kew growing into trees, where it attained about 30 feet.
Addisonia, 1917, p. 61. Poor.

In *Shrub Roses of Today* I included a chapter like this, devoted to oddments that did not fit elsewhere, and here I record a further hybrid of R. *roxburghii*, to add to the shrub-forms in my earlier book. As it is a climber it fits best here:

'Triomphe de la Guillotière'. Guillot, 1863. The raiser's name will immediately quash any suspicion that this rose is connected with the guillotine! An extremely interesting hybrid of R. *roxburghii* (R. *microphylla*) and one that may well be used again in our search for 'different' roses. The dainty leaves, pinnate or divided into neat small leaflets, indicate its ancestry. It flowers well on a west wall at the Roseraie de l'Haÿ; borne singly and in clusters the flowers are light rose-pink and fragrant, about 3 inches across, tightly filled with petals in the Old Rose style, with button eye. Buds large, round, downy; bark smooth. This is certainly a rose on its own, for preservation, and it should be quite hardy.

10

The Botany of Climbing Roses and the Derivation of Some Garden Climbers

by GORDON D. ROWLEY

Great families of yesterday we show,
And lords, whose parents were the Lord knows who.
Daniel Defoe, 1660–1731.

A CLIMBING as distinct from bush habit is characteristic of one of the most natural and readily recognizable Sections of the Genus *Rosa*—the Synstylae. It also occurs in four other small Sections of one to two species each: the Indicae, Banksianae, Laevigatae and Bracteatae. All these are diploids with fourteen chromosomes each, as are many of their garden progeny, and they have their centre of diversity in South-east Asia, the Synstylae extending thence along the southernmost limits of the genus to India, Arabia and North Africa, and Europe, with a single rather distinct species (R. *setigera*) native to the New World.

The characteristic habit, with a sharp distinction between long and short shoots, combines with other features to set the Synstylae apart from the remaining species of *Rosa*. The small, mostly white flowers are crowded into large flat or conical trusses. In the centre of each bloom the styles are tightly pressed together and exserted to stand up like the head of a pin, thus giving the name to the

Section. They often persist on the fruit, which is a small globular red hep unlike the large flask- or urn-shaped heps of other Sections. The Indicae differ mainly in the reduction of the inflorescence to a few large flowers, and the remaining three climbing Sections stand rather isolated and have deciduous, almost free stipules.

Opinions differ widely on how many species comprise the Synstylae. Most authorities accept between one dozen and two, but Hurst went so far as to reduce them all to a single species. This extreme view finds support in the *Rosa moschata* complex, which extends in an apparently continuous belt from Europe (*R. moschata sens. str.*) to North-west Africa and Arabia (*R. abyssinica*), India (*R. brunonii*), Manchuria (*R. maximowicziana*) and to a peak of variation in Central China, where the magnificent R. *sinowilsonii* displays the upper size limit of the Section, with leaves often a foot long. In Huxley's terminology, *Rosa moschata* is a clone shewing a gradient of characteristics throughout its distribution, although more field work is needed to ascertain whether or not clear discontinuities exist to justify recognition of several species. Meanwhile conservative botanists will tend to lump them all together, whereas horticulturists prefer to retain the names at least of those of garden merit. Just how much seedlings can vary I found out when Dr A. K. Janaki-Ammal sent me seed of wild Musk roses growing in parts of Nepal. The progeny ranged in foliage from glossy deep green to blue-grey and downy with an attractive purple flush below. Flower and truss size also varied from plant to plant.

The change-over from bush to climbing habit in wild roses led to a corresponding change in habitat preference. Thus we find the climbers on the margins of woods and copses where the necessary support is to be found, rather than out in the open where the shrubby and thicket-forming types grow. They tolerate shade in the early years, but flowering is usually confined to branches that reach up above the undergrowth.

Wild hybrids between climbing and bush roses are relatively rare, but the cross appears in the ancestry of many groups of garden roses. It leads to a blurring of the sharp difference between the two habits and the occurrence of many intermediates. The genetics of climbing habit has not been fully worked out, and a somewhat complicated inheritance seems likely. On the other hand, there is no doubt that straight mutation often leads to a climbing sport arising from a bush rose, or the reverse change, and this mutation can be stabilized by vegetative propagation, even though it may affect only the surface tissues, the core remaining unaltered. Propagation by root cuttings of certain climbers has produced bush roses only because the new plant arises solely from the core tissue, not from the skin as in budding or normal grafting. As yet we have no certain method of inducing the change from bush to climber or *vice versa*, and experiments at the John Innes Institute give no support to the popular belief that hard pruning or propagation from lateral instead of long shoots can make a climber revert to a bush.

Hurst noticed that in *Rosa* perpetual flowering is associated with dwarf habit, arising by mutation from a climbing species (R. *chinensis*, *sempervirens*, *multiflora*) in which new shoots that would normally climb produce inflorescences instead. However, this is not inevitably so, as has been shewn by the measure of success in selecting garden roses combining tall growth and long flowering season. Nor is repeat flowering confined to descendants of climbing species: we have it to some extent in *Rosa rugosa* and *damascena*.

The following tables illustrate some of the ancestry of garden climbers and ramblers:

MULTIFLORA DERIVATIVES

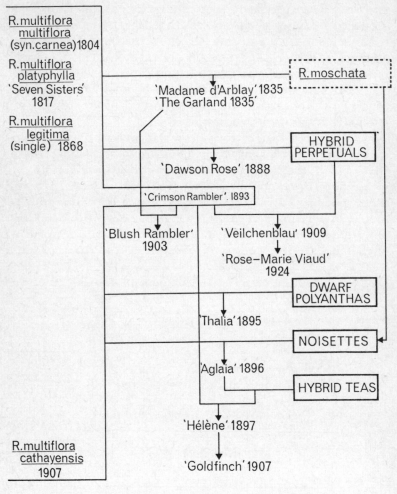

Rosa
multiflora
Thunb.

Ancestral varieties
and early introductions
from the Far East

R.multiflora
multiflora
(syn.carnea)1804

R.multiflora
platyphylla
'Seven Sisters'
1817

R.multiflora
legitima
(single) 1868

R.multiflora
cathayensis
1907

'Madame d'Arblay' 1835
'The Garland 1835'

R.moschata

HYBRID
PERPETUALS

'Dawson Rose' 1888

'Crimson Rambler'. 1893

'Blush Rambler'
1903

'Veilchenblau' 1909

'Rose-Marie Viaud'
1924

DWARF
POLYANTHAS

'Thalia' 1895

NOISETTES

'Aglaia' 1896

HYBRID TEAS

'Hélène' 1897

'Goldfinch' 1907

Broken lines indicate wild species.
Entire lines indicate cultivars.

LUCIAE DERIVATIVES

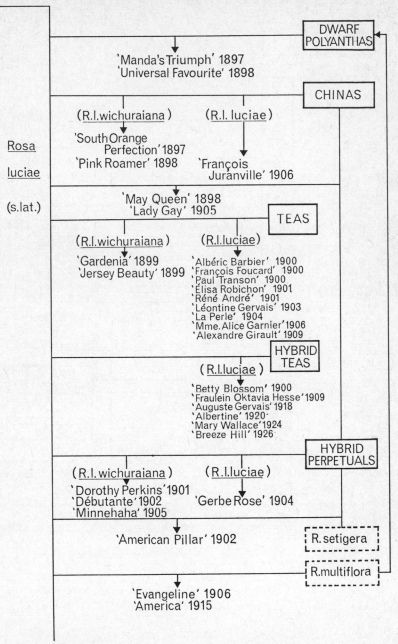

DWARF POLYANTHAS

'Manda's Triumph' 1897
'Universal Favourite' 1898

CHINAS

Rosa
luciae

(s.lat.)

(R.l.wichuraiana)

'South Orange
    Perfection' 1897
'Pink Roamer' 1898

(R.l. luciae)

'François
    Juranville' 1906

'May Queen' 1898
'Lady Gay' 1905

TEAS

(R.l.wichuraiana)

'Gardenia' 1899
'Jersey Beauty' 1899

(R.l.luciae)

'Albéric Barbier' 1900
'François Foucard' 1900
'Paul Transon' 1900
'Élisa Robichon' 1901
'Réné André' 1901
'Léontine Gervais' 1903
'La Perle' 1904
'Mme. Alice Garnier' 1906
'Alexandre Girault' 1909

HYBRID TEAS

(R.l.luciae)

'Betty Blossom' 1900
'Fraulein Oktavia Hesse' 1909
'Auguste Gervais' 1918
'Albertine' 1920
'Mary Wallace' 1924
'Breeze Hill' 1926

HYBRID PERPETUALS

(R.l.wichuraiana)

'Dorothy Perkins' 1901
'Débutante' 1902
'Minnehaha' 1905

(R.l.luciae)

'Gerbe Rose' 1904

'American Pillar' 1902

R.setigera

R.multiflora

'Evangeline' 1906
'America' 1915

NOTE: *Rosa luciae* Franch. & Roch. is interpreted here in the broad sense as including both
R. *luciae luciae* and
R. *luciae wichuraiana* (Syn. R. *wichuraiana* Crép.).
Precise parentage is indicated only where it is known or can be surmised with reasonable accuracy.

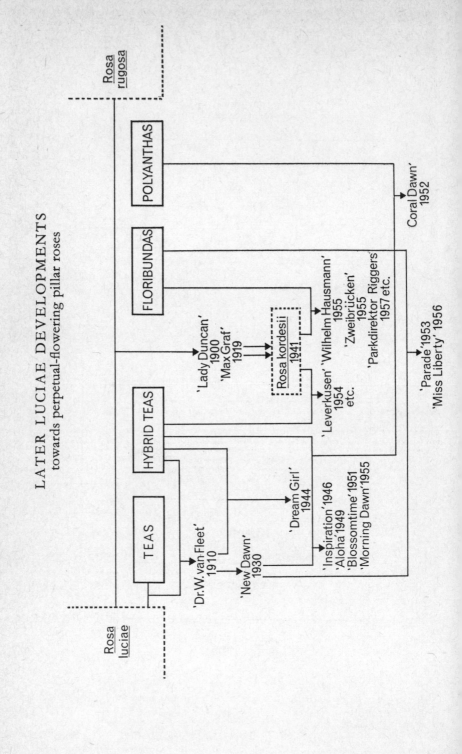

LATER LUCIAE DEVELOPMENTS
towards perpetual-flowering pillar roses

Rosa rugosa

Rosa luciae

POLYANTHAS

FLORIBUNDAS

HYBRID TEAS

TEAS

'Lady Duncan' 1900
'Max Graf' 1919

Rosa kordesii 1941

'Leverkusen' 'Wilhelm Hausmann' 1954 1955
'Zweibrücken' 1955
'Parkdirektor Riggers' 1957 etc.

'Dream Girl' 1944

'Dr.W. van Fleet' 1910

'New Dawn' 1930

'Inspiration' 1946
'Aloha' 1949
'Blossomtime' 1951
'Morning Dawn' 1955

Coral Dawn' 1952

'Parade' 1953
'Miss Liberty' 1956

1. The form of *Rosa filipes* known as 'Kiftsgate'.

2. The late Mrs J. B. Muir standing by her 'Kiftsgate' *Rosa filipes*.

3. *Rosa brunonii* 'La Mortola' at Kiftsgate, Gloucestershire.

4. 'Kew Rambler', whose greyish leaves shew the influence of *Rosa soulieana*. Fragrant pink flowers.

5. The Luciae Rambler
'May Queen' (1898).

6. 'Paul Transon', one of the Luciae Ramblers, which inherit glossy foliage
and sweet fragrance from *Rosa luciae*, and have occasional flowers after the
main crop.

7. 'Climbing Cécile Brunner' at the University Botanic Garden, Oxford.

8. Vigorous 'Claire Jacquier' (1888), a fragrant yellow Noisette Rose.

9. 'Lamarque' (1830) on a south wall at Knightshayes Court, Devon.

10. Another Noisette, 'Madame Alfred Carrière' (1879) in constant production at the Roseraie de l'Haÿ, near Paris. It is trained on ropes, leading up to posts.

11. 'Sombreuil' (1850), a productive and hardy Tea Rose in blush colour.

12. 'Devoniensis' (1851), another excellent Tea Rose, deliciously fragrant.

13. 'Dream Girl' (1944), exceedingly fragrant modern pillar rose demonstrating the value of nodding flowers on climbers.

14. A Musk Rose climbing into yew trees at Maidwell Hall, Northamptonshire.

15. Formal training of rambling and climbing roses at Bagatelle, Paris.

16. Formal training of ramblers and weeping standards at the Roseraie de l'Haÿ, near Paris.

PART 4

Practical Points

11

Cultivation, Pruning, and Training

The Twelve Months

Snowy, Flowy, Blowy,
Showery, Flowery, Bowery,
Hoppy, Croppy, Droppy,
Breezy, Sneezy, Freezy.

George Ellis, 1753–1815.

SCARCELY a month goes by without roses needing attention of some kind—even if it is only admiration! The tidier we want our roses to appear the more work there is to be done, but I must say I prefer a more lazy approach to them.

Cultivation

There are very few soils that will not grow a rose. We must except damp acid soils and really wet clays, and the hungriest of chalks, but otherwise roses will grow. They will do best where there is good drainage, a deep, medium soil, neutral or nearly so, and in full sunshine. We can do a lot to help our soils. Draining is important for all plants; only bog plants like soil permanently saturated with moisture. Drainage can be helped by ensuring that surface water is drained off—if hollows abound—by attention to the contours; by deepening ditches or creating them; by laying pipes, or laying cut heather in trenches instead of pipes. In lime-free soil the heather will last for several decades and water will percolate through it. It is no use digging a deep hole in too damp a spot and filling the base with rubble or clinker, replacing the

163

soil and planting the rose; the rubble will simply act as a sump and *collect the water*.

Drought is another matter, which can be partially rectified by other means such as leaving a hose on for a day. Very porous soils and also very sticky soils can be improved by any kind of open humus—leaves, chopped bracken, rotted straw, garden compost, wood shavings, etc. Lawn mowings and sawdust can also be used but are apt to 'cake' and should be stirred from time to time. Sawdust and wood shavings, when applied un-rotted, should be supplemented by a sprinkling of sulphate of ammonia (or nitro-chalk on acid soils).

Deep initial digging over as large an area as possible is the first prerequisite. Plant firmly at the right depth or a little lower, observing the 'collar' of the plant. Apply manure in a year's time to the surface; there is no need to dig it in or cover it except to make things tidy. See that roses are not baked at the root, give them a mulch or some lowly plants to help to gather together dead leaves, making a ground cover of growth and debris. Apply bone meal in autumn or a well-balanced fertilizer in spring; do not use fresh strong nitrogenous manure as it encourages sappy growth, which opens the door to diseases. Plant when the ground is in good workable condition; if necessary delay planting and put the roses into temporary quarters for a week or more, if they arrive by rail inopportunely.

A little hole, hastily dug in soil that has already been static for some years, is the worst preparation you can give for your rose.

These are the rules that I try to adopt; those who want further elaboration must look elsewhere, and I cannot do better than recommend the following books:

Roses for Enjoyment, by Gordon Edwards (Collingridge); *Gardening on Lime*, by Judith Berrisford (Faber), and *Gardening on Clay*, by H. H. Crane (Collingridge).

Greenfly and other insect pests: there are many proprietary brands of insecticides available in stores, to be applied on the foliage or on the soil and thus through the system of the plants.

'*Black spot*': this is a nuisance in some districts, in some seasons, sometimes, but not usually in large towns, where the sulphur in the air prevents its incidence. It attacks almost all roses, and there are different 'strains' of the fungus blowing about the country during the summer; hence one can never be sure where infection comes from. The spores take a fortnight to develop in the tissues of the leaves. Spraying with sulphur preparations is helpful. The disease does not very greatly affect strong-growing roses, but renders them unsightly in bad seasons, and may in very extreme circumstances actually kill plants. If the general health of the plants is fostered by mulching and the avoidance of strong nitrogenous manures, they will be more resistant to any fungus.

For fuller details of pests and diseases, pruning, etc. please refer to the publications of the National Rose Society, or to Mr Edwards's book, mentioned above.

Pruning

From the amount of space devoted to pruning roses, in books published during the last hundred years or so, we might conclude that it was a difficult subject, and also that every rose needed very full attention. When we get to know the idiosyncrasies of every rose and our own soil and climate, we can give devoted and individual care to every plant, but life is seldom long enough or sufficiently leisurely for this. There are, however, a few principal rules about pruning rambling and climbing roses which all of us must know before picking up the knife or secateurs; they are the rules which apply to the different flowering groups.

Broadly there is only one rule which applies to all roses and other hard-wooded plants, and that is: *Prune immediately after flowering.* This has three further qualifications:

(a) If the rose flowers only once in the growing season, the pruning should then be done immediately after the flowers are over unless we expect a display of berries or heps, in which case some shoots should be left; further pruning must be done in late winter after the heps have gone;

(b) If the rose goes on producing flowers through summer and autumn—i.e. is 'recurrent', 'remontant', 'repeat-flowering' or 'perpetual'—the pruning is left until late winter. February is usually a good month, but I do it whenever a mild day occurs from Christmas onwards;

(*c*) If subsequent heps or berries are expected from varieties in
(*b*) then we do not remove spent flowers, but as a rule
these are not varieties conspicuous in fruit, and spent
flowers are best removed to encourage later production
of buds.

The pruning for any rose consists of removing or shortening
wood that has flowered so that the plant can put its energies into
making new wood for the next year. In group (*a*) we *remove from
the base* all the oldest, weakest wood (leaving some for fruiting if
required and suitable); in (*b*) we *shorten side shoots* and occasionally
remove from the base very old wood, likewise.

Pruning (*a*) refers to roses in Chapters 2, 4 and 5. Those in
Chapters 2 and 5 really manage very well, after a little attention
during the first two years or so, without regular pruning, but give
them a clean-out every five years afterwards, or if you prefer they
may be left in a glorious tangle. Those in Chapter 4 benefit from
regular and drastic pruning. The recurrent varieties in Chapter 5
must be treated circumspectly.

Pruning (*b*): those in Chapters 6, 7, and 8.

The roses in Chapter 9 remain; the Banksian roses require
practically no pruning, as indicated in their chapter; R. *laevigata*
and its varieties come into group (*a*) above, but really need very
little pruning; R. *bracteata* and its hybrids are perpetual flowering
shrubs, and an occasional thinning out in late winter is all that is
required.

From the above it will be understood that only the garden
ramblers require any systematic attention. All the others, and even
these, can be left to themselves if the taste of the owner prefers.
By this I mean that, if we like free-grown tangles with rather less
flower, we need not bother about pruning except once in a while
to remove really spent old wood. If we are training ramblers on
supports in a neatly kept garden, pruning should be done regularly. Those ramblers which are given trees and hedgerows as
supports are best left to themselves, after the initial attention;
this consists of pruning away all the first few years' growth as
soon as a mighty shoot arises, when established.

The most frequent question about pruning roses is the treatment in the first spring of planting. If you are hard-hearted you

may cut all roses in Chapters 2, 4, and 5 to six inches above the ground in spring after planting, and the remainder may be shortened to about four feet. But I generally leave the whole lot as they are until after their first flowering, and then, when their roots are fully established, they can be treated properly, removing all weak growth.

Training

There is nothing difficult about training ramblers; the shoots are pliable and can be bent gently to any position. The climbing sports of Hybrid Teas are another matter, and the strong young shoots snap if handled too roughly. All of these sports—and the climbing Noisettes, Bourbons and Hybrid Perpetuals, Tea Noisettes, Teas and 'Mermaid'—tend to become 'leggy' at the base, and it is most important to keep the strong young shoots from growing straight up the wall. This can be achieved by two methods. In a restricted width of wall it is best to nip out the extreme tip when about two feet high and to train the subsequent branches in different directions. Later strong branches can be tipped likewise. Where there is greater width available the shoots should be spread out nearly horizontally; in later years shoots will arise along their whole length for training upwards. As a reminder and enforcer of these rules it is quite a good idea to plant *under* a window—so long as it is four feet from the ground level—rather than between windows; the resulting training of branches around the window will make a delightful picture.

12

Display

Le vrai but de la vie est d'améliorer
un coin du monde, ne fut ce qu'un arpent,
et d'y faire fleurir la paix des plantes.

Viaud-Bruant.

ALTHOUGH roses as a whole are flimsy plants—seldom being really dense and almost always deciduous—the ramblers and climbers enter very importantly into the design of the garden. As with all good gardening, the intending planter's question should be, 'What rose would be best there?', rather than the more frequent, 'Where can I put this variety?'. The importance of the ramblers and climbers is that as a rule they need artificial support, and the support must necessarily fit in with the house, paths, or walls, and all the main features of the garden. Therefore the rule should be first to decide where an arch, pillar, arbour or other erection would be an asset to the garden, next to decide upon what form would be most appropriate, and then select the most suitable roses for it.

However, all this presupposes a formal garden. Seldom do artificial erections look comfortable in a natural planting of shrubs and plants with paths of grass or gravel gently curving and accentuating the contours. In such gardens certain roses will display themselves naturally and superbly, and be a tremendous addition to the garden through the colour and fragrance they give, and their period of flowering will automatically prolong the display of flowering shrubs which in the main flower earlier. I recall 'The Garland' foaming over shrubs at Munsted Wood; R. *multiflora* arching over the path at Nymans; the trails of 'Daisy

Hill' and 'Lady Curzon' and 'Complicata' leading from the shrubs into trees in various informal gardens, and the vigorous species in the Synstylae Section climbing into trees at Nymans, Knightshayes, and elsewhere; the old apple trees disporting 'Madame Plantier' at Sissinghurst, and 'Rose-Marie Viaud', 'Albéric Barbier' and others growing likewise in Constance Spry's garden at Winkfield. To my mind there is nothing so beautiful as a living support for all sprawling or scrambling species

roses, whether they be called shrubs, climbers, or ramblers. The sports of Hybrid Teas and similar stalwart roses are unsuitable for such culture not only because of their stiff growth, but because their sophisticated flowers need, I think, association with buildings to make them acceptable.

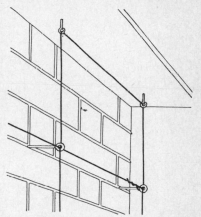

1. Wires stretched through vine-eyes, 3 inches from brickwork.

As there is normally a house in a garden it would be as well to consider the means of fixing roses to the walls before going round the garden to seek other opportunities to provide homes for them. The ideal method of securing climbers to house walls is to have 'vine-eyes' built into the brickwork, projecting some four inches, ready for wiring later (Figure 1) [1]. If the finish is brick, that is excellent, but if the finish is to be stucco or stone-dash or woodwork, which will need colour-washing or painting from time to time, then difficulties at once present themselves. When the plants are thoroughly established and have reached full beauty, thickly intertwined, it may be necessary to take them down to apply a fresh coat to the wall surface. The only means of achieving this is to have the wire arranged in panels 6 feet or so wide, attached only at the eaves and at the base, so that they can be let down and bent outwards complete with the plants when required. To facilitate this, only pliant growers can be used, and they must be kept to their own strips of wire. But the whole job is so awkward

[1] The figures cited refer to drawings in this chapter.

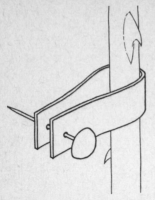

that on such wall-finishes it is best to avoid climbing plants and grow a few shrubs; alternatively to be severe so that when the evil day arrives we can cut the climbers down and let them grow up again. Sometimes this produces wonderful refreshment for the plants, but of course it will be two or three years at least before they are fully restored.

When wiring a building it is best to have perpendicular and horizontal wires securely fixed—the mesh may be 9 inches or 1 foot square for roses. Pig wire is very suitable for restricted spaces. The bare wire will not hurt the roses, and is nearly invisible when once the foliage arrives—in fact against some walls it is unnoticeable at any time. Some people hammer nails into the wall, but this is not good for the wall neither is it as good or secure for the rose, because the nail must have a leather or stout webbing loop (Figure 2) to wrap round the stem of the plant, and in due course these give way. On no account should nails be hammered into stucco or stone-dash. On certain types of building, panels of trellis, preferably rectangular and not diamond-shaped, are appropriate and even decorative. They should be of seasoned wood (well steeped in a preservative non-toxic to plants) and about 1 inch by ½ inch securely fixed 4 inches from the wall, and securely joined at every crossing (Figure 3).

2. Large-headed nail and leather or plastic strap.

The other matter to consider at the outset of planting around the house is the position of drains, extensions of footings, and the projection of eaves. One of the driest places in the garden can be the north or east wall, where

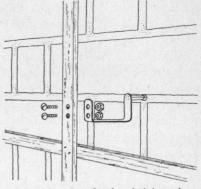

3. Metal bracket fixed to brickwork, to support wide-mesh wooden lattice.

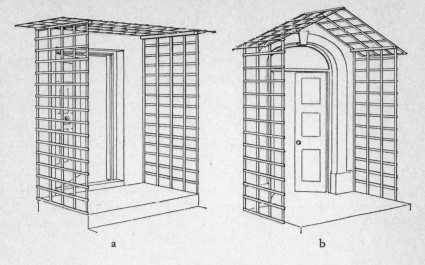

4. Various traditional arches for doorways:
(a) and (b) wooden lattice, (c) galvanized wire.

the eaves project perhaps a foot and
where no summer rains borne on south-
west winds can fall. Footings are not
usually a nuisance with modern buildings,
but both these, drains, and manholes can
ruin planting schemes around old houses.
A paved path also can lead all water away
from the narrow border along the house
wall, especially if the paving is set in
concrete—as it should be if permanence
and ease of work are considered.

Immediately adjoining the house is the
first artificial extra we have to consider
—the possible arch over the door. This must be designed in
relation to the house (Figure 4) and the only rule left to
planters is to choose a thornless scented rose of graceful habit;
the colour must of course tone in with the paint on the door
and windows. Sometimes a view will focus on to an insignificant door or window, which can be immeasurably enhanced
by a surround of trellis, suitably designed—a *trompe l'œil*—and

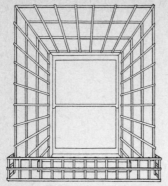

5. *Trompe l'œil* of wooden lattice fixed flat on wall, which can support a climbing plant, to enhance a plain window.

gracefully enshrined by roses or other climbing plants (Figure 5).

Fences and walls surrounding the garden usually follow the boundaries, and provide support for a great variety of roses and other climbers. The ideal is to have wires or trellis as for the house walls; close-boarded fences should have a final rail added at the top, as roses can be very heavy, and if the boards project above the main top rail, as is usual, pieces of board often get broken in storms. These remarks refer to walls and solid fences, but in some places open fences (Figures 6, 7) may be chosen; they can look very well in the country if of cleft rail and posts, or in built-up areas posts and rails of prepared and painted wood (white or near white is really the only acceptable colour) can look very smart and also charming. It is an American idea, and an open fence of any of these materials hung informally with roses is a delightful method of defining an area without erecting too substantial and

6, 7. Various fences of open wood-work, described in text.

private a barrier. Quite unimposing, long-lasting, and effective
is split chestnut paling. Near some period houses with a Chinese
interior a Chippendale style of fence-pattern might be chosen,
in natural oak or painted, or a neat white fence of straight boards,
spaced evenly apart. On sloping ground walls may be built to
retain soil, and for these roses can be chosen to hang down. Open
fences dividing one part of
the garden from another are
best made in the cleft style so
that the rails are not all on
one side of the posts, which
gives a 'front' and 'back'
appearance, and these in-
terior fences must serve a
definite purpose and be connected with the house or
solid hedges or buildings.
Transparent preservatives
can be obtained for use
when wood is preferred in
its natural colour.

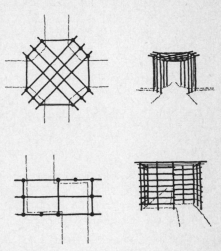

   Summerhouses and
arbours can provide excellent positions for ramblers
and climbers. The summer-
house can be quite a cheap
8. Elaborate arches or arbours at junction
of paths, or to give reason to a twist in
a path.

plebeian affair if dense-growing ramblers are chosen, so that it
becomes completely smothered—with close boarding inside to
keep out the earwigs! Without boarding it would be an arbour,
constructed of open poles and crossbars. An arbour can be a place
to sit, and also can be used for passing through. At a junction of
paths, for instance, two crossing arches can be made diagonally,
each of two or three posts, and the whole top can be covered.
Or if a path should change direction or alignment, a similar
arbour can disguise it and turn its accident into an embellishment
(Figure 8). These are all important features of a garden to be
given positions which govern other features such as arches, pergolas, pillars, and pyramids.
   An arch arbitrarily placed along a path to provide a home for a

couple of roses will always be a superfluous adornment, better removed; it should mark an entry or an exit or have some such purpose. But a series of arches down a path is a different matter and can be very enjoyable, either separately spaced or connected in the form of a pergola. Even so, there should be a definite feature or view at each end to give a reason for such an important series of arches. Arches of single poles look rather insignificant, but two poles each side with crossbars and two poles across the top complete also with crossbars, turn a wooden arch into a

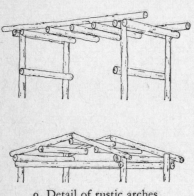

9. Detail of rustic arches.

stronger unit both aesthetically and practically (Figure 9). An alternative is to erect metal pipes connected with wires and wire mesh, longer lasting but less pleasant. If wood is used, trouble occurs usually just at ground level where rot sets in; the best preventative is to char the base or apply a preservative; either treatment should extend from the base to a height of six inches above the ground level, the bark having been removed if natural wood is used. Every few years it is as well to remove a little soil and re-treat the length of wood from just below soil level to just above it. I find bedstead irons, L-shaped in section, ideal for supporting weakened posts, when hammered in behind them. They are fairly inconspicuous. Another good idea is to sink wide pipes into the soil to take the size of wooden pole chosen, so that, when the wood rots, new posts can be inserted into the pipes without disturbing the climbing plants. If metal pipes are used for the entire uprights they can be disguised by tying stout canes around them for the whole of their length (Figure 10). Curved metal arches supported on wooden pillars are very charming.

Pergolas need big material if they are to be successful: nothing less than 6-inch-square timber if they are to be of this material. Pillars of masonry are best, with heavy timber crossbars; the masonry can be rubble with rough plaster covering, rounded or square with fairly straight branches laid across; brick to match

the house, or brick tinted with a wash after building, with rough-
hewn beams or beams out of old barns; or fancy work of brick,
stone, and tile with prepared wooden beams—each scheme is
progressively more sophisticated. Occasionally the dignity of the
house and the means of the owner may permit the use of Doric
columns.

The minimum width for brick pillars is a brick and a half, or

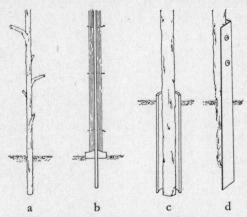

a   b   c   d

10. Examples of different materials for posts to
support roses as 'pillars': (a) rustic post, (b)
metal pipe covered with canes, (c) post inserted
into drainpipe, (d) post which has rotted below
ground being supported by angle-iron.

14 inches square, except in very tiny gardens where one brick
square might be permissible. The lowest three courses should be
2 inches wider all around to form a plinth, and a concrete capital,
cast easily by any intelligent builder, should fit the top, with a
hole for a dowel pin left in the centre to pass through the cross-
beam, which should cross the path and project beyond the edge
of each capital. In a pergola these first cross-beams should support
the next which follow the length of the path, thus revealing the
sky between them when we look down the pergola (Figure 11).
If the first beams run down the length of the path, connecting
the pillars at the sides of the path, and the next beams are all *across*
the path, we get the effect of a wooden ceiling, which to me is
heavy and unattractive (Figure 12). It is of course necessary, in

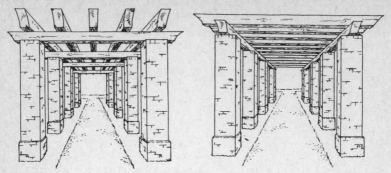

11, 12. Construction of pergolas: brick pillars supporting wooden beams.

erecting such a fine feature as this can be, to ensure that adequate foundations are made to support the masonry. Nothing is so irritating and disappointing as a post or pillar which is not perpendicular from all angles.

Pillars on their own may be of wood, prepared and painted, or of larch with 9-inch side shoots retained, or of brick, or actual classical pillars of stone (Figure 13). The more beautiful they are the less invasive roses should be chosen. Isolated pillars to take 'pillar' roses can be connected with a wooden beam—when I believe they become a 'peristyle' if surrounding a court or alcove —or chains or ropes. Chains hang best, but thick rope about

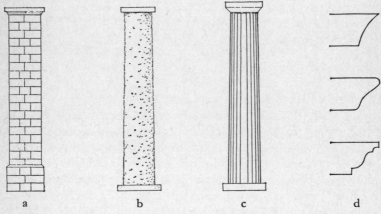

13. Pillars: (a) brick, (b) roughcast, (c) stone; (d) some alternative finishes for ends of cross-beams.

¾-inch diameter makes a good substitute; only very pliant roses will
achieve the graceful effect that is
desired.

The width for any arch is dictated
by the width of the path, and the
minimum width for a path to take
two people abreast (the only hospit-
able and pleasant way of walking
around; how I have hated following
an otherwise kind host because of
his narrow paths!) is 6 feet between
arches; 7 feet is preferable. Remem-
bering that climbing plants will hang

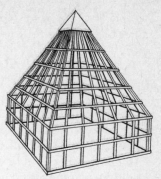

14. Pyramid of wooden lattice
to add temporary height to a
garden.

from the crossbars, 7 feet is also the minimum height. For the
sake of proportion I should make the arch 8 feet minimum width,
and thus qualify what I wrote earlier about its being an important
garden feature.

Another way of displaying our roses is on pyramids. Newly
designed gardens are apt to appear rather flat for some years, and
pyramid-shaped structures of wood can speedily be covered with
roses to give height and substance along a formal walk within two
or three years. In a long straight walk, such pyramids can be
helpful in creating interest, or simpler structures can be made as
tripods with three strong posts (Figures 14, 15).

It will be seen that there is a great variety of material and erection to provide homes for our rambling and climbing roses, and

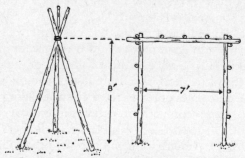

15. Tripod and simple arch of stout poles,
shewing proportions.

I hope that the descriptions, drawings, and lists will provide answers to most questions that greet the beginner when selecting roses.

We have still to consider rose hedges. While these are usually composed of shrub roses, ramblers are also suitable, but they need initial support, either a post-and-rail fence, or just a couple of wires at about 2 feet and 4 feet from the ground on stout posts every 10 feet or so. (It is best to plant roses *between* the posts along any sort of fence; there is then less disturbance to the roots if new posts have to be put in later.) The roses of the lax-growing classes should be planted about 10 feet apart, or closer if a mingling of colours and shapes is required. There is no limit to the possibilities of ramblers for display in the garden; the contrasts of colours, shapes, and styles is almost infinite, and a very long display can be achieved if early and late flowering varieties are included.

It remains to consider companions for roses. Earlier in this book and in my previous writings, I have said how I prefer roses mixed with other things; they are often desperately dull on their own. Even though they may be our favourite flower, their planting should not be carried to excess. No meal would be acceptable if given entirely to caviar and no symphony would be enjoyed which was composed entirely for clarinets. To me the most interesting gardens are those where a wide selection of plant form and flower is used for effect through the entire year. If roses are planted to excess, then the areas devoted to them will be dull for seven months of the year, and exhibit a fussiness for the remaining months, since their leaves are small and the effect of the flowers— whether large or small—is 'spotty'.

Rose beds—by which I mean the conventional geometrical designs prescribed in lawn or paving for the reception of Hybrid Teas and Floribundas—are dull areas for most of the year; especially as the general method of culture is to leave the soil bare beneath them, a custom evolved in days when 'bedding' roses were too weak to stand competition from ground-covering plants. Arches and other supports for ramblers and climbers can be bare of blossom for very much longer. Of course the foliage of roses has its beauty, but I do not think we should tolerate it on its own as much as we do.

Companions in any walk of life are best if they provide contrast or complement. Considering colour first, if we want contrast it is best provided by blue, all other colours being found in roses, though mauve and purple are scarce among ramblers and climbers. There are many blue, mauve, and purple border plants, though few shrubs in these tones; some that come quickly to mind are buddleias, lavenders, ceratostigma, and caryopteris; sages, hardy geraniums (rather too early-flowering), echinops, eryngiums, and delphiniums; agapanthuses, stokesia, catananche, with many clematises among climbers. I should seldom look for plants of similar colours to roses as companions for them unless the contrast in size, texture, and shape of blooms was sufficient, such as escallonias, fuchsias, and honeysuckles, or the larger blooms of hollyhocks and lilies.

As a rule roses are so delightsome in themselves, and are such universal favourites, that I consider their companions most valuable when they not only provide colour before the roses start to flower but also have good foliage as a contrast to the roses. Here again we can choose soft or strong characters. No background for roses in my opinion is so good as a first-class yew hedge. If you can bear your ramblers and climbers to hang over such a hedge you will have a picture that none can but praise. (Photograph, Plate 14.) The velvety uniform dark green will shew up all but the darkest of roses and enhance the purity of the clearest colours. Other hedges, through the evergreens to the deciduous, are less good. For the arches and pergolas some of the vines, providing large flat solid leaves, are the very best of contrasts; of greyish tinge in its greenery is 'Black Cluster', a hardy black grape, while the 'claret vine', *Vitis vinifera purpurea*, is well known for its similar clusters of fruit borne among foliage that from August onwards assumes an ever deeper wine-colour. *V. coignetiae* is the largest-leaved, but rampageous, and most brilliant in autumn; for smaller arches the 'Dutchman's pipe', *Aristolochia sipho*, can provide equal magnificence of greenery, without the autumn colour.

Roses are best displayed in growing trees when these have comparatively small leaves. Most of the big-leaved trees are too coarse, dark, and luxuriant. I like climbing roses appearing out of columnar cypresses; from ancient apples and pears, thorns and laburnums; the strongest foaming out of pines; but there are certain trees which may be considered too dignified to be the host for roses, and among them I would number the magnolias, trees of great majesty and character of line. There are many colour contrasts that come to mind, such as a purplish rambler in a silver weeping pear; a scarlet, white or yellow climber peering out from a coppery-leaved prunus; a brilliant yellow rose enhancing a golden holly or maple—or just the white scented trails of R. *longicuspis* hanging out of any greenery, wafting fragrance through the garden.

> . . . strength may wield the ponderous spade,
> May turn the clod, and wheel the compost home;
> But elegance, chief grace the garden shows,
> And most attractive, is the fair result
> Of thought, the creature of a polished mind.
>
> William Cowper, 1731–1800.

13

Selections of Ramblers and Climbers for Various Positions and Purposes

Much like the summer's bee am I,
A thousand flowers before his eyes,
He, knowing each one's power to please,
No sooner settles than must rise.

W. H. Davies, 1871–1940.

THE FOLLOWING lists, I hope, will help intending selectors who might otherwise waste hours searching for what they want for a given purpose. There are so many roses available that none of us, given a little care, need choose a variety unsuitable for its position. One must consider height, foliage, style, tractability, season, fragrance and colour, and also the background and complementary planting if we want to select the ideal variety.

The varieties selected are, in my opinion, the best in their groups. Every variety mentioned in this book is not necessarily included. As nearly every rose makes an exception to some rule or other the selections should only be broadly interpreted. The lists of varieties are not in any particular order. Generally the width to allow to each variety is approximately the same as its height, depending on how much height of wall or fence is available.

* Denotes roses described in *The Old Shrub Roses*, and † those described in *Shrub Roses of Today*; though shrubs, they are of lax growth and are equally at home with some support.

1. Graceful ramblers for arches, ropes, chains and 10-foot pillars; also for trees up to 18 feet. Grace is their great attribute: they should therefore be used so that this character can best be appreciated.

   All varieties in Chapter 4, except Félicité et Perpétue, Francis E. Lester, Lykkefund, Paul's Himalayan, Patricia Macoun, Phyllis Bide, Rambling Rector, Spectabilis, and Venusta Pendula.
   wichuraiana
   multiflora
   * Mme Plantier

   All varieties in Chapter 5, except Albertine, Breeze Hill, City of York, and Gerbe Rose.

   ---

2. Roses for walls, fences, pillars, up to 8 feet.
   Less graceful, and shorter growers, which are none the less tractable.

Dream Girl	Gerbe Rose
Cocktail (short)	Breeze Hill
Laure Davoust	Allen's Fragrant Pillar
Spectabilis	Paul's Single White
† Hermosa, Climbing	Star of Persia
* Zéphirine Drouhin and the	† Gruss an Teplitz
more vigorous Bourbons.	Most varieties in Chapter 8
Phyllis Bide	

   ---

3. Sprawlers for ground cover, hanging over low walls, and covering low hedges, logs, and stumps.

† Max Graf	Little Compton Creeper
† *paulii rosea*	† *polliniana*
† *macrantha* and varieties, except	Félicité et Perpétue
Harry Maasz	* Mme Plantier
† Schneelicht	† Lady Curzon
wichuraiana	Sanders' White
Magic Carpet	† *paulii*

   ---

4. Shrubby sprawlers, more vigorous and bushy than in List 3, for use as graceful informal shrubs, for growing over hedgerows, large stumps, low fences, and in general rather wild conditions.

* Complicata	Goldfinch
† Harry Maasz	Blush Noisette
† Daisy Hill	Félicité et Perpétue
† Lady Curzon	Francis E. Lester
Rambling Rector	Kew Rambler
The Garland	Flora
† *setigera*	Albertine
† *soulieana*	Maigold
multiflora	Most varieties in Chapter 8

5. Roses needing the protection of a warm wall in Surrey.

Aimée Vibert	Rêve d'Or
moschata Autumnalis	William A. Richardson
The Old Musk Rose (R.	Belle Portugaise
moschata)	La Follette
bracteata and varieties	Sénateur Amic
banksiae and varieties	Fortune's Yellow
laevigata	Lady Hillingdon, Climbing
anemoneflora	Reine Marie-Henriette
anemonoides	Solfaterre
gigantea	Sombreuil
gigantea cooperi	Souvenir de Léonie Viennot
sempervirens	,, d'un Ami
sinowilsonii	† Cramoisi Supérieur
brunonii	Madame Sancy de Parabère
,, La Mortola	Devoniensis
Céline Forestier	Maréchal Niel
Lamarque	Bush Tea Roses in Chapter 6

6. For densely covering arbours, unsightly sheds, etc.

Félicité et Perpétue	May Queen
Albéric Barbier	Little Compton Creeper
Francis E. Lester	Wedding Day
Kew Rambler	Rambling Rector
François Juranville	† Lady Curzon
New Dawn	*longicuspis*
Albertine	Lykkefund
Many varieties in Chapter 8	Sanders' White

7. Excessively strong roses for training into trees, making shoots up to 30–40 feet.

brunonii   ⎫ for sheltered
   ,,   La Mortola   ⎭ districts only
Paul's Himalayan Musk Rambler
filipes Kiftsgate
rubus

8. Very vigorous, hardy roses for training into trees, making shoots 20–30 feet.

longicuspis see also page 190	François Juranville
Polyantha Grandiflora	New Dawn
helenae	Rose-Marie Viaud
mulliganii	Réné André
Wedding Day	Silver Moon
Bobbie James	Madame d'Arblay
Albéric Barbier	Claire Jacquier
La Perle	Lykkefund
Cécile Brunner, Climbing	Ayrshire Splendens

9. Hardy large-flowered climbers for house walls, rather stiff in growth and generally bare at the base, where a shrub or short-growing clematis will be an added asset.

All varieties in Chapter 7	Madame Alfred Carrière
Mermaid	Paul Lédé, Climbing
Gloire de Dijon	Tallest varieties in Chapter 8

10. Single-flowered ramblers and climbers.

All wild species in Chapter 2	Silver Moon
Wedding Day	*anemonoides*
Kew Rambler	Sénateur Amic
Hiawatha	Cupid
Evangeline	Soldier Boy
Francis E. Lester	Dainty Bess, Climbing
Little Compton Creeper	Mermaid
Jersey Beauty	Paul's Perpetual White
laevigata	*gigantea*
banksiae lutescens	Una
banksiae normalis	

11. Thornless roses (ramblers, climbers and shrubs).

multiflora Simplex ⎫	* Chloris
„ Cress ⎬ under-	* Blush Hip
and Danieli ⎭ stocks	* Mme Legras de St Germain
canina Brog's	* Mme Plantier
† de la Grifferaie	* Prince Charles
* Zéphirine Drouhin	† Mrs John Laing
* Kathleen Harrop	*moschata* Autumnalis
* *gallica* (wild species)	Aimée Vibert
* Cosimo Ridolfi	† *foliolosa*
* Duchesse de Buccleugh	† *pendulina*
* Antonia d'Ormois	Amadis

† Morlettii	Goldfinch
Mme de Sancy de Parabère	Rose-Marie Viaud
† *dupontii*	Violette
† *blanda*	*banksiae*
† *sericea denudata*	Lykkefund
† „ *polyphylla*	

12. Roses for north walls, except in very exposed areas. This is a preliminary list of roses that have been observed thriving and flowering reasonably well without sun. They would flower better with sun. Any hardy rose will provide a number of blooms on a shady wall, provided it is not overhung by trees.

Gloire de Dijon	Mme Grégoire Staechelin
Mermaid	May Queen
† Conrad F. Meyer	Albéric Barbier
† Nova Zembla	Souvenir de Claudius Denoyel
Félicité et Perpétue	Paul Lédé, Climbing
Soldier Boy	Danse du Feu
Paul's Scarlet	Leverkusen
Purity	* *alba semi-plena*
New Dawn	* *alba maxima*

13. Roses suitable for growing as weeping standards: this is a term to describe ramblers which are propagated by budding high up on a stem of wild rose, to weep down like a fountain or umbrella.

† Raubritter
Graceful varieties from Chapters 4 and 5

14. Purple- and mauve-coloured ramblers, climbers, etc. It is not always realized that this colour is available.

Rose-Marie Viaud	Russelliana
Veilchenblau	Aschermittwoch
Bleu Magenta	* Zigeuner Knabe)
Violette	* William Lobb } shrubby
Amadis	* Tour de Malakoff)

15. Modern shrub roses suitable for walls, fences and pillars.

† Kassel	† Gloire de Ducher
† Buff Beauty	† Hugh Dickson
† Moonlight	† Souvenir du Dr Jamain
† Francesca	† Cécile Brunner, Climbing
† Pax	† Rosenwunder

† Scarlet Fire   † Düsterlohe
† Till Uhlenspiegel   * Complicata
† Gruss an Teplitz   † Constance Spry
† Harry Maasz

Many of these approximate the growth of varieties in Chapter 8 which are also suitable.

---

16. Old roses of lax growth, described in *The Old Shrub Roses*, suitable for training on walls, fences and pillars.

Blush Hip   Kathleen Harrop
Tour de Malakoff   Zéphirine Drouhin
Jeanne de Montfort   Madame Legras de St Ger-
William Lobb   main
Bourbon Queen   Madame Plantier
Madame Ernst Calvat   Blairi No. 2
Madame Isaac Pereire

BIBLIOGRAPHY

Addisonia, New York Botanical Garden, 1916 et seq

AITON, William, *Hortus Kewensis*, 1789

American *Rose Annual*, 1917 et seq.

ANDREWS, Henry C., *Roses*, 1805–28

BAILEY, L. H., *The Standard Cyclopedia of Horticulture*, 1927

BAIRD, Bessie Marie, *Roses for Southern Gardens*, 1948

BAUHIN, Caspar, *Pinax*, 1671 ed.

BEAN, W. J., *Trees and Shrubs*, 1949

Belgique Horticole, La, 1851–85

BERRISFORD, Judith, *Gardening on Lime*, 1963

BOIS, E., and TRECHSLIN, A.-M., *Roses*, 1962

BONNET, E., et BARRATTE, G., *Catalogue raisonné des plantes vasculaires de la Tunisie*, 1896

Botanical Cabinet, Conrad Loddiges and Sons, Vols. 1–20, 1818–30

Botanical Magazine, The, 1787 et seq.

Botanical Register, The, 1815–47

BOWLES, E. A., *My Garden in Summer*, 1914

BRAAM, A. E. VAN (artist C. H. B. Ker), *Icones plantarum sponte China*

BROUGHAM, Henry Charles, 3rd Baron Brougham and Vaux, *List of Roses in Cultivation at Château Éléonore*, Cannes, 1898

BUNYARD, Edward A., *Old Garden Roses*, 1936; also in *The New Flora and Silva*, Vol. 2

Choix des Plus Belles Roses, Paris, 1845–54

COCHET-COCHET and MOTTET, S., *Les Rosiers*, Paris, 1896 et seq.

CRANE, H. H., *Gardening on Clay*, 1963

CURTIS, Henry, *Beauties of the Rose*, 1850–3

DARLINGTON, Hayward Radcliffe, *Roses*, 1911

DESFONTAINES, Renato, *Flora Atlantica*, 1798

DRAPIEZ, P. A. J., *Herbier de l'amateur de Fleurs*, 1828–35

DUHAMEL DU MONCEAU, Henri Louis, *Traité des arbres et arbustes*, 1819

DUMONT DE COURSET, G. L. M., *Le Botaniste Cultivateur*, 2nd ed., Vol. V, 1811

EDWARDS, Gordon, *Roses for Enjoyment*, 1962

ELLACOMBE, Henry N., *In a Gloucestershire Garden*, 1895

——, *Plant Lore and Garden Craft of Shakespeare*, 1896

Floral Magazine, The, 1861–71 and 1872–81

Flore des Serres et des Jardins de l'Europe, 1845–67

Florist and Pomologist, The, 1862–84

Garden, The, founded by William Robinson, 1871 et seq.

Gardeners' Chronicle, 1841 et seq.

Gartenflora, 1852 et seq.

Garten-Zeitung, Berlin, 1882–5

GAULT, S. Millar, and SYNGE, Patrick M., *The Dictionary of Roses in Colour*, 1971

GERARD, John, *The Herball*, 1597
GORE, Mrs, *The Rose Fancier's Manual*, 1838
HARIOT, Paul, *Le Livre d'Or des Roses*, 1904
HERRMANN, Johannes, *Dissertatio inauguratis botanico medica de Rosa*, 1762
HIBBERD, Shirley, *Garden Favourites*, 1858
HILLIER AND SONS, Winchester, England, *Rose Catalogue*
HOFFMANN, Julius, *The Amateur Gardener's Rose Book*, 1905
HOLE, Dean S. Reynolds, *A Book about Roses*, 1870
Horticulteur Français, L', 1851–72
HU, HSEN-HSU, *Icones Plantarum Sinicarum*, 1929
HURST, Dr C. C., in *The Old Shrub Roses* (G. S. Thomas), 1955
Illustration Horticole, L', 1854–96
Illustrirte Rosengarten, (M. Lebl, Editor), Stuttgart, 1875(?)–79
IWASAKI, Tsunemasa (edited by Ida Kuratavo), *Phonzo Soufo*, 1921
JACQUIN, N. J. von, *Florae Austriacae*, 1773–8
——, *Plantarum rariorum horti Schönbrunnensis*, 1797–1804
JÄGER, August, *Rosenlexicon*, 1960
JAHANDIEZ, Émile, and MAIRE, Dr René, *Catalogue des Plantes du Maroc*, 1931
JAMAIN, Hippolyte, and FOURNEY, Eugène, *Les Roses*, 1893
Jardin Fleuriste, Le, 1851–4
JEKYLL, Gertrude, and MAWLEY, Edward, *Roses for English Gardens*, 1902
Journal des Roses, 1877–1914
KEAYS, Mrs Frederick Love, *Old Roses*, 1935
KINGSLEY, Rose, *Roses and Rose Growing*, 1908
KOMLOSY, *Rosenalbum*, 1868–75
LAWRANCE, Mary, *A Collection of Roses from Nature*, 1799
LAZARO E IBIZA, *Compendio de la Flora Española*, 1921
LEROY, André, *History of the Rose*, 1956
LINDLEY, John, *Rosarum monographia*, 1820
LOBEL, Matthias de, *Plantarum seu stirpium icones*, Antwerp, 1581
LOUDON, *Hortus Britannicus*, 1830
LOWE, Richard Thomas, *A Manual Flora of Madeira*, 1868
McFARLAND, J. Horace, *Modern Roses*, V, 1952
——, *Roses of the World in Colour*, 1937
Meehan's Monthly, 1891 et seq.
MEEHAN, Th., *Native Flowers and Ferns of the United States*, Vols. 1 and 2, 1897
MILLER, Philip, *The Gardener's Dictionary*, 1768
MULLIGAN, B. O., in R.H.S. *Dictionary of Gardening*
Nestel's Rosengarten, E. Schweizerbartsche Verlagshandlung, 1866–9
New Flora and Silva, Vols. 1–12, 1929 et seq.
NIEDTNER, Th., *Die Rose*, 1880
PARK, Bertram, *Guide to Roses*, Collins, 1956
PARKINSON, John, *Paradisi in Sole Paradisus Terrestris*, 1629
——, *Theatrum botanicum*, 1640
PARSONS, Samuel B., *The Rose*, 1847
PAUL, William, *The Rose Garden*, 1848, 1872 et seq.
Paxton's Magazine of Botany, 1834–49

Plus Belles Roses au début du vingtième siècle, Les, Société Nationale d'Horticulture de France, 1912
PRINCE, William, *Manual of Roses,* 1846
RAY, John, *Historia plantarum,* Vol. II, 1688
REDOUTÉ, P. J., *Les Roses,* 1817–24
Reeves' Drawings of Chinese Plants (R.H.S. Library), 1812–31, Vol. 2
REHDER, Alfred, *Manual of Cultivated Trees and Shrubs,* 1947
Revue de l'Horticulture, Belge et Étrangère, La, 1875–1915
Revue Horticole, La, 1846 et seq.
RIVERS, Thomas, *Rose Amateur's Guide,* 1843 et seq.
ROESSIG, D., *Les Roses,* 1802–20
Rose Annual, The, National Rose Society of Great Britain, 1907 et seq.
Roses et Rosiers, Paris, 187–?
ROWLEY, G. D., 'Some naming problems in *Rosa*', in *Bulletin van de Rijksplantentuin,* Brussel, 30 Septembre 1959
Royal Horticultural Society, *Journal,* 1856 et seq.
SABINE, Joseph, in *Transactions of the Horticultural Society,* 1822
SCHLECHTENDAL, D. F. L. von, and LANGETHAL, L. E., *Flora von Deutschland,* 1880–8, 5th ed.
SHEPHERD, Roy E., *History of the Rose,* 1954
SIEBOLD, Philipp Franz von, and ZUCCARINI, Joseph Gerhard, *Flora Japonica,* 1835–70
SIMON, Léon, and COCHET, Pierre, *Nomenclature de tous les Roses,* 1906
SINGER, Max, *Dictionnaire des Roses,* 1885
SINGLETON, Esther, *The Shakespeare Garden,* 1922
SMITH, Tom, *Rose Catalogues,* Daisy Hill Nurseries
SOWERBY, James, and SMITH, Sir James Edward, *English Botany,* 1790–1814, etc.
STEP, Edward, *Favourite Flowers,* 1896–7
STEVENS, G. A., *Climbing Roses,* 1933
STRASSHEIM, C. P., *Rosenzeitung,* Verein deutscher Rosenfreunde, 1886–1933
SWEET, Robert, *The British Flower Garden,* 1st and 2nd series, 7 vols., 1823–9 and 1831–8
THOMAS, G. C., *The Practical Book of Outdoor Rose Growing,* 1920
THOMAS, G. S., *The Manual of Shrub Roses,* 4th ed., 1964, Sunningdale Nurseries, Windlesham, Surrey
——, *The Old Shrub Roses,* revised ed., 1961
——, *Shrub Roses of Today,* 1962
WALLICH, Nathaniel, *Plantae Asiaticae Rariores,* Vol. II, 1831
WILLMOTT, Ellen, *The Genus Rosa,* 1910–14
WILSON, E. H., *If I were to make a garden,* 1931
WILSON, Helen Van Pelt, *Climbing Roses,* 1955
WYLIE, A. P., in *Journal of the Royal Horticultural Society,* Vol. LXXIX, page 555 et seq., December 1954
——, 'The History of Garden Roses', in *Endeavour,* Vol. XIV, No. 56, October 1955
YOUNG, Wing Commander N., in *The Rose Annual,* National Rose Society, 1962

'**Colcestria**'. B.R. Cant, 1916. A strangely neglected rose which has a good first crop and repeats modestly later. It has good foliage and is vigorous. It is the flowers that are remarkable; silvery rose-pink, very full with rolled petals. Very fragrant. A worthy companion to 'Paul's Lemon Pillar'.

'**Princesse Louise**'. 1829. This is of the same origin as 'Félicité et Perpétue' and 'Adelaïde d'Orléans', q.v. The flowers are between the two in shape and fullness, opening creamy-blush-white from pink buds. Equally hardy and floriferous.

Rosa chinensis is not in cultivation. The species is a native of central China and is a tall climbing rose, leaves with 3–5 leaflets, flowers single, usually crimson, sometimes pink, produced in summer only. In this book—and many others—the R. *chinensis* usually quoted is one of four hybrids that were introduced to Europe around 1800, particularly 'Parson's Pink' which is now usually called 'Old Blush'.

ADDENDA FOR 3RD EDITION, 1983

R. *bracteata* and R. *clinophylla*. Apparently it was R. *clinophylla* which Kingdon Ward found in Burma, not R. *bracteata*.

R. *longicuspis*. When Mr. Desmond Clarke and I were working on the revision of the genus *Rosa* for *Trees and Shrubs Hardy in the British Isles*, by W. J. Bean, Eighth edition, he drew my attention to the fact that the rose which for years I have grown and distributed as R. *longicuspis* is not that species but identical with, or allied very closely to, R. *mulliganii*. Two learned botanists had identified my plant as R. *longicuspis*, but it seems they did not take into consideration the large hep of this species (R. *mulliganii* has small heps) and some other characters. R. *longicuspis* does not seem to be in cultivation.

R. *moschata* and R. *brunonii*. While the old writers had always observed and described the true old R. *moschata* under that name, towards the end of the 19th century French botanists decided that R. *brunonii* was in fact the type of R. *moschata*; hence the subsequent confusion in botanic gardens. In fact, having examined Dr. Hurst's herbarium specimens at the University Botanic Garden, Cambridge, I find that he accepted R. *brunonii* as R. *moschata* and that all his observations therefore apply to the former species. It is possible that the recurrent flowering habit of the old R. *moschata* (R. *brunonii* was not found and named until 1822) was transmitted not only to the Autumn Damask but also to the first Noisette, 'Champney's Pink Cluster'. Further notes of mine occur in the Royal National Rose Society's *Annual* for 1983.

Luciae Roses. It was during work on the same book as above that further light was shed by Mr. Clarke on this group of roses. We both think now that the real reason for the general difference between the roses in Chapters 4 and 5 is that while those in the former are hybrids between Synstylae roses and the Old Garden roses, those in Chapter 5 owe their glossy foliage and yellowish colouring to an admixture of the Tea roses in their parentage. Therefore the suspected influence of R. *luciae* is not as great as I had thought and in any case R. *luciae* and R. *wichuraiana* are considered synonymous by botanists today.

'Brenda Colvin'. Sunningdale Nurseries, 1970. This is a seedling from R. *filipes* 'Kiftsgate' which occurred spontaneously in the garden of the famous landscape architect at Filkins in Oxfordshire, after whom it is named. Miss Colvin gave it to me for introduction when I was manager at Sunningdale Nurseries. It makes immense growths, with coppery red young foliage, turning to glossy dark green. The flowers are borne in large trusses, single, clear pink fading nearly to white, with a delicious scent. It brings some colour into the many gigantic climbers of the Synstylae Section.

'Princesse Marie'. 1829. This is another of the roses raised by M. Jacques, head gardener to the Duc d'Orléans, and obviously of similar parentage to 'Félicité et Perpétue', 'Adélaïde d'Orléans' and 'Princesse Louise'. Truly was M. Jacques a lucky raiser!— all would have been open pollinated at that date, as hybridisation was not fully understood. It is extraordinary that only in recent years have I met this rose. My first acquaintance with it was at Nymans; Lady Rosse had brought cuttings from Ireland a few years ago and today the plant ascends to some 30 ft., dripping out of a tall holly. Since then I have received blooms for naming from various parts of the country. Struck with its general resemblance to the varieties mentioned above, I think there is no doubt that it is this old variety. Descriptions by old authors mention "red" but this is common among roses of rich pink colouring when there were no reds available—wishful thinking and nurserymen's licence! The blooms, in small and large trusses, are cupped and do not open widely, rich pink in bud turning to clear rose, exhaling a sweet scent. The foliage glossy and dark. I think there is no doubt that *Rosa sempervirens* as well as R. *arvensis* had a hand in this group of roses. With 'Treasure Trove' this brings welcome colour to these tree-scramblers.

'Treasure Trove'. Treasures of Tenbury Wells, Worcestershire, 1979. *Rosa filipes* 'Kiftsgate' seeds itself fairly liberally in gardens where it is grown and then often shows a pinkish tinge to the petals, the result of being hybridised with a modern rose. This particular plant cropped up some ten years ago in Mr. John Treasure's garden and grew strongly, exhibiting the brownish-ruby young foliage of 'Kiftsgate'; it has extraordinary vigour and in 1979 had made a great pile over shrubs and trees, achieving some 33 ft. in width and 20 ft. in height. It is still growing. The foliage turns to mid green on maturity. After a few years' growth it produced flowers; in recent years it has been covered with bloom, casting its delicious fragrance afar. The blooms average about 20 in a truss; they are semi-double, about 2 inches across, cup shaped on opening, of warm apricot and showing a cluster of yellow stamens. As they age the flowers turn to delicate pink and later to blush, the numerous tints blending well together. It flowers at midsummer. See also colour plate and description in the Royal National Rose Society's *Annual* for 1979.

Index

Main entries are denoted by heavy type. For notes on descriptions see p. 23.

ARBOURS for roses, 173
Arches for roses, 181 et seq.
Attar of roses, 38

Bacon, Sir Francis, 49
Bagatelle, 20. Photograph, Plate 15
Banks, Lady, 146
Barbier et Cie, 79, 80
Bitton Grange, 53
Bodnant, 21, 45
Borde Hill, 45
Bowles, E. A., 53
Breeding, 141
Brougham and Vaux, Lord, 103, 108, 145
Bunyard, E. A., 34, 66
Busby, Mr, 103

Calcutta Botanic Garden, 147
Cambridge Botanic Garden, 36, 48, 94
Cant, Benjamin, 80
Chains, ramblers for, 182
Champneys, John, 88
Château Éléonore, 108, 145
Chelsea Physic Garden, 53
Chinese Rose Tree, the, at Ispahan, 51
Clark, Alister, 103
Classification of roses, 139 et seq.
Climbers, definition of, 16
Clone, definition of, 23
Collet, Sir Henry, 95
Comber, James, 88, 107
Companions for roses, 178
Conservatory roses, 183
Cooper, Mr, 95
Coroneola, the, of Parkinson, 37
Cultivars, 23
Cultivation, 163, et seq.

Daisy Hill Nursery, 38
Dartington Hall, 99
Descriptions, notes on, 23
Diseases, 164
Display in garden, 20, 21, 22
Distribution of species, 27, 156
Dog Brier, 31, 49
Drummond, Robert, 146

Ellacombe, Canon, 53

Farrer, Reginald, 30
Fauque et Fils, 80
Feast, Messrs, Baltimore, 60
Fences for roses, 172
Fleischmann, Mrs Ruby, 109
Foliage, good, 141; see also *R. sinowilsonii*, 45
Fragrance of green apples, 80
    of musk, 56
    of roses in Synstylae Section, 18
    of tea, 94
Frances Burney, see under 'Madame d'Arblay', 69

Graces, the Three, 63
Graft hybrid, 112
Greville, Sir Charles, 42, 71
Ground-cover, roses for, 18

Hakluyt, Richard, 36
Hanbury, Sir Thomas, 147
Harkness, Peter, 104
Hedges of roses, 178
Henry, Dr Augustine, 34
Hesse, Herm A., 80
Highdown, 30, 47, 104, 148
Hole, Dean, 12, 99
Hopkins, W. B., 97
Horvath, 44

Hunt, W. L., 145
Hurst, Dr C. C., 18, 87, 94, 156

Jacques, M., 59, 62, 68
Janaki-Ammal, Dr A. K., 156
Jekyll, Gertrude, 13
John Innes Institute, 94, 107, 151
Johnston, Major Lawrence, 131

Keats, John, 49
Kerr, William, 146
Kew, Royal Botanic Garden, 21, 36, 48
Kiftsgate Court, 30, 33, 34, 100, 148
Kingdon Ward, F., 151
Knightshayes Court, 30
Kordes, Herr Wilhelm, 58, 74, 129

La Mortola, 147
Laburnocytisus adamii, 112
Law, Mrs Nigel, 93
LeGrice, E. B., 141
Lisbon Botanic Garden, 103
Loudon, Earl of, 59

Macartney, Lord, 150
MacKenzie, W. G., 53
Mammoth rose tree, Santa Anna, 100
Manda, W. A., 80
Manza Botanic Garden, 93
Melford Hall, 64
Messel, Lt-Col. Leonard, 88
Messel, Mrs, 88
Moschus moschiferus, 56
Muir, Mrs J. B., 33, 34
Munstead Wood, 168
Musk, 27; also Chapter 3
    deer, 27, 56
    (*Mimulus moschatus*), 27
    scent in roses, 56
Mutation, definition of, 23
Myddelton House, 37

National Rose Society's Trial Ground, 95, 131
Noisette, Louis, 88
Noisette, Philippe, 88
North walls, roses for, 185
Notes on descriptions, 23
Nour Jehan, Princess, 38
Nymans, 39, 74, 88, 104, 107

Orléans, Duc d', 59, 68
Ottawa, Central Experimental Farm, 69
Otto of roses, 38
Oxford Botanic Garden, 96, 107

Page, Courtney, 95
Pam, Major Albert, 150
Parks, J. D., 146
Pelargonidin, 13
Pergolas, 176
Periclinal chimera, 112
Perpetual flowering, definition of, 24
Photinia serrulata, 54
Pillars, roses for, 176, 186
Polesden Lacey, 21, 66
Posts for roses, 174
Powis Castle, 21, 148
Pruning, 165 et seq.
Purple ramblers and climbers, 60, 62, 185
Pyramids for roses, 176

Queen Mary's Rose Garden, 21

Ramblers, definition of, 16
    for various garden features, 182
Rampant growers, 100, 130, 145, 183
Recurrent roses, definition of, 23
Regent's Park Rose Garden, 21
Remontant roses, definition of, 23
Rendall, Mr, 100
Repeat-flowering, definition of, 23
Rogers, John, 54
Ropes, ramblers for, 182
Rosa abyssinica, 156
    alba, 50
    alba odorata, see under *R. bracteata*, 151
    anemoneflora, 149
    anemonoides, 153
    arvensis, 17, 27, 28, 30, 31, 49, 51, 58 et seq.

    banksiae, 17, **148**
    banksiae albo-plena, see *R. banksiae banksiae*, 146, 148
    banksiae banksiae, 146, **148**
    banksiae flore-pleno, see *R. banksiae banksiae*, 146, **148**
    banksiae lutea, 147, **148**
    banksiae lutescens, 147, **148**

Rosa banksiae lutescens spinosa, 149
  banksiae normalis, 146, **149**
  banksiae rosea, 149
  blanda, 123
  bracteata, 17, **150**, 190
  brunonii, 17, 22, 27, 30, 31, **33**, 37, 38, 43, 52, 55, 156
  brunonii 'La Mortola', 22, **33**. Fig. 1. Photograph, Plate 3.
  brunonii, hybrid of, known as R. *moschata*, 36–7, 190

  canina, 31, 49, 62
  cantabrigiensis, 64
  carteri, see R. *multiflora nana*, 41
  cathayensis platyphylla, see R. *multiflora platyphylla*, 42
  centifolia, shape of, 67
  centifolia muscosa, 27 n.
  cerasocarpa, 17, **33**
  cherokeensis, see R. *laevigata*, 152
  chinensis, 17, 34, 55, 190
  chinensis × R. *pendulina* (Boursault), 123
  chinensis mutabilis, 137
  cinnamomea, connected with R. *moschata damascena alba*, 55
  clinophylla, 152, 190
  cooperi, see 'Cooper's Burmese', 95
  corymbifera alba hispanica, see under R. *moschata plena*, 38
  crocacantha, 17, 29
  cymosa, 147

  dupontii (R. *moschata nivea*), 55

  ernestii, see R. *rubus*, 43

  farreri persetosa, 11
  filipes, 17, 30, 31, **34**
  filipes, growing wild in China, 30
  filipes 'Kiftsgate', 22, **34**, 35, 36. Photographs, Plates 1 and 2
  foetida, influence on breeding, 131, 132
  fortuneana, 149

  gallica, 48
  gentiliana, see under 'Polyantha Grandiflora', 35, **43**
  gigantea, 17, 89, 94, 95

Rosa gigantea erubescens, 95
  gigantea 'Macrocarpa', 94
  glomerata, 29

  helenae, 17, 22, 27, 29, 31, **35**, 36, 43, 62
  helenae, Barbier's form, 69
  henryi, 17, 29, **35**
  highdownensis interplanted with R. *multiflora*, 40

  involucrata, see R. *clinophylla*, 152

  kordesii, 19, 46, **129**

  laevigata, 17, 95, **152**
  leonida, see 'Marie Leonida', 151
  leschenaultiana, 29
  lheritierana, 124
  lindleyana, see R. *clinophylla*, 152
  longicuspis, 17, 22, 27, 29, 31, 34, **35**, 39, 45, 190. Fig. 2
  lucens, see R. *longicuspis*, 35
  luciae, 17, 29, 31, **46**, 80, 81, 113, 191
  luciae, distinction from and confusion with R. *wichuraiana*, **46**, 81, 191
  lucida duplex, see R. *clinophylla*, 152
  lyelli, see R. *clinophylla*, 152

  maximowicziana, 17, 29, 156
  microphylla, 154
  moschata, the Old Musk Rose, 17, 27, 30, 31, **36**, 46, 58, 60, **156**. Fig. 2
  moschata, the Old Musk Rose, confusion with R. *brunonii*, 33, 36, 37, 190
  moschata, the Old Musk Rose, influence on breeding in past, 31; in future, 55
  moschata, the Old Musk Rose, rediscovery of, 48 et seq.
  moschata 'Autumnalis', **38**, 46. Fig. 4
  moschata 'Botanic Garden form', or hybrid of R. *brunonii*, 36–7
  moschata damascena alba, a form or hybrid of R. *cinnamomea*, 55
  moschata flore semi-plena, 38
  moschata major, **37**, 50

Rosa moschata minor, 50
  moschata minor flore-pleno, 37
  moschata nastarana, 39
  moschata nepalensis, 33
  moschata nivea (R. *dupontii*), 55
  moschata plena, **37**, 38
  moschata semi-plena, see R. *moschata plena*, **37**, 38
  moyesii interplanted with R. *multiflora*, 40
  mulliganii, 17, 27, 30, 31, 35, **39**, 190
  multiflora, 17, 28, 29, **39**, 47, 60, 88, 168
  multiflora, introduction of, 31
  multiflora, purplish ramblers derived from, 60, 62
  multiflora carnea, **41**, 60
  multiflora cathayensis, **41**
  multiflora 'Cress and Danicli', 40
  multiflora 'De la Grifferaie', 40
  multiflora japonica, **40**
  multiflora multiflora, 60
  multiflora nana, 41
  multiflora platyphylla, 41, **42**
  multiflora polyantha, a name given to R. *multiflora nana*, 41
  multiflora simplex, 40
  multiflora thunbergiana, see R. *multiflora*, 39
  multiflora watsoniana, 28, 29, **42**

  napaulensis, see R. *moschata nepalensis*, 33
  nepalensis, see R. *moschata nepalensis*, 33
  noisettiana, 87 et seq.

  odorata gigantea, see R. *gigantea*, 95
  odorata pseudindica, see 'Fortune's Double Yellow', **105**, 149

  pendulina × R. *chinensis* (Boursault), 123
  phoenicea, 17, 28, 31, **42**, 51
  pissartii, see R. *moschata nastarana*, 39
  polyantha, see R. *multiflora*, 39, 43
  polyantha grandiflora, 30, **43**

  reclinata, 124
  roxburghii, 154

Rosa rubifolia, see R. *setigera*, 60; also 44
  rubus, 17, 22, 30, 31, 39, **43**
  rubus nudescens, 44
  rubus rubus, 43
  rubus velutescens, 44
  ruga, 32
  rugosa, used through R. *kordesii* in breeding climbing roses, 129

  sempervirens, 17, 28, 30, **44**, 51, 58, 88
  sempervirens, influence on Ayrshire Roses, 59
  sempervirens, introduction of, 31
  sempervirens latifolia, 44
  setigera, 17, 28, 29, 41, 44, 59, 60, 62
  setigera, confusion with R. *rubifolia*, 60
  setigera, influence on breeding of Prairie Roses, 59
  sinica, see R. *laevigata*, 152
  sinica 'Anemone', see R. *anemonoides*, 153
  sinowilsonii, 17, 28, 30, 31, 35, **45**, 156
  soulieana, 17, 28, 29, 31, 37, **45**, 62, 75, 82

  triphylla, see R. *anemoneflora*, 149

  watsoniana, see R. *multiflora watsoniana*, 29, **42**
  wichuraiana, 17, 29, 31, **45**, 80, 113, 129. Fig. 5
  wichuraiana, confusion with and distinction from R. *luciae*, 46, 81
  wichuraiana, influence on breeding, 61
  wichuraiana variegata, 46

Rose Adélaïde d'Orléans, 12, 44, 59, **62**, 75. Plate I
  Aglaia, 61, **63**
  Agnes, 64
  Aimée Vibert, 19, 88, **91**
  Aimée Vibert à fleur jaune, 91
  Alba odorata, see under R. *bracteata*, 151

Rose Albéric Barbier, 31, 46, 79, **81**, 130, 169
Albertine, 5 1, **81**, 113
Alchymist, 129, **133**
Alexandre Girault, 80, **82**. Plate IV
Alister Stella Gray, 12, 39, 62, **95**, 97. Plate V
Allen Chandler, 19, 115, **116**
Allen's Fragrant Pillar, **116**
Allgold, Climbing, 129, **133**
Aloha, **133**
Altissimo, **133**
Amadis, 60, **63**. Plate III
American Pillar, 15, 21, 44, **62**
Anemone, see R. *anemonoides*, 153
Anna Olivier, 105
Apeles Mestres, 115, 117
Aschermittwoch, see 'Ash Wednesday', **134**
Ash Wednesday, 130, **134**
Auguste Gervais, 80, **82**. Plate IV
Austrian Copper, 132
Autumnalis, see R. *moschata* 'Autumnalis', **38**, 46. Fig. 4
Ayrshire, 32, 58, **59**
Ayrshire Splendens, 58, 184

Ballet, Climbing, 130, **134**
Baltimore Belle, 44, 60, **64**
Banksian, 12, 15, **145**
Banksian, see R. *banksiae banksiae*, 148
Banksian roses, pruning, 147
Bantry Bay, 130, **134**
Beauty of Glazenwood, see 'Fortune's Double Yellow', **105**
Beauty of the Prairies, 44, 60
Belle Amour, 58
Belle Portugaise, 103
Bennett's Seedling, 58
Bettina, Climbing, 116
Bleu Magenta, 60, **64**. Plate II
Bloomfield Abundance, Climbing, 96
Blossomtime, **134**
Blush Boursault, 64
Blush Cluster, see 'Blush Noisette', 90
Blush Noisette, 19, 62, 88, 89, **90**. Plate V
Blush Rambler, 31, 60, **65**

Rose Bobbie James, **47**, 62. Fig. 6
Bouquet de la Mariée, see 'Aimée Vibert', 91
Bouquet d'Or, 99
Bourbon, 19, 182
Bourbon, of lax growth, 186 (No. 16)
Boursault, 60, 63, 64, 123
Boursault, Crimson, see 'Amadis', 63
Breeze Hill, 81, **82**
Brenda Colvin, 191
Burnet, 11

Calypso, see 'Blush Boursault', 64
Camellia, see R. *laevigata*, 152
Caroline Kuster, 105
Casino, 116, 129, **134**
Catalunya, see 'Gruss an Teplitz', 120
Catherine Mermet, 105
Cécile Brunner, Climbing, 11, **96**, 111. Photograph, Plate 7
Céline Forestier, 89, **96**. Plate V
Champneys' Pink Cluster, 87, 88, 90
Chaplin's Pink, 15, **62**
Charles Lefèbvre, 13
Château de Clos Vougeot, Climbing, 115, **117**
Cherokee, see R. *laevigata*, 152
China, 19, 48
Christine, Climbing, 115, **117**
City of York, **83**
Claire Jacquier, **97**. Photograph, Plate 8
Colcestria, 190
Compassion, 130, **134**
Complicata, 169
Constance Spry, 58
Cooper's Burmese, **95**
Cooperi, see 'Cooper's Burmese', 95
Coral Dawn, 130, **134**
Crimson Glory, Climbing, 114, 115, **117**
Crimson Rambler, see 'Turner's Crimson Rambler', 31, 42, 60, 73
Crimson Shower, 61, **65**
Cupid, 113, **117**. Plate VII

Rose Daily Mail, see 'Madame Édouard Herriot', 182
Dainty Bess, Climbing, 114, **118**
Daisy Hill, 168
Danse du Feu, 12, 130
De la Grifferaie, 40
Débutante, 61, **65**
Desprez à fleur jaune, 89, **97**
Devoniensis, Climbing, **105.** Photograph, Plate 12
Direktor Benschop, see 'City of York', 83
Dog Brier, 31
Dog Brier, White, 32
Donau, 65
Dortmund, 129, 130, **135**
Dorothy Perkins, 15, 21, 31, 46, 61, 62, **65**
Doubloons, 44, **118**
Dr Van Fleet, 15, 129
Dream Girl, 113, 129, 130, **135.** Plate VIII. Photograph, Plate 13
Dreaming Spires, 130, **135**
Duchesse d'Auerstädt, 98
Duchesse de Cazes, 89
Dundee Rambler, 58

Easlea's Golden Rambler, 113, **118**
Eden Rose, Climbing, **118**
Elegance, 115, **119**
Élisa Robichon, **86**
Ellen Willmott, 118
Ellinor LeGrice, 115, **119**
Emily Gray, 81, **83**
Ena Harkness, Climbing, 114, 115, **119**
Engineer, The, see 'Turner's Crimson Rambler', 73
Erinnerung an Brod, 60
Étendard, 130, **135**
Étoile de Hollande, Climbing, 12, 115, **119**
Euphrosyne, 63
E. Veyrat Hermanos, **105**
Eva Corinna, 60, 64
Evangeline, **66**
Excelsa, 15, 61, **66**

Félicité et Perpétue, 42, 44, 59, 66, 75. Plate I

Rose Fellemberg, 88, 89, **92**
Fiteni's Rose, 95
Flaming Sunset, Climbing, 114, **119**
Flammentanz, **138**
Flora, 59, **67**
Florida, see 'Blush Boursault', 64
Flying Colours, 103
Fortune's Double Yellow, **105**, 149
Francis E. Lester, 29, 61, **67**
François Foucard, **86**
François Juranville, **83**
Franziska Krüger, see 'Mademoiselle Franziska Krüger', 105, **107**
Frau Karl Druschki, 115
Fräulein Oktavia Hesse, 80, **83**
Frensham, 19
Frühlingsgold, 64
Frühlingsmorgen, 11

Gail Borden, Climbing, 116
Gardenia, 80, **83**
Garnette varieties, 111
Général Schablikine, 106
Gerbe Rose, 80, **84**
Gioia, see 'Peace', 125
Gloire de Dijon, 12, 13, 15, 89, **98**
Gloria Dei, see 'Peace', 125
Gold of Ophir, see 'Fortune's Double Yellow', 105
Golden Dawn, Climbing, 115, **119**
Golden Rambler, see 'Alister Stella Gray', 95
Golden Scepter, see 'Spek's Yellow', 127
Golden Showers, 19, 115, 129, **135**
Goldfinch, 31, 61, 63, 67. Plate II
Grand'mère Jenny, Climbing, 116
Gruss an Aachen, Climbing, 113, **119**
Gruss an Teplitz, 113, **120**
Guinée, 12, 115, **120**

Hamburger Phoenix, 129, 130, **135**
Handel, 130, **136**
Helen Patricia, 62

Rose Hiawatha, 61, **68**
  High Noon, 115, **120**
  Himalayan Musk, see R. *brun-onii*, 33
  Himalayan Musk, Paul's, 70
  Homère, 105
  Hume's Blush Tea-Scented China, 94

  Iceberg, Climbing, **136**
  Independence, Climbing, 114, **120**
  Independence Day, Climbing, 121

  Jaune Desprez, see 'Desprez à fleur jaune', 97
  Jaune Sérin, see under R. *banksiae normalis*, 149
  Jean Ducher, 105
  Jean Lafitte, 44
  Jersey Beauty, 80, **84**
  Josephine Bruce, 11
  Josephine Bruce, Climbing, 116

  Karlsruhe, **136**
  Kassel, 130, **136**
  Kathleen Harrop, 113
  Kew Rambler, 29, 61, **68**. Photograph, Plate 4
  Kiftsgate, see under R. *filipes*, 22, **34**, 35, 36. Photographs, Plates 1 and 2
  Kitty Kininmouth, 103
  Kordes' Sondermeldung, see 'Independence', 120

  La Belle Marseillaise, see 'Fellemberg', 92
  La Follette, 103
  La France, Climbing, 114, **121**
  La Mortola, see R. *brunonii* 'La Mortola', 22, 27, **33**. Fig. 1. Photograph, Plate 3
  La Perle, 80, **84**
  Lady Curzon, 169
  Lady Forteviot, Climbing, 115, **121**
  Lady Gay, 61, **68**
  Lady Godiva, 66
  Lady Hillingdon, Climbing, 11, 106. Plate VI
  Lady Sylvia, Climbing, 114, **121**

Rose Lady Waterlow, 114, **121**
  Lamarque, 89, 99. Photograph, Plate 9
  Laure Davoust, 60, **68**
  Lawrence Johnston, 128, **131**. Plate VII
  Le Rêve, 128, 131, **132**
  Léontine Gervais, 80, **84**
  Léopoldine d'Orléans, 62
  Leverkusen, 129, 130, **136**
  Lilac Charm, 11
  Little Compton Creeper, 84
  Long John Silver, 44
  Lorraine Lee, 103
  Lykkefund, 62, **69**

  Macartney, see R. *bracteata*, 150
  Madame Abel Chatenay, Climbing, 11, 114, **121**
  Madame Alfred Carrière, 100. Photograph, Plate 10
  Madame Alice Garnier, 12, 80, **84**
  Madame Antoine Mari, 107
  Madame Bérard, 105
  Madame Bravy, 105
  Madame Butterfly, Climbing, 114, **122**
  Madame Caroline Testout, Climbing, 114, **122**
  Madame Constans, 86
  Madame d'Arblay, 13, 60, **69**, 130
  Madame de Sombreuil, see 'Sombreuil', 109
  Madame Édouard Herriot, Climbing, 114
  Madame Falcot, 107
  Madame Gabriel Luizet, 65
  Madame Grégoire Stæchelin, 113, **122**
  Madame Hardy, 11
  Madame Henri Guillot, Climbing, 114, **123**
  Madame Lambard, 105
  Madame Legras de St Germain, 92
  Madame A. Meilland, see 'Peace', 125
  Madame Pierre S. Dupont, Climbing, **123**
  Madame Plantier, **92**, 169
  Madame de Sancy de Parabère, 12, 113, **123**, 185. Plate III

Rose Madame Willermoz, 105
Mademoiselle Claire Jacquier,
    see 'Claire Jacquier', 97
Mademoiselle Franziska Krüger,
    105, 107
Magic Carpet, 129, 136
Magnolia, see 'Devoniensis', 105
Maigold, 130, 136
Manetti, 93
Maréchal Niel, 13, 100
Marie Leonida, 151
Marie van Houtte, 105, 107
Marjorie W. Lester, 69
Mary Wallace, 80, 81, 85, 113
Masquerade, Climbing, 137
Max Graf, 129
May Queen, 12, 80, 85. Photo-
    graph, Plate 5
McGredy's Ivory, Climbing, 115,
    124
Meg, 130, 137
Memorial Rose, see R. wichu-
    raiana, 45
Mermaid, 12, 13, 16, 62, 115, 130,
    151
Michèle Meilland, Climbing, 114,
    124
Minnehaha, 61, 69
Morlettii, 64
Mrs Arthur Curtiss James, 115,
    124
Mrs Herbert Stevens, Climbing,
    12, 108, 115. Plate VI
Mrs John Laing, 11
Mrs Sam McGredy, Climbing,
    114, 124
Multiflora Polyantha, a name
    given to R. multiflora nana, 41
Muscate Perpetuelle, 38
Musk, the Double, 37, 38
Musk, the Old English, 19, 27,
    48 et seq. Fig. 3
Musk Rose, the Himalayan, see
    R. brunonii, 33
Myrrh-scented, Ayrshire, 58, 59

Nancy Hayward, 103
Nepal Musk Rose, see under R.
    brunonii, 33
Nevada, 13
New Dawn, 16, 62, 124, 129, 130,
    137

Rose New Dawn Rouge, see 'Éten-
    dard', 135
Niphetos, 108
Noisette, 19
Noisette Ayez, see 'Spectabilis',
    72
Noisette 'Flesh Coloured', see
    'Blush Noisette', 90
Noisette 'Repens', 88
Nymphenburg, 130, 137

Old Spanish, see 'Russelliana', 71
Ophelia, Climbing, 114, 125

Papa Gontier, 108
Parade, 130, 137
Parkdirektor Riggers, 129, 137,
    138
Parks's   Yellow   Tea-Scented
    China, 89, 94
Patricia Macoun, 69
Paul Lédé, Climbing, 102
Paul Transon, 12, 80. Photo-
    graph, Plate 6
Paul's Carmine Pillar, 15
Paul's Himalayan Musk Rambler,
    22, 60, 70
Paul's Lemon Pillar, 113, 125
Paul's Scarlet Climber, 15, 128,
    138
Paul's Single White, 129, 132
Peace, Climbing, 19, 125
Pennant, 103
Perfecta, Climbing, 116
Phyllis Bide, 61, 70
Picture, Climbing, 114, 125
Pillar of Gold, see 'E. Veyrat
    Hermanos', 105
Pink Chiffon, 58
Pink Perpétue, 130, 138
Polyantha Grandiflora, 30, 43
Prairie Rose, the, see R. setigera,
    44
President   Herbert   Hoover,
    Climbing, 114, 125
Princesse de Nassau, 39
Princesse Marie, 191
Princess Louise, 190, see also under
    'Baltimore Belle', 64
Purity, 113, 115, 129, 138

Queen Elizabeth, Climbing, 116
Queen of the Prairies, 44

Rose Rambling Rector, 62, **70**
Ramona, 153
Raymond Chenault, 130, **138**
Reine des Violettes, 11
Reine Marie Henriette, **108**
Réné André, 80, **85**
Repens, Noisette, 88
Rêve d'Or, 102
Reveil Dijonnais, 128, **132**
Ritter von Barmstede, 130, **138**
Rose de l'Isle, see 'Blush Boursault', 64
Rose-Marie Viaud, 70, **71**, 169. Plate II
Roseraie de l'Haÿ, 11
Rosy Mantle, **138**
Royal Gold, **126**, 129
Rubens, 105
Ruga, 32
Russelliana, 62, **71**
Russell's Cottage, see 'Russelliana', 71

Salut à Teplitz, see 'Gruss an Teplitz', 120
Sanders' White, 61, 182, 183
Santa Catalina, **138**
Scarlet Fire, 130
Scarlet Grevillia, see 'Russelliana', 71
Schneezwerg, 152
Schoolgirl, 130, **139**
Seagull, 62, **72**
Sénateur Amic, **104**
Seven Sisters, 60; see R. *multiflora platyphylla*, 42; sometimes confused with 'Félicité et Perpétue', 42
Shakespeare's Musk, 53
Shi-Tz-Mei, see 'Turner's Crimson Rambler', 73
Shot Silk, Climbing, 114, **126**
Silver Moon, 153
Single White China, see R. *bracteata*, 150
Soldier Boy, 130, **139**
Solfaterre, 109
Sombreuil, Climbing, 109. Photograph, Plate 11
Sondermeldung, see 'Independence, Climbing', 120
Soraya, Climbing, 114, **126**

Rose Souvenir de Claudius Denoyel, 114, 115, **126**
Souvenir de Madame Léonie Viennot, 109
Souvenir de la Bataille de Marengo, see 'Russelliana', 71
Souvenir de la Malmaison, Climbing, 11, 113, 114, **126**
Souvenir d'un Ami, 105, **109**
Spectabilis, 44, 59, **72**. Plate 1
Spek's Yellow, Climbing, 11, 115, **127**
Splendens, Ayrshire, 58, **72**
Star of Persia, 128, **132**
Super Star, 13
Susan Louise, 103
Swan Lake, **139**
Sweet Sultan, 130, **139**
Sympathie, 130, **139**

Ten Sisters, see 'Turner's Crimson Rambler', 73
Thalia, 62, 63, **72**
The Engineer, see 'Turner's Crimson Rambler', 73
The Garland, 13, 60, **73**, 168. Fig. 7
The Hon. Edith Gifford, 105
Thé Maréchal, see 'Maréchal Niel', 99
Thelma, 73
Thoresbyana, 32, 58
Treasure Trove, 192
Triomphe de la Guillotière, 154
Turner's Crimson Rambler, 73

Una, 62, **73**
Universal Favourite, 74

Valentin Beaulieu, 86
Veilchenblau, 60, **74**. Plate II
Venusta Pendula, 58, **74**
Vicomtesse Pierre de Fou, 110. Fig. 8
Violette, 12, 60, **74**. Plate II

Wedding Day, 30, **47**, 62
White Dog Rose, see R. *arvensis*, 32
White Dorothy, 75
White Rambler, see 'Thalia', 72
Wickwar, **75**

Rose Wichmoss, 75
    Zéphirine Drouhin, 107, 113
Rose-water, 38
Roseraie de l'Haÿ, Paris, 20, 34, 64, 82, 98. Photograph, Plate 16
Roses, Ayrshire, 32, **59**
    Banksian, 145
    bedding, 16, 139
    botany of climbers, 155 et seq.
    Bourbon, 19, 182
    Boursault, 123
    Burnet, 11
    Cherokee, 152
    Climbers, Hybrid Tea style, 111
    Climbers, the New, 128
    Climbing, definition of, 16, 139, 155
    Damask, 28, 31, 48, 55
    Damask, Autumn, 31, 50, 55
    Dwarf polyantha, 19, 31, 140
    Floribunda, 16, 19, 31
    Floribunda Climbers, 128, 140
    for arbours, covering sheds, etc., 183
    for climbing into trees, 22, 169, 179, 183, 184
    for covering hedges, stumps, etc., 182
    for ground cover, 182
    for road verges, 40
    for walls, north, 185
    for walls, sunny, 184
    for weeping standards, 185
    for wild gardening, 182
    Hybrid Musk, 31
    Hybrid Perpetual, 19
    Hybrid Tea, 16, 19, 20, 93, 112 et seq., 140
    in trees, 22, 169, 179, 183, 184
    late-flowering, 141
    Luciae Ramblers, **79**, 140, 191
    Macartney, 150
    Moss, 27 n.
    Noisette, 19, 31, 48, **87** et seq., 140
    Polyantha, 19, 31, 140
    Polypoms, 140
    ramblers and climbers for gardens of old roses, 139
    Ramblers, old and new garden, 58
    Ramblers, the wild Musk, 27
    rambling, definition of, 16, 139, 140
    scrambling, 16
Roses, selections of, for various purposes, 181
    shrub, 16, 139
    sprawling, 182
    Synstylae, 27
    Tea, 89, 93, 98, **104** et seq.
    Tea Noisette, 19, 89, 94, **95**, 115, 140
    thornless, 184
    uses in the garden, 20
Rosier Banks Épineux, 148
    de Philippe Noisette, 90
    Musqué, Le, 38
Rowley, Gordon, 70, 123
Royal Botanic Garden, Kew, 21
Royal Horticultural Society, Wisley, 21, 96, 103, 104, 131

Sabine, Joseph, 59
Saint Felicitas and Saint Perpetua, 66
St Nicholas, 47, 97
St Paul's Waldenbury, 126
Santa Rosa, mammoth rose tree at, 100
Scent, of green apples, 80
    of Musk, 56
    of Tea, 94
Scramblers, 16
Shakespeare, 49
Shalimar Bagh, 101
Sissinghurst, 100
Slocock, Mrs Ashley, 70
Smith, Mr T., 90
Southill Park, 104
'Sport', definition of, 23
Standards, weeping, roses for, 185
Standish and Noble, 106
Steadman, Keith, 75
Stearn, Dr W. T., 54
Stern, Sir Frederick, 47
Summerhouse, 173
Sunningdale Nurseries, 9, 106
Synstylae Section, species of, 17; botany of, 155 et seq.

Tea roses, 104 et seq.
Tender roses, 183

Tintinhull House, 123
Training roses, 20, 21, 22, 167
Trees, roses for, 183, 184
Trelissick, 150
Tripods for roses, 177

Understock, R. *manettii*, 93
Understock, R. *multiflora* as, 40

Van Fleet, 81

Wakehurst, 45
Wall, north, roses for, 185

Wall supports, 169
Walls, roses for, 182, 183, 185, 186
Walsh, M. H., 61
Weeping standards, 185
Wisley, rose garden, 21
Woodall, E. H., 146
Wormley Bury, 150
Wylie, Miss Ann, 112, 113

Xanthoceras sorbifolia, 54

Young, Wing-Commander, 107